Rules for the Road

A Traveling Man's Guide to Avoiding Sexual Indiscretion

William Hanna

iUniverse, Inc.
New York   Bloomington

iUniverse books may be ordered through booksellers or by contacting:
iUniverse

1663 Liberty Drive
Bloomington, IN 47403
www.iuniverse.com
1-800-Authors (1-800-288-4677)

ISBN: 978-1-4502-1604-3 (sc)
ISBN: 978-1-4502-1606-7 (hc)
ISBN: 978-1-4502-1605-0 (ebook)

Printed in the United States of America

iUniverse rev. date: 04/27/2010

Preface

The stories contained in this book are intended to be humorous and are fiction, although some elements of each are true. The stories told are designed to highlight thoughts and memories of various situations I encountered while on the road.

I have traveled extensively, primarily on business, and many of my travels were to Asian countries during the 1990s. As a result, I came to the conclusion that, regardless of what one does, a person is occasionally going to be swept up in the events of the moment, whether or not those events were of their making. Emerging unscathed from what happens always requires all of one's wits to accomplish.

These events have occurred over the course of dozens of trips to all parts of the world. The fact that this book condenses them into a single trip is only to keep the book reasonably sized. Each event could be expanded to become a book on its own.

I trust that all who read the book will find it entertaining because that is what it is meant to be. Just to make sure we're all on the same page, however, I feel honor bound to state that the book is purely fictional, and comparisons to people or events cannot and should not be made. Any suggestions to the contrary are baseless and unwarranted.

General Rule For Remaining Faithful To One's Significant Other While Away From Home On An Extended Business Trip

This book contains ten rules to be observed, should one wish to avoid infidelity while away from home on extended business travel. Each rule follows a detailed narration of the events that inspired it.

All this notwithstanding, there is one general rule to follow for those who do not wish to take the time to study the following text in detail.

In my experience, I have found that a chastity belt is still the best way to promote faithfulness, although fitting it for males may require some redesign of the original concept, such as using extra-strong materials, especially when the male is particularly well hung.

While chastity belts are the only true method of controlling the female Homo Sapien, there are additional ways of insuring that the male will remain true to his love back home. Unfortunately, these can only be discussed in a private setting where decorum is not an issue.

Nevertheless, controlling the beast in all of us is to everyone's benefit, since it demonstrates in real time how slender the bonds of holy matrimony really are.

I hope that the reader will commit the entire text to memory so that they may avoid the mistakes of famous world travelers such as Bill Clinton, president of the United States, NASA astronaut Lisa Nowak, vice presidential candidate John Edwards, New York State governor Eliot Spitzer, Prince Charles of England, Governor Mark Sanford who has displayed a tremendous love for Argentina, Tiger Woods who allegedly displays a desire to have a girl in every port, and Clara Harris who solved the problem of her husband's infidelity by running over him three times with her Mercedes in the parking lot of the Clear Lake, Texas, Hilton.

One
Interior China from a Train

There were two things that William Hanna hated about China. The first was the heat of summer—worse than Houston, Texas, where a lot of Vietnamese war refugees had settled because it was the closest thing to the Mekong Delta that they could find in America. The second was that Chinese trains had no air conditioning while they were stopped in the station. Some local dufuss a long time ago had decided that the generators that ran the damn things could depend on the movement of the wheels down the track to generate the power to run the cooling system—there was no juice to power the cool air during station stops.

Although the windows on Chinese trains opened to let in a breeze, it was so superheated that it was of no help, especially for Hanna. August in Shanghai, China; August in Houston, Texas. Weather-wise they were the same.

Hanna had long since written off train travel in America, but in China, it was frequently the only way to get from point A to point B unless you preferred to walk. Air service in China, if it existed, meant flying at thirty-five thousand feet on some Russian Ilysian II jet that was about to explode because of the fuel leaking from the belly tanks. Unfortunately, it was too far from Shanghai to Nanjing (a five-hour train ride) to walk. Hanna could only sigh quietly, knowing that in China every train was a local unlike the

5:37 express to Greenwich out of Grand Central that, once upon a time, he commuted on. That train always got him home from Grand Central in forty-five minutes with Hanna enjoying the complete solitude, martini in hand, looking forward to an evening of baseball practice with favorite son who swung wildly at every pitch in T ball or an hour at a recital listening to his favorite daughter as she missed every second key.

All that had happened before he had been transferred to Houston. Sometime thereafter, he had made a personal note to dispose of forever the person who had given him Houston's October Chamber of Commerce tour of the town and had him moved in before the heat arrived in April of the following year. He frequently mused as to whether or not six ounces of arsenic in a glass of water would do the trick.

Hanna had brought three colleagues from the office with him on this trip at the suggestion of his boss, Mr. Jason Llewellyn, president and chairman of the board. They all had individual reasons for being along, which were as different as night and day or a third alternative, if there was one, and, like Hanna, they all reported independently to Mr. Llewellyn. The company they worked for was a conglomerate making everything from engines and automotive spare parts to electronics; however, its flagship product, and the one Hanna spent most of his time involved with, was a new design form of electric automobile.

Clifford Harrison was the executive vice president in charge of all automotive sales and marketing. Cliff had proven many years ago that he could sell the proverbial refrigerators to the Eskimos, and as a result, he was now in charge of the entire sales and marketing staff of twenty three scattered around the world. He didn't know what the word "no" meant, and he carried a golf handicap of two. He was medium height and had a full head of hair with a wave in it, which he combed back on the sides. There wasn't an ounce of fat on his body as a result of the robust sex life of a traveling salesman and walking a golf course every other day.

No one complained about his mastery of golf, however, since

he was personally responsible for a couple hundred million in sales every year. All the others on his staff were lucky if they made a hundred million, and they needed his help most of the time to do that. It wasn't difficult to have sales of these amounts when you were in the automotive and airline business.

Rudolf Van Neys was the vice president of engineering. He was quite religious and let everyone know that he wouldn't stand for what he described as, "any sinful activities." He was overweight almost to the point of being obese, about five foot seven, and going bald prematurely.

Rudolf's inability to tolerate sinful activities resulted in his frequent early departure from the evening round-table discussion of the day's events, which was always held in the bar. After the second drink, the language always got a little rough and occasionally terribly rough. The rest of the guys didn't really worry about this. Rudolf ate his meals with them, because he had to eat like everyone else, and he refused to go anywhere by himself because "it was too dangerous." He had trained himself to take a drink with dinner, however, since in this part of the world it was regarded as an insult to refuse the host's offer to have one.

Rudolf was quiet and reserved, saying little. Hanna always pegged him as the kid at school who had been constantly bullied by the big kids. Rudolf had little imagination. Everything in his world could be assessed and quantified with a slide rule. Rudolf had never graduated to the twenty-first century: for him, the slide rule was all that he needed to work his engineering magic. For Rudolf, entertainment in these circumstances, on a flight to Hong Kong from San Francisco, was provided by an old, outdated, tape player with huge headphone speakers playing Brahms.

Hanna could work with Rudolf and Clifford, but his heart lay with the vice president of finance, Jaime Maldonado. He was born of illegal Hispanic immigrants from Vera Cruz and, as a young man, was superbly educated by his parents. Jaime was a Harvard MBA, his education paid for half by the university because his surname gave him minority status and half by his parents who both worked several jobs at once, seven days a week for years, to insure he would have the opportunity to excel. Jaime was about thirty years old and as handsome as young Hispanic males get. His English was perfect. He was on his way up the corporate ladder.

Jaime had taken the challenge of being the child of illegal aliens and run with it. Although he wasn't yet married, it was just a matter of time. He was currently dating about the prettiest thing Hanna had ever laid eyes on, and the two of them adored each other. He also had all the great characteristics of a true Hispanic. He was hard working, had an unquestioning love for his family, and had deep religious convictions that never failed him. Plus all that, he walked around with a constant smile on his face. Hanna loved Jaime. *Hell*, Hanna thought, *he loved all Hispanics*.

Jaime had two faults. He was a puppy dog, always wanting to be with the crowd and do everything they did. This meant that he would try anything, and he always ended up drinking more than he should have trying to keep pace with the old pros like Hanna. Jaime never won this game, but at the same time, he never stopped trying.

His second fault was that he never shut up: he was born talking.

Starting the trip in Houston, the group had caught a flight to San Francisco, where they boarded a 747 non-stop flight direct to Shanghai. They were all in first class (the company allowed that if the flight was over four hours in length), and as soon as they became airborne, the service reserved for those whose employer was willing to pay twelve-thousand dollars for a round trip ticket began. Everyone was in a good mood.

The evening in first class started off with fine wine of which everyone partook. That was followed up with beluga caviar on wafers, a few grapes if one was so inclined, and, of course, the mandatory chilled Russian vodka. Hanna usually had two chilled vodkas. Service continued with a salad of the traveler's choice; Hanna usually had a wedge of iceberg lettuce with blue cheese. Not the blue cheese that one bought in the local grocery store but the kind aged in French caves, which all you had to do to serve was take the lid off the jar and the dressing would crawl out and set itself down like a sacrificial lamb on the top of the lettuce bed. It wasn't really blue cheese, it was Limburger. Hanna loved it. It would hang on your breath for days regardless of how often you brushed your teeth. The entrée came next. Hanna usually had lamb chops with mint jelly and asparagus on outbound flights. He had no reason why; he just did. He'd take an occasional bite of bread but not a lot. As far as Hanna was concerned, bread was fattening.

Dessert was different for every first-class passenger, as near as Hanna could discern. He usually ordered a crème **brûlée,** which he followed up with more fine cheese combined with green grapes, coffee, and an Amaretto Sarrono. After that, everyone was on their own. Hanna usually started with a Chivas Regal, neat. He could drink that stuff all the way to Hong Kong if he chose to.

On this flight, Hanna was seated with Clifford, not by luck but rather by design. This forced Rudolf and Jaime to sit together, a situation for which Jaime privately expressed his loathing to Hanna later. Of course, there were movies playing constantly. Hanna and Clifford more or less ignored the first movie, preferring instead to discuss the trip and the goals they had established for themselves. Clifford was a good man. He largely kept his private life to himself and that included his private, on-the-road dalliances. By the time the flight attendant picked up the dinner-service utensils, they were well into the second movie. Cliff was tired. Within minutes, he was in a deep sleep, having been plied with more fine booze than he had been accustomed to.

Hanna looked over at his two traveling mates. Jaime had passed by a couple of times on his way to the bathroom, during the second trip of which he expressed his dismay at being seated next to Rudolf. Hanna's only response was, "Jeeezzz, Jaime. Why can't you just be friends?"

After the second movie finished, Rudolf got up for the third time and headed for the toilet. After he returned and started to get comfortable, Hanna couldn't stand it any longer. He got up and walked over to where Rudolf and Jaime were sitting.

"It's been a pretty long flight don't you think, Rudolf?"

"It sure has, Hanna. I'll be glad when we land. I'm claustrophobic, and this cabin is starting to get to me."

"Don't worry Rudolf. In another hour, we'll be half way there."

Rudolf hadn't realized the flight to Shanghai took fifteen and a half hours.

None of the support troops had been to China previously, and they were all excited by the adventure even though they tried to hide it from Hanna. Regardless of how he assessed their personalities and traits, they were all the best in their respective fields of expertise, and Hanna respected them all for the talent they brought to the table. He only had two concerns with their presence on this trip. Could he keep them from a mutiny when they were out of town in a foreign country for two weeks where no one understood a word of the English language and could he keep them from screwing up the negotiations by saying or doing something that blew everything out of the water?

After landing in Shanghai and sleeping overnight, they boarded a train taking them from Shanghai to Nanjing. It was somewhat less aggravating than most since he had selected the group's seats and put himself on the aisle. This seat provided Hanna with an unobstructed view of a family of five and the crotch of the oldest of three daughters who was sitting directly across the aisle from him. He estimated she was somewhere around eighteen years of age. Her father and mother were totally engrossed in arguing about something, probably their escape route out of the country since their arrest for breaking the one child rule per couple was imminent. Obviously, this nymphet had decided that it would be a good time for her to do a little testing to determine what reaction she might evoke from a good-looking stranger from the West if she stretched her legs straight out in front of her, let her *mini ride up, and waved a little yum yum at him. Hell,* Hana thought, *as far* as Chinese women were concerned, no man was ever too old or too decadent if he could get them out of this hellhole and into America. Hanna's antenna immediately began to rise. It was impossible to approach a fully mature female in China, let alone a child, without the promise of swift retribution from a defender of morals for the People's Republic. This usually involved something similar to some Bedouin out of *Lawrence of Arabia* burying you up to your neck in the sand and then having some samurai come racing by on horseback with the sole intent of swinging his sword in an arc and grinning as your head rolled slowly across the sands.

Oh well, he thought, as long as she didn't throw a blanket over her lap and start to masturbate while she fondly looked him in the eye, he could probably choke down his Chinese freeze-dried noodles provided by the coolie who had magically appeared and then disappeared.

Chinese freeze-dried noodles, soaked in boiling water for thirty minutes, were the only thing any Westerners could eat in most public places in China with a modicum of assurance that they would not catch some life-ending disease within the next forty-eight hours.

Ah, what the hell—she was still drilling holes in him with her eyes and the noodles had some flavor.

Life was good.

"Hey guy," Cliff said. The greeting shook him out of his revere. "Have you noticed that little darling sitting across the aisle? I could sure punch that clock."

"No crap," Hanna replied. "I'm surprised you even looked, being so engrossed in your game of checkers and all." Everyone in China traveled with board games designed to dull the senses as to how long the trip would take or how bored they were becoming—a billion-plus brain-dead ninja mutants. His crew was becoming the latest casualty.

All the people traveling with Hanna on this expedition were there because of some field of expertise (engineering, design, expediting, etc.), however, none of them were ever going to get it because they hadn't read his e-mail about "Doing Business in

China for Dummies." In his company, Hanna was the guru of the Far East—which was the reason why these people kneeled down in front of him to repeatedly chant their unworthiness. *Ah, what the hell*, he thought, *once a day would be fine.* (There was no conceit in Hanna's family: he had it all.)

Hanna had been traveling into the country for some time, trying to establish a new auto manufacturing operation by negotiating a partnership with a Chinese counterpart. The associates with him on this trip were all specialists who could cite six-sigma crap and those kinds of western concepts that had the innate ability to glaze over the eyes of the listeners, especially a bunch of Chinamen who had to hear every word translated for them. The translation usually was provided by some "couldn't care less" little darling who completely destroyed their concentration and forced them keep their hands in their pockets all the time. (It was nice to know that there was at least one shred of commonality that Chinese and American males shared.)

There was a second hurdle in addition to the translation issue. As near as Hanna could figure, most translators were part time: their main profession had to be actress or cheerleader for the Chinese Olympic ping-pong team. As Hanna had frequently observed, they all wore their clothes too tight and their skirts too short, and they all wanted to go down to the hotel cabaret in the evenings to sip coke with their countrymen after they realized their American bosses had drunk too much to get a hard-on.

It normally took several attempts to make cognitive thought understood among the Chinese. Even when they nodded their heads, one still wondered if anything the American was saying, as related by the translator, was permeating the bone structure of the person she was addressing. It never appeared to be that way.

The train finally began its approach to Nanjing. Hanna knew this because he heard the city's name stuck in the middle of an announcement in Chinese that went on forever by what had to be the train's conductor. In addition, Hanna had also noticed that the donkeys pulling two-wheeled carts had been replaced by more modern two-cycle, piston-engine tractors that sounded like old beat-up lawn mowers. It was lucky the country had more population than it could keep track of. A head count sufficient to manually overrun every country on the planet was the only way China would ever achieve world dominance.

Two
Houston on One's Mind

Hanna thanked God he was wearing an open-necked, short-sleeved dress shirt, which his wife always insisted was a contradiction in terms, since there was no such thing as a short-sleeved dress shirt. Nevertheless, in this part of the world it was the only thing one could consider wearing if they didn't want to sweat to death.

Despite everything happening around him, Hanna's mind momentarily drifted back to the wife he had left behind only a couple of days previously. Over the course of the thirty years they had been together, first in a long-distance relationship, followed by a period of living together, and then getting married, Hanna's feelings had never changed about what was now Mrs. Hanna. She was the love of his life and the best thing that had ever happened to him. She had more of everything than any other woman he had ever known. When she walked into a room, it went silent as people looked at her with desire and at Hanna with envy. She was always better turned out than any New York runway model, she always smelled like heaven, and she was the sexiest thing he had ever known. In public, she was a perfect lady, and in private she made Hanna feel like he was the most fortunate man in the world.

Mrs. Hanna attended gym at least three times a week, and she had one of the hardest bodies Hanna had ever gotten to know. She was tall, slim with no more than a twenty-two inch waist, long legged, and her gorgeous blond hair fell to her shoulders gleaming when the sun's rays hit it right.

The first time they made love, Hanna couldn't figure out how he had come to be so lucky. To this day, he still felt the same way. *Back to real world now.*

Hanna realized that it wasn't just hot on the platform: it was stifling. Hanna had heard that the Chinese formed a cloud of noxious body odor whenever they gathered in large groups. The sea of Chinese in the railroad station yard, none of whom could have had a shower in the last seven days or had no idea what a scented underarm deodorant was, only added to his misery and discomfort.

He could tell his associates' thoughts paralleled his own since they appeared to be silently cursing the 105 degree heat, 96 percent humidity, and the dirt in the air. The dirt, provided courtesy of the million coal-fired power plants located around the country, soaked into everyone's skin and made it impossible to take a deep breath. The Chinese took no notice of this, perhaps because they all smoked and were likely to die by the age of forty three.

Hanna's group was in the middle of the mandatory introductions to the entire management of the company with whom they were about to restart merger negotiations for the nth time, all having turned out because of the sanctity of the occasion. Hanna's translator, Sheu, was taking everything with fake aplomb and grace as the sweat dripped down the ass of her pants just the same as it was doing with all of his group. Because she was from somewhere to the far north of China, her body had never adjusted to the unrelenting heat of the South. Hanna reflected on the humor of the situation, only because it was the wetness of her clothing that gave her away: Chinese women didn't have asses.

"Ah, Mr. Hanna, please meet Mr. Pong. He is an economist for Nanjing Motor Works."

All accountants in China had become "economists" in the late 1940s after Mao Tse Dung wiped out the accounting profession at the beginning of his reign. He believed the decadent western ways of this portion of China's population did not sufficiently benefit the well-being of the peasantry. They also ate food that was at a premium, which withheld it from others that Mao believed were much more deserving. He therefore took care of the profession through the barrel of a gun.

Hanna smiled as he shook the weasely hand of the five-foot-six man with bad breath standing six inches in front of him, bowing from the waist and occasionally spitting on him as he expressed his delight at meeting again.

"Ah so, Mr. Hanna, chei chei, ah, ah, ah so chei, chei."

Round and round they went as heat stroke was beginning to set in.

Memo to self: Be sure to use hand wipes just as soon as possible and do not, under any circumstances, touch a cigarette when lighting up until after using a cleansing wipe.

Something foul and greasy had just come off of Pong's hand onto Hanna's.

He turned to their translator. "Hey, Sheu, ask these butt heads to get us into something frickin' air conditioned before I die." Instantly, he saw the terror in Sheu's eyes.

"Ah, Mr. Hanna, I'm not familiar with the word 'butt head'? What does this mean?" Hanna could tell that she was expecting the knife to appear momentarily that would forever end life as she knew it because of her inability to translate these words.

Hanna turned, and in a very sympathetic manner with his arm over her shoulder, apologized. "I'm sorry Sheu. 'Fricking' is a derivative of an intensely profane word that was invented by women for use in polite company when they can't reveal their true feelings like men do. We can discuss it and the other words later in my room where there will be plenty of time to not only define them but to also demonstrate their meaning. Meanwhile, let's just have our hosts take us to our cars where we can get out of the heat and back into the comfort of some air conditioning. I'll die if I don't locate some cool soon."

"Ah so, you want air conditioning. I will ask your hosts to take us to your car. Also, I will be very pleased to have you define new English words for me. Possibly, we can do that tonight?"

Despite the fact that Hanna didn't know a word of Chinese, he expected his translators to be American born and fluent in English. At three-hundred dollars an hour, there was no reason why he should demand less.

Sure, darling. Possibly we do it tonight, he thought.

Memo to self: Be sure to check this evening's itinerary and set aside some time for an English tutorial.

Jesus Christ, what the hell was he thinking? He had a beautiful wife at home who adored him just as much as he adored her and who was living solely based upon the promise of his quick return.

Actually, the second reason they were standing on the station platform was because one of his associates was pointing out to the coolie crew, who were also employees of the host company, which of the luggage stacked in the vestibule of the train was theirs. These bags would be loaded in the van that would follow them to the hotel. It simply would not be appropriate for the Americans to carry their own luggage. In addition, since they were here on the far side of the world for two weeks, each of them had brought at least three bags for which they had each paid extra since it was over the airline's weight limit, despite the fact that they had flown first class.

Just as he was about to turn to follow the Chinese company's president and the translator to the waiting, cool car, he caught a movement out of the corner of his eye. The body was gorgeous, a fact that was apparent despite the drab clothing it was wearing, and it had an ass, the first one he had seen since his arrival in country. When it turned towards him, it smiled one of those pure, generous, virginal smiles, and the 102-pound frame it was mounted on only showed more evidence of a desire to meet and become friends with him. She was carrying (not pulling) his bag even though it had wheels, the largest bag he had packed, the one that weighed in at eighty-five pounds.

"Mr. Hanna, my name Liu. I will take your luggage to hotel."

Jesus Christ, Hanna thought, *She speaks English, too!*

"Liu," Hanna responded, "A great pleasure to meet you, but you mustn't carry that."

He gently but firmly retrieved the bag from her tiny hand. *God, the bag weighed almost as much as she does*, he thought.

Sheu had turned as this happened, as had the president, and both were at his side in an instant.

"Mr. Hanna, you will please come with us to the cool car. We will talk more inside. Don't worry about the bags. Our employees take care of them. You need to rest. Come. Come."

Hanna looked at them, then turned back towards the girl who had introduced herself as Liu. She was gone: swallowed up in the sea of stinking humanity that milled around on the platform.

Hanna let himself be escorted to the car. He hoped Liu didn't expire before she made it to the van.

Overindulging

The Chinese feel a strong need to entertain their foreign guests at banquets and toast their mutual fondness for one another. Foreigners have gained a reputation during these events for being unable to hold their liquor, since they tend to arrive for work the following day disheveled and hung over. Actually, a closer examination of circumstances surrounding these events reveals that it is not the toasts with local Chinese liquor that cause this problem. Rather it is that, after returning to their hotel room, most foreigners require at least three full glasses of scotch to wash the taste of the food and booze out of their mouths before retiring for the night.

Unpublished works by William B. Hanna, circa 1996

Three
Steering Negotiations

Chinamen did everything by rote. That was how their system worked. Children were taught that death was the option if they did not heel to the credo. Variations on any theme were not tolerated. Clocks ruled the world. You were not late. You were not early. You were on time—exactly on time.

Business in China worked the same way.

Breakfast was at seven am. There was always one dignitary, a management type from the Chinese firm, who joined them for this event. Everything was an event, whether a meal or otherwise. The food always came off a hundred trays served by the coolies of the kitchen, and you picked what you wanted. Hanna always pointed to things that looked as though they were overdone since anything cooked at less than 250 degrees for at least ten minutes carried with it the threat of an agonizing death. This also went for lunch and dinner.

He was the only one in his organization who had traveled to China more than a dozen times without being laid up for three or four days with some form of stomach upset. The rest of the guys challenged caution when eating the crap they were served, and it never occurred to any of them what might be passed on to them when they were shaking hands. As a result, some unknown kind of germ to which they had never previously been exposed invaded their bodies. The lack of acquired immunity caused violent reactions within the white man's body. The shivers, the shits, and other diabolical symptoms usually convinced the sufferer that death was the only option available, and the sooner it came, the better. It was worse than its Mexican counterpart, Montezuma's revenge.

Hanna had noted two things early on during his travels to China. First, the Chinese all wanted to act like Americans, so they tried to do everything Americans did. The second was that, despite all that was holy, they could not bring themselves to eat anything using normal eating utensils. Chopsticks were the only way to go.

It only took Hanna one day in China to decide what he had to do: he ordered fried eggs sunny side up. This order took fifteen minutes for his translator to describe to the waiter and presumably make them understand. Hanna had pretty much written off any hope of having eggs (or whatever they were likely to substitute for eggs) served to him in the manner he had described. His group's attending Chinaman followed suit by ordering the same, having no idea what he had just done.

The eggs arrived as ordered. As best Hanna could recall, a first! Nevertheless, there they were, all shiny, loose, and runny. Hanna couldn't wait. He dove into his order with toast in one hand and utensils in the other, forking down the eggs. Out of the corner of his eye, he watched their corporate baby sitter for the day, the economist, anticipating his disgust with what he had unknowingly ordered.

The Chinaman, Pong, looked as though he was about to panic, and you could just see the smoke coming out of his ears as he thought, *How the hell am I going to eat this thing?*

Hanna spoke with him through the translator who could hardly hold back from giggling.

"This is a fine five-star hotel, Pong. You'd better eat up. We're going to have to get to the plant soon."

Pong grabbed his chopsticks and gulped. As he bent over his plate, there was a gasp and then a slurp. Hanna watched as the yolk began to quiver and break. The yellow went this way and that, ending up on the tablecloth, Pong's face, and his shirt. The translator had to excuse herself, since it was not polite to openly break out in laughter at the sight of a countryman's plight. Hanna was only amused to the extent that this activity had become a noble demonstration of how closely this country could still be linked to the hairy cavemen in the Geico commercials. *Christ, he thought, the guy had eaten it all in one bite.*

Every day the schedule was the same. The Americans were met at seven for breakfast. At precisely eight, the bill was paid, and everyone was escorted to the waiting van to travel to the Chinese company for negotiations. They arrived at the plant at precisely eight thirty. At precisely twelve noon, negotiations broke for lunch. Lunch always took one and a half hours. The first fifteen minutes were devoted to karaoke, during which the local employees sang a combination of 1950s American hit songs played on an old record player, interspersed with an occasional aaaahaaaahiiiieeeeeeeee Chinese folk song, accompanied by a one-stringed instrument that was designed to forever destroy one's appreciation for music. The biggest problem with this arrangement was that all the American songs were produced by some form of voice recognition technology (probably in Taiwan or Thailand), which, from time to time, misinterpreted words, rendering senseless what was being sung.

Hanna had once taken particular enjoyment in pointing this fact out to one tiny Barbie doll with the voice of an angel. She just merrily sang along regardless of whether the words made sense or not. In actual fact, she didn't know a word of English. Hanna spent hours trying to think of a way to pork her. He never did figure out how to do it.

Dinnertime was a problem for the Chinese. They had to eat by themselves in order to determine their strategy for the next day's meetings, all the while knowing that at the same time their visitors (the ugly Americans with a delightful translator in tow) were invading some restaurant within their city to consume vast quantities of very expensive spirits and wines, eating like gluttons, and becoming loud and obnoxious until they were an embarrassment to the host company. Because of this perceived problem of their visitors' excesses, the local company's management made arrangements to hold banquets every other day and always on Friday evenings.

This created problems for both negotiating teams. The Americans hated the food, which was half awful and half life threatening. The local booze served at these events and the endless rounds of "gumbis" (toasts) only ensured that everyone would have a cracking headache in the morning. Friday nights meant the weekend, and all the guys wanted to do was be rid of all these people they had been negotiating with all week. The other side's desire, Hanna thought, was only to get to a state of drunken stupor as fast as they could, since these were state-sanctioned functions and therefore their actions were justified.

Oh, well, Hanna thought, *they would have to stay with protocol even though he had an uneasy feeling about the evening that could only be described as visceral.*

Four
Hannasan, Please Meet Suzie Wong

Hanna could feel it coming.

The Chinese executive assigned to provide breakfast coverage made the announcement, even though he probably shouldn't have. "Ah so, Hannasan, we eat together tonight. We send car to pick you up at hotel at six pm."

For about the tenth time, Hanna wondered why his Chinese hosts nearly always addressed him as "san," when he had always thought that was a Japanese term, but they had done so on every one of his previous trips, so he had come to accept the practice.

The Chinese knew that Americans would have to come back to the hotel first before dinner, since they could not tolerate going out for the evening without an opportunity to freshen up with a shower to wash off all the crap that had accumulated on their bodies during the day's activities.

All banquets were held at the company's offices in the dining rooms provided for the company's staff. While the Chinese culture demanded togetherness of the workers because they were all equal, Hanna noticed that he never saw any actual greasy workers stepping into the executive dining hall. Nevertheless, everyone was equal. Hanna's translator, who was being paid an incredible three-hundred dollars per hour, bragged loudly and frequently about her husband who drove a motorized rickshaw in Shanghai.

Hanna didn't really care about the Chinese philosophy, since he had demonstrated to himself more than once that all you had to do was wave a couple of grand at these consecrated butt heads and they immediately departed from their beliefs. Every time someone began to expound on this garbage, he nodded a sympathetic all-knowing understanding and changed the subject to anything that made sense within the realm of civilized society.

It was Friday, and so, at lunch (as had been advised at breakfast) Zhang, the company's president announced, in a manner that said "you shall attend," an invitation to everyone to attend the evening's banquet. Hanna sighed inwardly and acknowledged his pleasure and that of his group of associates at being allowed to accompany the president of the company to such an event at a time when the president should be devoting his time to his wife and family. He went on to express his hope that all was well with the family of the president and asked the forgiveness of Zhang for any difficulty this intrusion by Hanna and his group into Zhang's personal time caused him.

Hanna began to think about how long it would take to extricate his negotiating team from the phony, gushy, sweetness of these pricks and allow them all to escape for forty-eight hours to relax for the weekend without all the formality.

The van arrived at 5:59 pm and everyone loaded up. Within seconds, they were off to the banquet. Hanna was amazed when they arrived at the party room on the company's premises at precisely six thirty pm. The facilities were large, contained a cabaret, with communal restroom facilities, which required the male visitors to walk through the female area that, to his amazement, had curtains hiding all but the lower half of the women's calves and their three-inch heels. No one seemed to be bothered with this arrangement, which allowed the women to proceed in privacy behind the curtain with doing whatever women do while sitting on the can. This total lack of privacy just about killed Hanna, and he wondered to himself why the arrangement wasn't reversed with the women walking by the men's urinals on the way to their john. The communal bathroom would never have been tolerated anywhere else in the world, and Hanna felt sorry for the girls. At the same time, it occurred to him that the women had been doing this all their lives, and it probably never occurred to them that maybe they should be embarrassed by the set up.

As with all Chinese banquets, the food was terrible. Hanna participated in about five entrees of the hundred or so offered to them at about a dozen a time. When the cook brought out the live snake so that everyone could admire how impotent it was in its ability to strike while being held by the tail, he took orders for those who might desire a shot glass of its blood. Cliff, the vice president of sales and marketing, raised his hand and was immediately applauded by the hosts. Zhang leaned over and with a sly wink told Cliff through the interpreter how virile he would become because he had accepted the Chinaman's offer. Hanna immediately leaned over to Cliff from the other side of the table and let him know that he would puke if he had to watch him drink that crap. He also expressed his hope that the vice president didn't mind if he excused himself and went to the john while this course was being served.

Even though Hanna had been to China many times, he had never been able to come to grips with formal oriental dining. It was obvious that these people in the simple process of growing into adults in China had immunized their bodies to the point where there was nothing except for the most aggressive forms of disease that could give them an upset stomach. The Chinese food served in America bore absolutely no resemblance to the Chinese food served in China—and it demanded all of Hanna's staying power not to retch at least once during the course of one of these meals.

Surprisingly, Hanna was doing well this time despite these attempts to upset his stomach.

The next course was the turtle. It was alive, weighed in at about ten pounds, and was brought out on a large serving tray for all to admire.

"Would anyone enjoy a shot glass of bile from his gall bladder?"
was the question. It took a good ten minutes to ask and to solicit responses
to this invitation, during which time the animal took a dump
in the middle of the tray. This time, not only did Cliff respond
affirmatively, Rudolf, the vice president of engineering, did as well.
Hanna couldn't believe it. He lowered his head and slowly shook
it.

It was only a matter of time.

Dinner ended precisely at eight pm after a series of toasts using
the local quack-grass liquor designed to completely destroy one's
brain cells when it was not being used to put criminals to death
by injection. Zhang then announced (via the interpreter) that they
must all move to the next room for some entertainment. After all,
he pointed out, it was Friday night.

Zhang and the interpreter escorted Hanna into the extremely
low-lit room. After his eyes adjusted to the dimmer lights, he
realized that there were women assembled in the room who had not
joined them for dinner. He had no sooner sat down holding a glass
of Chivas Regal to wash the taste of dinner out of his mouth when
he recognized Liu sitting with a couple of friends on the far side of
the room. He sat his drink down, got up, and asked the interpreter
if they could be introduced. Smiles were bestowed on him from
every corner of the room. Zhang was absolutely ecstatic.

"Of course this is possible, Hannasan. Have you met Liu
before?"

Hanna's only response was to mumble that they possibly might
have exchanged pleasantries at the train station upon the arrival of
their delegation in town.

"Ah so," was the response. "Then let me formally introduce
you to Liu."

Liu was dazzling in a traditional white Chinese print silk dress
with a high neck and a slit up the side of one leg almost to her hip.
She looked even smaller than the day Hanna had first spotted her
at the railroad station, but now that she was formally dressed she

was radiant. She rose and looked into Hanna's eyes, and there was no mistaking that she had exactly the same hunger for his body that he had for hers. She extended her hand to shake Hanna's, and the feeling was as though a bolt of lightning had just passed between them. *This woman has an agenda,* Hanna thought. He just hoped that she would have as much fun disclosing it to him as he was going to have in determining what it was.

"Liu! You will please meet Hannasan!" Zhang said. As near as Hanna could figure, it wasn't a request. It was an order.

"Hannasan, very pleased to meet you," Liu said in English as she stood up and curtseyed. Zhang smiled. To him this diabolical force from the West appeared as though he was completely taken in by his offering, and she was an employee!

"Hannasan," Zhang said, "You must dance! Enjoy some fun. Appreciate the time you have devoted to us living in China, the mother of creation, where you have come in a furtherance of our mutual goals and prospects."

Zhang turned to Liu and said, "Come to appreciate what it is that Hannasan has to offer." Liu told Hanna later what he had said. At the time, the translator made no attempt to interpret Zhang's remarks.

Liu thanked Zhang for giving her the opportunity to assist in this great endeavor by the two companies and pledged her undying effort to assist in its successful conclusion. She then took Hanna's hand and led him out to the dance floor.

The music was out of old movies and off old LP records. The sound came over loudspeakers strategically placed around the dance floor: mainly U.S. artists who wowed their fans in the 1950s and 60s. Current American music in the twenty-first century was considered too decadent for sensitive Chinese ears to listen to it. As far as Hanna was concerned, it was the best of what America had created: Frank Sinatra's "I've Got You Under my Skin" and Billy Joel's "A New York State of Mind." He loved every piece, and they were all extremely danceable. More than that, the room was relatively quiet and dark allowing them to enjoy the sound and their dance together.

The floor was an "L" shape. Moving onto it and around to the left put them out of sight of his negotiating crew, plus Zhang and his cronies, because all the executive chairs, cushioned to the extreme, were located down at the far end close to the bar. It really didn't make any difference at this point. A lot of people were dancing, which blocked Hanna's view of that end of the room and the people down there from seeing him. Liu danced him over to the far end of the room in about thirty seconds. Her poise and the way she held his hand to dance spoke to this being the first dance between new friends. She was the perfect lady.

Once around the corner, everything changed.

Hanna could not believe what was happening, it came so fast. Liu wasn't dancing with him any longer. She had completely melted into his body. He would have guessed that he was dancing by himself except that occasionally Liu made a movement that he could feel, and every time she did it, the hard-on he had developed upon seeing her again became harder—as if that were possible.

They made a good-looking couple. It wasn't just a case of Liu being beauty pageant material, which she was. While no Brad Pitt, Hanna could hold his own in the handsome, good looks department. Six foot one, a hundred ninety pounds, muscular, full head of hair, infectious smile—they all combined to stimulate very naughty thoughts in any woman.

Hanna was suddenly oblivious to everything. All that mattered any longer was taking advantage of Liu with this thing between his legs.

Liu had not said a word since they began to dance. Hanna couldn't stand it; he had to say something, if only to allay the suspicions of the Chinese company's management.

"Liu, you are a very pretty young woman."

There is no way Hanna could have described this, but somehow, Liu moved closer to him. He could feel her motor running down below, keeping time with his.

"Hannasan, I don't want to marry any Chinaman. I want an American man like you. I want someone like you to cook for, to have children with, to spend my whole life with, and to make love with forever."

"Hannasan," she was whispering, "take me with you. I will be yours forever."

"Liu," Hanna said. "In the first place, I am very happily married to someone who means the world to me. Secondly, all my children are older than you are. Thirdly, you can't just come with me to America. It is a little bit more complicated than that. It would not be possible to consider anything of that sort without a lot of thought."

Hanna realized he had a problem with this protestation since they were still dancing as tightly as ever. Furthermore, Hanna was as hot as a pistol, and as near as he could determine, so was Liu.

It was at that point that he postulated a new theory:

It does not matter under what circumstances or where a female of the species is born, the characteristics of the gene pool never vary.

He could sense some disappointment in what he had just said, but it just seemed to make Liu more determined. She was gorgeous, and in an effort to let her down politely, Hanna said, "Liu, you look so much like Suzie Wong, do you mind if I call you Suzie when no one else is around?"

"Oh, Hannasan, you know Suzie Wong? She is a woman in old movie. I love to watch old movies. She is one of my favorites. She is very beautiful—the most beautiful person in the world. Yes, yes, I would feel honored if you called me Suzie. There is only one difference between Suzie Wong and me."

Score one for Hanna, he thought.

To keep the conversation going until someone came to his rescue he added, "Well, you are as beautiful, if not more beautiful, as she, so what could possibly be different between the two of you?"

Liu pulled the hand he had around her waist down to where

her gorgeous leg appeared below the slit in her dress that ran almost to her hip. She brought her lips up to his ear and sighed.

"Suzie Wong was prostitute, Hannasan. I am virgin."

Hanna was in trouble.

Five
The Agony of Defeat

Zhang was announcing through the translator that it was nine pm and that everyone must go home to get a good night's sleep. Hanna couldn't believe what was happening. In the first place, it couldn't have been more than ten minutes since he began dancing with Liu, and that was at eight o'clock. Secondly, even if it was nine pm, he still didn't want to go home. Liu had transformed his body into a red-hot poker, and he didn't want it to end.

Sheu, the translator, sensed Hanna's distress and was making her way across the room.

"Hannasan," she said, "Mr. Zhang always concludes his evening activities at nine pm. We must all get to the van to be driven back to the hotel."

Hanna was outraged.

"Driven back to the hotel?" he almost screamed the question. "I don't want to be driven back to the hotel. I want to stay right here. I want the music to continue. I want to keep on dancing. Tell Zhang to stop this crap and put the music back on. Tell him negotiations are over right now if he doesn't do as I say. Tell him I know where he lives."

Sheu with all her female instincts in play took Hanna's arm. "Come," she said. "You must thank Zhang for a wonderful evening and wish that he have very lovely weekend. We must bid him farewell and tell him we look forward to seeing him again on Monday."

Hanna revolted. "Zhang can kiss my ass. I'm going to get that coolie to turn the lights back off and turn the music on. For me, the night is NOT over."

Hanna turned back to grab Liu.

She had vanished.

Hanna turned around to look at Sheu with one of those "What the hell is going on?" looks in his eyes, and Sheu's response was instant.

"Liu lives with her parents, Hannasan," Sheu said. "She must be home by nine thirty pm, and she has six kilometers to ride her bike to get there."

Hanna finally shrugged his shoulders, giving up the struggle. He would never understand Chinese culture. He then turned again and looked at Sheu. The slight hint of a smile on her face told Hanna exactly what she was thinking. With Liu out of the picture, Sheu now had Hanna to herself. He could see her mind scheming, and Hanna was ready to bet she was going to try and talk him into having a drink in the bar at the hotel after they got back there in an effort to divert his attention.

Sheu had told Hanna in a weak moment earlier in the week that her husband was a womanizer, which meant that by now he had probably finished work and was in the process of undressing something on one of the park benches in Shanghai in advance of making himself comfortable with the body, regardless of whose it was.

Hanna sensed that Sheu was just a horny as he was, and the thought of her husband's infidelity became the justification for her pursuit.

Bring it on, Hanna thought. He was ready.

By this time, Hanna had mumbled through all of the damn pleasantries demanded of these occasions and was headed for the door and the van. He got in the passenger seat up front with the driver and leaned back.

Some day he was going to have someone kill Zhang, Hanna thought to himself, (as Johnny Cash had said in Folsom Prison Blues) *just to watch him die.*

His three fellow negotiators climbed into the rear of the van along with the Sheu, the translator, and they were immediately off at raceway speeds with the horn blaring to warn the people up ahead. It had a very tinny sound that most horns on Chinese driven vehicles had. The fact that a large part of Chinese driving instruction was how to keep one hand on the horn at all times gave this driving instrument a half life of about ten-thousand miles. The one in this van was obviously approaching its limit.

One shouldn't drive fast in China in the middle of the night because you could easily kill a dozen bike riders you couldn't see since they never wore anything reflective on their person or on their bike that might reveal to a driver that the biker was using half the car's space. *Besides,* thought Hanna, *by now most of the bike riders were drunk and using up most of the road as they weaved along, having been squatting on their haunches since four thirty this afternoon, drinking some vile Chinese beer concoction.* Hanna didn't really hate the Chinese, as far as he was concerned it was a case of "to each his own." However, if it wasn't for the 200 hundred-million-dollar size of the deal, which would allow Hanna's company to gain a foothold that potentially put them in a dominate position in the largest consumer market in the world, he would have long since written off the prospect of doing business here.

Hanna took one final look around before he closed his eyes. There was Liu again, quietly smiling at him and waving a fond goodbye.

Jesus, she is gorgeous, he thought to himself, as he put his head back to take a quick nap. *Well, it's too early for the night to end. I guess I'll have to move to the fall-back position (plan B),* he thought. He hoped Plan B had climbed on the van with the guys.

He didn't turn around to verify if his concerns were real. He knew she was back there.

Rule One For Avoiding Infidelity While Away From Home On Extended Business Travel

Age and the wisdom of our elders are to always be respected. Therefore, one should always ensure that the host assigned responsibility for entertainment is an old man whose gonads have long since gone dormant because of the overuse of the local liquor which, from time to time, becomes an alternative fuel source for powering diesel engines, coupled with a lifetime devoted to sucking on unfiltered cigarettes. Long-term use of the drugs described allows the old fart to develop a mental immunity to the desires of his guests, bringing him to be concerned only with the thought of getting a good night's sleep.

Six
A Disaster Compounded

The driver and their management escort accompanied Hanna's crew to the front door of the hotel, their beat up van looking like it ought to be towed, sitting there under the portico of a five-star hotel where Mercedes, Jaguars, and Cadillacs comprised the bulk of the automotive population. *Hell, who cared,* he thought. The most incredible vision of all the time he had spent in China had just pedaled off down a dark road on a beat up old bicycle and disappeared into the gloom of a lightless night on the far side of the world.

There was one upside to the evening however—he could drink the bar dry tonight because tomorrow was Saturday. He could sleep in a bit, although he seldom did, and he and the guys could spend a relaxing Saturday sightseeing and sitting in small, expensive tea rooms down on the river's bank. Sheu would be there to brighten events. *What the hell, things weren't so bad that he had to go up to the roof and jump.*

He suggested a nightcap in the bar, but the boys knew that Hanna wanted to be alone with Sheu, so they made their perfunctory excuses and trundled off to the elevator "to retire for the night," as they said. Actually, they were just going up to the skyline bar that rotated on top of the building.

Hanna didn't care. He made for the lobby bar at the end of the room away from the band. The band was playing solid American music, sometimes as good as that which he had been dancing to earlier with Liu, and these guys were live. The Chinese could mimic anything, they just couldn't invent.

Hanna knew most of the songs by heart, since many were from his generation, and in some cases, the band was doing a better job than the original release. There were three horns, a muted trumpet, a saxophone, a clarinet, two guitars—one rhythm and one Hawaiian—a piano, drums, and a singer with a terrific voice and a body to match. Under other circumstances, Hanna would have taken a seat at the edge of the dance floor where they were playing, but for now, all Hanna wanted was a quiet, peaceful corner where he could discuss "business" with Sheu. As they walked along he noted, contrary to everything that his grandmother had ever taught him, that there was not one starving Chinaman in the place.

The hotel lobby was huge, at least three stories high, very wide, and half a block long. It was furnished with fascinating period furniture, and the place had been decorated to look old English countryside. Hanna always wondered where the Chinese got this stuff. The walls were paneled. People (there had to be at least a hundred and fifty in the lobby enjoying after dinner aperitifs, coffee, and such) all spoke quietly, almost in whispers. Shops ringed the outer perimeter of the upper two floors, all European or New York boutiques and almost all of them still open since it was only nine thirty on a Friday night. *Crap*, Hanna thought, *no American woman traveling with her husband would have begun to consider dinner while Coco Channels was still open.* The place was bustling, a microcosm of quiet bedlam.

Hanna was pretty international himself because of all his travels. He spoke three languages, and he must have recognized at least twenty-five different languages being spoken as he strolled across the lobby with Sheu on his arm. His mind drifted back to his homeland where most people spoke only English. The joke was: What do you call a person who speaks three or more languages? (Multilingual). What do you call a person who speaks two languages? (Bilingual). And what do you call a person who only speaks one language? (American). If you walked into the lobby of any five-star hotel in a foreign land be it Paris, Rome, Berlin, or Moscow you would hear all the major languages of the world being spoken at once. About the only place you would experience that in the U.S.A. was in New York.

To his pleasant surprise, Sheu did not appear to be at all uncomfortable with the way she was being accommodated. Her slim frame, obvious mastery of languages (after all she was on the arm of either an American or a Russian), her tailored look in a suit that, if it wasn't, sure looked like an Oscar de la Renta, cut knee length to reveal extremely well formed gams, and a walk on three-inch heels that gave just a hint of sex being (how did the questionnaires always put it) "somewhat important" to her lifestyle, all spoke to her maturity and a healthy lust for "the best" however one might define that term. Liu had begun to dim in Hanna's mind as he began to assess the situation more closely.

The bartender or waiter, whatever you wanted to call someone working a room in China where the least expensive thing you could order ran about fifteen dollars a drink (with no upside limit), helped them onto the divan and arranged the cushions before they sat down. *The Chinese, Hanna thought, could earn more here in one night because of the international crowds over tipping than the automotive guy down at the factory where he had just come from could in a year.* In addition to his loathing for the suck-up attitude the Chinese had, he had trouble dealing with the constant smile and decaying yellow or green teeth of probably close to half the male population due to their chain smoking and indifference to utilizing a tooth brush.

Usually, they spoke English perfectly, even though they uttered only a few words of it, and usually they were quietly observing every movement you made and recording every word you said in some unobtrusive part of the hotel on instructions from the local government. These people could speak English better than his translator.

Visiting Westerners may not have understood that Zhang was a member of the local government, because it was never mentioned. Most Westerners didn't realize that, in Communist countries, the inner circle comprised all of the political brownnosers to the national party in the capital of the country. Thus, the guys who ran the country also had the best jobs as a reward for their loyalty to the party. Hanna had begun to notice that with each successive trip it didn't matter what city you were in you always had a room on one of two floors, so, beginning with his third trip, he just began to assume that these rooms were wired. After that, things got real easy. If he wanted to keep something confidential, he just discussed it during a walk in the park. On the other hand, if he wanted the local politburo to know how supremely pissed off he was, he just talked in his sleep and everybody fell all over themselves trying to fix his problem the following day. Sometimes you could see they were having a problem trying to avoid disclosing how they had learned about his issues.

The president of every company in town was a member of the local politburo. The fact that there were five-hundred members in town was the reason why no decisions had ever been made in the history of the community and also the reason why eyeglasses were the last thing the world could recall the Chinese inventing.

The waiter's sole duty was to make sure that you over drank and that the directional recorder in his vest pocket caught every word you said during the course of the evening. Your entire conversation, on tape, would be sent to a central bureau office, where it would be translated and analyzed overnight. By the following morning, everyone in town knew everything you had said over the course of the previous evening. The waiter never left a corner alcove built strategically to the rear of the seating area. He handed all drink orders to a female coolie, who brought them out to serve.

Hanna decided against talking about some phony plot to overthrow the government, preferring instead to concentrate on porking the translator, who, he suspected, was just as horny as he was. She sure had exuded body heat at each chance to grab his arm as they walked along into the hotel.

"What will it be Sheu?" he asked. "It's Friday night, and we're both out of town. Coffee and a liqueur? A glass of wine perhaps? The world is your oyster, and Hannasan is here to make sure there is a pearl inside of every one you open."

Sheu smiled and ordered wine, the most expensive on the list as near as Hanna could recall. He ordered a double Chivas Regal (twenty years old), his long-time favorite. *What the hell,* he thought, *this was all going on an unlimited expense account.*

Sheu was no different than any other Chinese woman—in Hanna's view, she was no different than any other woman, period. Somehow he sensed that Sheu was going to demonstrate some mood tonight. It was in the way she moved. She began to speak.

"Hannasan," she said, placing her hand on his knee, "I know you are attracted to Liu. She is beautiful, young, and innocent, and she wants an American for a husband. But, she could be dangerous for you. She is better known in this town than you realize, and if you become the first for her—she's a virgin— you might have to explain to her Chinese boyfriend. He's a heavyweight wrestler training for the Chinese Olympic team, and he's very, very strong."

The drinks had arrived. Hanna reached over, grabbed both glasses, handed her glass of wine to her, toasted to their evening just beginning, and took a long sip of his twenty-year-old scotch. This woman was more insightful than he realized. More than that, he observed, she was absolutely right. He had to start giving her more credit despite the fact that he was going to put some heavy moves on her before the evening was over.

Sheu returned the toast, put down her glass, and returned her hand to his knee. *She is looking better all the time,* Hanna thought, and it wasn't just a case, as Willie Nelson used to put it, of all the girls getting prettier at closing time. Hanna decided to explore the background of this woman a little bit farther.

"Sheu," he said, "I don't mean to be offensive, but you don't really look Chinese. What I mean to say is, you look a little Chinese but you don't have many Chinese features. For instance, your face. It is not round, but rather it is more an oval like many European women."

Her expression told Hanna that she took the remark as a complement.

Sheu smiled an intriguing smile.

"The reason for that is simple, Hannasan. Even though I live in Shanghai and teach English at the university, I was born in northeastern China in the city of Dandong."

She didn't have to go any further. Hanna already knew the answer. Dandong lay in the very northeast coast of China across the Yalu River from North Korea. Hanna had been there a number of times, and half the people in that part of the country had European features like Sheu. This part of China had, from time-to-time over the centuries, been overrun by everything from the Russians and Mongols to the Japanese. One other fascinating feature of the city was the old bridge that the U.S. Air Force had bombed to oblivion during the Korean War. The piers still stood, running across the river. The Chinese had just ignored them and built a new bridge to North Korea.

In that part of the world, half the population had some Russian blood in them, and to a certain extent, all things considered, that was not all that bad.

"You have Russian blood in you," Hanna said.

The reply was instantaneous. "Yes, Hannasan, I do. My father is Russian."

Jesus, Hanna thought, *I'm not just going to seduce a Chinese Communist tonight; I'm going to pork a Russian one as well.* Hanna couldn't believe his luck.

Life was good.

Their glasses were approaching empty. The waiter reappeared and suggested they might enjoy a refill. Both Sheu and Hanna agreed. They were both beginning to feel the body heat. Sheu was no longer just holding her hand on Hanna's knee, she was stroking it. Hanna's arm, which he had placed up on the back of the sofa, began to slowly drift down—first to Sheu's shoulder, then to her back, her waist, and ultimately to what ass she had.

God, why didn't she have a bit more ass? Hanna thought, *she would be perfect if she did.*

One thing Hanna did notice: Sheu had not protested the slow encroachment upon her body, and as a matter of fact, her stroking of his knee began to extend to the upper part of his leg almost up to his crotch. *She's sitting right on the cusp,* Hanna thought. *Another half an inch, and she is going to be stroking more than my leg and from that point on, there is no turning back.*

Sheu leaned towards him, and Hanna just let her come. He loved her ruby red lips. Chinese women always wore makeup on dates, and Hanna just assumed that Sheu was beguiled by the fact that it was Friday night with a handsome foreigner at her side.

You have such a fascinating way of reading women, Hanna thought in that vain way he had, as Sheu very slowly began to move closer. Hanna started doing the same. Suddenly there was no space left between them, and the only thing saving them from what should have been the shocked stares of others in the room was the fact that Hanna had chosen the perfect seat for just such a development.

The embrace got longer and harder. Sheu's back began to arch to the point where Hanna no longer had to pull her toward him; her back was arching all on its own. Sheu was so hot she was about to go orgasmic. Hanna pulled away slightly, moved his hand up to the base of her neck, pulled her close to his cheek so that his lips were right at her ear lobe.

"Why don't we retire for the night?" he asked.

Sheu was immediately on her feet. She grabbed his hand and made for the elevator. All Hanna could do was follow.

His last words were to the waiter whose name he had noted from his tag when he served the second round of drinks. "Tang, please close out our tab and add 50 percent for yourself."

Tang grinned like the proverbial Cheshire Cat. "Thank you

Hannasan. You have wonderful evening." The guy was salivating as he took a second hard look at Sheu.

The wait for the elevator was interminable. There were several couples ahead of them, and Hanna was beginning to wonder if they could all get on at one time. Sheu kept moving from side to side, standing first on one foot then switching to the other. She was breathing heavily, almost to the point where she could be heard, and her chest kept rising and falling. She kept her arm wrapped closely around Hanna's waist as though she needed him to maintain her balance. Hanna knew exactly what was happening. She was just about to come all by herself.

The elevator door opened, and everyone got on. Hanna made a move for them to get on as well, but Sheu grabbed him tightly and stepped back. All the Chinamen and their wives looked at him questioningly, so he bowed and quietly said that they would catch the next one. All the women scowled as soon as they looked at Sheu. One Chinaman grinned. The others all appeared to be completely disinterested.

The bell announcing a second elevator going up chimed before the doors to the first had closed. Sheu quickly grabbed him, hopped on, hit the "close door" button, pushed the forty-fourth floor button, and practically nailed him to the wall.

Christ, Hanna thought, *how am I going to get us to my room before she gets naked?*

Fortunately, the elevators were fast and they arrived before she let him out of the lip lock. She raced down the hallway hauling Hanna behind her, and then stood at the door breathing hard while Hanna fumbled with the key to get into the room.

The door opened.

Services

The word in Chinese for "ice" is "no ice."

Unpublished works by William B. Hanna circa 1996

Seven
Jesus! Why Did Mother Give Birth?

Sheu was hauling him over to the bed and dragging him down on top of her when she suddenly jerked upright. She was still panting, but she managed to say, "Hannasan, please excuse me one second," as she rose up and ran for the bathroom.

Hanna decided to relax. He took his jacket off, the upper half of an Armani suit, recently purchased in New York where he did most of his shopping for outerwear and lit a rare cigarette. He then wandered over to the window where the drapes were still wide open and took in the view of the city spread out before him for miles until it hit the edge of the Yangtze River. From there, one could see the lights of the river traffic moving up and down in a never ending line; those heading eastbound towards Shanghai and the ocean moving twice as fast as those moving upstream to the west, fighting the massive currents of the river which were twice as strong as the Mississippi.

Sheu was still in the bathroom, so Hanna decided to open the minibar and pour a split of champagne for her. He then opened and poured a Chivas Regal for himself and added a little water from the bottled stock also in the miniature cooler. He looked to see if there was any ice, but as with all Chinese establishments, there was none. The fun thing about drinking from the minibar in a Chinese hotel room was that nothing you picked came at a charge of less than thirty dollars a bottle, including the water. Champagne and fine scotches were much more than that.

Hanna went back to the window and took a last look then sat down in one of the huge stuffed chairs every room contained. He loved five-star hotels. He took one last draw on the smoke, butted it out, and began to wonder what Sheu was doing. She had been in the bathroom for at least twenty minutes now, and he had only heard a sound once or twice. They almost sounded as though they were moans and he hoped that nothing was wrong.

God, he hoped not.

He moved towards the bathroom door and was about to knock and inquire as to her well-being when the door opened. Sheu was standing there looking about as despondent as a PETA lover whose favorite dog had just been shot. She had gone completely cold.

"Sheu," Hanna said, "Whatever is wrong?"

Tears welled up in Sheu's eyes. "Oh, Hannasan," she said, "I'm so sorry."

"For heaven's sake, sorry about what?" Hanna said.

"I just began my period," Sheu said. "We can't make love now."

"Hold on, Sheu, what do you mean we can't make love? Having a period does not mean you can't make love. Just put your arms around me and hold me tight, and everything will be just fine," Hanna said.

He was in a panic. What the hell was he going to do with this hugely enlarged organ between his legs if she didn't allow him to get it off?

"No, Hannasan, no. I cannot do this. My period is too much. We must wait until it ends. Maybe next weekend. Can you do that?"

Hanna realized that the woman was distraught, and her mind was made up.

"Of course," he said smoothly, lightly kissing her brow, as he said, "We can wait until next weekend." Sheu was not going to be talked into bed tonight.

It occurred to Hanna that at this moment something chivalrous was probably appropriate.

"Why don't you enjoy this glass of champagne that I just poured for you? After all, we don't want to throw everything out the window now that we have restored caution to its place."

Hanna knew Sheu would never get that. The Chinese had little sense of humor, no appreciation for satire or sarcasm, and dry humor was completely lost on them.

Hanna could see that Sheu was despondent. Not that she would ever tell him to his face, but Hanna sensed she wanted his body badly enough that she was ready to forget her mother's remonstrations and climb in under the covers with him. Hanna could see, however, that she wasn't going to do it.

"I can't, Hannasan. I must go to my room. The next week won't be nice for me. Besides, right now I don't feel well."

Hanna could see that Sheu was telling the truth. She didn't look well. Hanna could see that a good night's sleep was the only thing that was going to help her.

"Can you take me to my room, Hannasan?" Sheu asked.

Always the gentleman to the end, Hanna agreed.

Never slam the door on tomorrow's opportunity, he thought. Besides, not doing this is what ended up putting a close friend of Hanna's on parole for three years when he was young. The buddy and a girlfriend got together one night, they made out, and his buddy fell asleep. The girlfriend did not like being ignored, so she screamed rape, and he never made it beyond the judge's preliminary hearing. Better to be a gentleman than face the possibility of going to jail especially in China.

The problem was Hanna had no Plan C.

It didn't take long to get to Sheu's room, which was just two floors below his, and the hour was growing late, so they had little delay at the elevators. When she got her door unlocked, she turned around longingly and gave Hanna a huge, tight hug.

"I'm sorry, Hannasan. As soon this over we will make love. For now, I must go to bed. Goodnight, Hannasan."

Hanna kissed her gently on the cheek, and with his hand upon her ass (such as it was), he slowly eased her into the room, backed away, and closed the door.

Goodnight, Sheu. Now what do I do? Hanna thought. He shook his head and climbed back on the elevator. The spell had been broken. All he wanted now was a bottle of the most alcoholic liquor that had ever been distilled in the history of the world.

Back in his room, Hanna swilled down what was left of the drink he had poured before Sheu came down with the monthlies. He grabbed the door of the fridge or minibar and extracted another Chivas Regal. He was about to slam it shut when he thought, *what the hell,* and grabbed a second miniature. It was time for a double.

He mixed it with some water and took a sip. *Goddammit,* he thought, *I want some ice.* He picked up the phone and hit the button for room service.

"Ah so, good evening, Mr. Hanna, how can I be of service this evening?" the sickly, smooth, sugary voice came back over the phone.

Hanna was in no mood for pleasantries. His evening had been destroyed twice within a matter of hours by events that no one should ever have to endure.

"I want some ice," Hanna practically screamed into the phone. "I am sick and tired of being served drinks in this so-called five-star hotel without ice!"

"Ah, Mista Hanna, you want ice?" was the reply. "So sorry, no ice."

Hanna smashed the phone down.

He cast his eyes towards the ceiling. "Jesus Christ, give me strength."

He said it so softly a lesser god would have actually thought he was praying.

Rule Two For Avoiding Infidelity While away from Home on Extended Business Travel

Fertile women in their child-bearing years represent the hope for the future of mankind. Unfortunately, a contradiction in terms arises with women possessing this capability since certain conditions go hand in hand with it that limit their ability to fornicate, notwithstanding their desire to be with child. Therefore, the business traveler in an effort to avoid infidelity at all costs should always concentrate on attempting to seduce this type of woman. The woman's status ensures that the odds of being struck by lightning are more likely than any sexual gratification the traveler may be contemplating.

Eight
What to Do When Left to
One's Own Devices

Hanna woke up Saturday morning with a bit of a headache. Not a bad headache, since he had practiced closing the bar (or emptying the room's minibar) far too many times over the years for the booze to have much effect on him. Besides, he was a fan of Foster Brooks (renowned for his ability to act like the consummate drunk) who had once opined that he would never be able to understand how anyone could wake up in the morning knowing that was the best they were going to feel all day.

My kind of man, Hanna thought.

He reflected on several things, finally deciding that the events of the previous evening confirmed as an irrefutable truth God's hatred for him. It was, he had concluded, the only reason why every opportunity that fell into his lap last night had disintegrated before his eyes. Those thoughts out of the way, he decided to make some coffee on the in-room coffee machine in the hope that it and a cigarette would improve his mood. While the coffee brewed, he decided he would call the troops and discuss some preliminary arrangements for them to all get together later for breakfast and to spend some time in Nanjing being tourists.

His mind wandered over the group of ragtags that were

accompanying him on this trip. Clifford, his vice president of sales and marketing was the most likely to be up at this hour. His job was filling the golf course with prospective customers, and many a morning he was on the tee box with a foursome at seven. It was now eight thirty. He should be up.

Hanna had the operator connect him to Cliff's room.

The phone rang seven times before it was picked up.

"Hello," the voice said with a groan. There was an echo in the room and he thought he could hear something like water running. Hanna guessed he had to be in the bathroom.

"Hey man! What's going on?" Hanna said. "Time to rise and shine. We got a whole basket of goodies waiting to be handed to us out on the boardwalk or whatever that wooden thing is down by the river. When you going to be ready to go down and get some breakfast?"

No sooner had Hanna said the word "breakfast" than he heard a horrific sound; something like a volcano erupting.

Jesus Christ, Cliff had a case of the Chinese banquet blues, Hanna thought.

"I can't make it man." The words came strictly from the mouth; the nose was completely jammed with something. "I feel like crap. As a matter of fact that's probably all that I am. I've been on the john since midnight."

Hanna thought, *the guy had ignored his e-mail and now he was going to pay the price.*

"You butt head," Hanna said, "I told you not to drink that live crap. Oh well, don't worry; you'll be back on your feet by Wednesday. Everything usually clears up in about five days."

Hanna hung up and scratched the guy from the itinerary for the day. There was no sense trying to call him back before tomorrow. Hell, he thought, he's not going to have the strength to hang up the phone for at least that long. His vice president for sales and marketing had just gone incommunicado for the next forty-eight hours.

Hanna took a sip of coffee. *Days like this are so refreshing,* he thought. *Time to restore one's soul.* He had the operator dial the VP for engineering's room. Rudolf was a poor substitute for Clifford; however, Hanna's theory always was any port in a storm. It was just that, if Rudolf was going to be in the group, Hanna wanted someone else to enjoy the day with when his engineer started acting like he was wall paper. The phone rang a dozen times with no answer. He hung up and called the operator to have her dial the room a second time. Hanna assumed she must have dialed a wrong number for a room from which the guests had already left. The phone continued to ring a second time, and he was all but ready to hang up and try again when the receiver was lifted from the phone.

The almost inaudible voice on the other end said, "Who is it?"

Hanna's response was to say, "Who do you think it would be butt head? How many other people in Nanjing would be calling your silly ass on a Saturday morning, other than me? Sorry about that, Rudolf, I was just calling to see when you might want to meet for breakfast? It's Saturday morning, we have the day off, the sun is shining, for some odd reason the sky is actually a dull blue, and we need to get up and get going!"

All he heard on the other end of the phone was a moan. As near as Hanna could figure, the comment back was "Let me die in peace." Rudolf hung up.

Jaime had the same problem as the other two.

After Jaime had finished pleading for mercy and a swift death, Hanna said, "I didn't think you had drunk any of that crap like the other two. How come you're in the same condition?"

Jaime's response was, "You remember those drunken shrimp they were serving?"

Oh Jesus! Hanna thought. Those things were skinned live from their shells, then set on a flat plate while a small glass of that local alcoholic witches' brew was splashed over them. It was supposed to cook them, but there was no way they could have cooked (marinated actually) unless they were completely submerged.

Those damn things were still wiggling around on the plate when people grabbed them with their chopsticks. Even though Jaime deserved everything he got, Hanna felt sorry for him. Hanna could never grasp the stupidity of mankind, and you didn't have to be Chinese for him to feel this way. At the same time, Jaime was too young to die.

"I suppose you didn't use the handiwipes after you shook everyone's hand before sitting down to dinner either, did you?" Hanna said.

All that seemed to emanate from the phone was a quiet sob.

Hanna hung up.

Let me see, he thought. *That leaves Sheu and me. Hey, there is nothing like having your own personal guide, plus she is not unattractive, and who knows, maybe her travails of the previous evening were only momentary. One could hope.* He picked up the phone and once again asked the hotel operator to dial a room for him.

For the fourth time this morning Hanna heard a groan. "Herrow" was the response to the ringing. It then slipped into Mandarin but he thought that he heard something that sounded like "doctor" somewhere along in the sentence.

"Sheu," he said. "Is that you? What's the matter? I have been waiting all morning to hear your sunny voice."

"Oh, Hannasan" was the response. "I am so sorry, but I am very sick. A doctor is coming soon to give me medicine."

"Well golly, I hope the medicine works, we have a lot of sightseeing to do today. When do you think you will be up and around?" Hanna said.

"Oh, Hannasan," Sheu said, "I cannot go with you today. I can't even stand up right now I so cramped. You will have to go without me today. I am so sorry, Hannasan, but I must sleep today. Can you call me tonight to see how I am, Hannasan? I will miss you if I don't hear from you before nighttime comes. Good bye, Hannasan. Please call me later."

The phone went dead.

Nine
The Agony of Defeat

Hanna sat there in the big padded chair and looked at the phone for a full thirty seconds. He couldn't believe it. He was oh for four on a beautiful Saturday morning. All dressed up and no place to go.

Actually, he was still wandering around in his underwear.

He poured himself another cup of coffee and decided to get cleaned up. He always had his best ideas in the shower. Maybe some divine intervention would occur while he was in there this morning. If nothing happened, he could always break the window to his room and jump. Life would end instantly, and he would then be able to extract revenge on the four butt heads he was traveling with. *He'd teach them a lesson*, he thought.

He brushed his teeth, shaved, and climbed into the shower. He took a long one, trying not to swallow too much water, which was the reason why most places in China didn't serve ice. If it wasn't bottled, it was contaminated. It didn't matter where you were.

"Oh, you can drink water," the front desk clerk would tell you. "This is a five-star hotel. We purify all water. May won tee (no problem)" they would say.

Of course, what you didn't know was that the whole system had been down for three days, the purified water supply was exhausted two days ago, and you were sucking up crap direct from the Yangtze River, the biggest cesspool in China and, by extension, the world.

He had just started to dress, when he realized he was really hungry. *Screw it*, he decided and called room service. He didn't have anyone to sit and enjoy breakfast with in the morning room downstairs anyway, so why not eat in his room and let the solitude and loneliness of the whole ugly mess slowly seep into his bones and make him fill with self pity at the lot in life he had drawn.

"Very good, Mr. Hanna. Your breakfast will be served at ten thirty am," said room service on the other end of the line.

He finished dressing, lit another cigarette (his second of the day), poured another cup of coffee (his third since waking up), and stood at the window.

He was just about to start complaining to himself about the slow room service when there was a quiet knock at the door. *Ah, finally*, he thought and three minutes early as he walked quickly towards the waiting meal of eggs, bacon, toasted English muffins, orange juice, hash browns, and plenty of jams and marmalade. Moreover, he had ordered everything double, and he closed the door to the bathroom just going by it to open the door to the room. That way the butt head doing the serving would think there was some gorgeous thing waiting in anticipation to come out and enjoy her swain once the guy left.

Screw these bastards, Hanna thought. A guy had to have some fun now and again, and he found it an enjoyable sidebar screwing with their minds.

He grabbed the door knob and swung it wide—

Liu was standing in front of him, smiling that radiant smile she had.

Time

The setting of the atomic clock in Washington, DC, to account for the nano-seconds of time lost as a result of the slowing rate of the earth's rotation is actually performed by marking the precise instant at which a Chinaman will knock on your door to announce it is time for lunch.

Unpublished works by William B. Hanna circa 1996

Ten
The Thrill of Winning

"Hello, Hannasan. May I come in?"

She didn't wait for an answer.

Closing the door slowly behind her, she quietly walked up to Hanna, put her lips an inch from his, closed her eyes, and waited.

It didn't often happen, but Hanna realized he was unable to talk. It was a beautiful morning, and it was going to be a wonderful summer day, not like the one they found themselves in the day they had arrived. He had dressed in tourist chic: a soft knit golf shirt open one button at the neck and a pair of five-hundred dollar Armani slacks, double pleated, with Ferragammo shoes and a matching Gucci belt that perfectly complemented his outerwear.

All that said, Liu had out done him. She was wearing expensive denims with a midriff blouse that revealed between the two a waist of no more than eighteen inches. She had boosted everything by wearing a pair of three-inch heels that lifted her body and arched her back. She was also wearing a not inexpensive necklace and matching earrings. She had to have every dollar she had earned over the past year in this outfit. Everything about her was absolutely pristine, virginal, and magnetic. She stood in front of Hanna, and the look said it all: I'm yours if you want me.

Hanna did the only thing that any experienced reprobate

would do. He slowly dropped his hands to her waist, gently closed them around it, pulled her to him, and in the process, locked her lips onto his. Once again, her body melted into his, except that this time they weren't dancing and there was nobody around to stop the party.

They both broke away from each other for a second to catch their breath and were instantly together again. The feelings they passed to each other were more than passion, more than lust. They were absolutely inside each other, and the feelings were electric. They were a train moving a hundred miles an hour. There was no stopping them.

The doorbell rang.

"Ah so, room service," said a voice.

They both ignored him.

The bell rang again, this time accompanied by a loud knock.

"Ah so, room service, Mr. Hanna,"

The third time the bell didn't ring; the knocking just became more insistent.

Hanna gave up. He looked at his watch. It was ten thirty am.

For the moment the spell had been broken.

"Let's have breakfast Liu."

He slowly let her go and walked reluctantly to the door, and jerked it open with a glare at the coolie with the tray on wheels delivering two exquisite breakfasts.

Liu had gone over to one of the huge overstuffed chairs and sat quietly on the arm, while Hanna directed the waiter on how he wanted him to set up the meal. His ardor had cooled, but that would not be a problem. They had all day to get to know one another. *Everything would be fine,* Hanna thought to himself.

Hanna signed the check, adding 25 percent. The son-of-a-bitch would have gotten 50 percent if he had just left without insisting on serving the meal when the people in the room refused to answer the door. But, the coolies working the menial jobs in these hotels had absolutely no imagination and no ability to think circumstances to their logical conclusion. After all, it was probably a consortium of these guys who had invented the four way on-off switch and the single speed rheostat, both of which Hanna had run into during his travels in China.

When he turned around, Liu was sitting there, smiling broadly and admiring the array of food set in front of her.

"Hannasan, how did you know to order breakfast for me?" she asked.

"Liu, you wouldn't believe me if I told you. Let's just sit and talk and enjoy the meal. If I told you I ordered it solely on the basis of a prayer that you might appear to enjoy it with me, you wouldn't believe me. Please sit and eat up."

The aroma coming off the food made Hanna realize just how hungry he was. Liu had obviously not eaten either, and she competed with him in seeing who could devour their serving the faster. The most important thing, however, was the fact that she ate with the flatware that came with the meal rather than chopsticks. The thing that amazed him the most was the way she was putting away the food, considering the exquisite body she fit it into.

Idly, Hanna asked how long she had been on the bus to get to the hotel this morning. The answer gave him the answer to his earlier question.

"Oh, I did not take the bus, Hannasan. I rode my bike. It only took two hours to get here."

No wonder the Chinese lived as long as the Westerners if they didn't smoke, Hanna thought. There probably wasn't one ounce of fat on her frame and every fiber of her being was muscle.

Hanna couldn't wait for later.

Rule Three For Avoiding Infidelity While Away From Home On Extended Business Travel

The fact that there are millions of underfed and malnourished in Africa and the Far East currently having insufficient food to keep them in good health represents a blight upon the face of the earth. Consequently, it is recommended that the business traveler use this concept as a model for life away from home. Remaining underfed at all times improves the odds that hunger pangs will overwhelm the traveler's ability to distinguish between the most basic needs of the body, causing him to order food when he should be concentrating on sexual gratification. It is also advisable, should the traveler mistakenly conclude that food is required to sustain bodily function, to order room service for delivery three hours late.

Eleven
Saturday in the Park

The tenor of the moment had changed. Good food, a perfect day, and intimate conversation had made them enamored of one another but the closeness they felt for each other begged for some air and a freshness the room did not contain.

"Let's walk down to the river Hannasan. It is very beautiful down there and there are many shops where you can buy souvenirs, have something to eat, and just sit and enjoy the scenery."

Hanna thought it was odd how her language could become so much better when she took the time to think about what she was saying. Her knowledge of the English language was almost flawless.

"Let's do it Liu. Show me what I don't know. Let's explore."

They kissed, put their arms around each other, and headed for the elevator.

There was plenty of time for the really serious muscle stuff later, Hanna thought. For the moment, being together was enough. And, at this moment, they were the best-looking couple in all of China.

The elevator reached the main floor, and they got off and walked across the lobby toward the exit. Once they were outside, they both took in a breath of fresh air and admired the day. The sky was blue, the breeze was light, and the dirt and pollution from a million power plants was gone. They looked at each other and began to walk—first, across the very wide portico where luxury automobiles and limousines arrived to drop their passengers. Heavy carved stone marked steps and exit sidewalks that continued from there on down to the street.

In a Chinese tradition that had been translated down through the generations, nothing in China was ever completely finished. Something was always there in the way of what would otherwise be a pristine view. This was ordered by some Chinese quack holding himself forth as some guru who knew how to avoid evil spirits while constructing the building.

At this point, it was a two-foot trench in the ground running three quarters of the way across the sidewalk, dirt, and small stone laying on the finished portion of the walkway, and absolutely no sign or a sawhorse to protect people from stepping right into the hole. Hanna took one look at it, and with Liu in hand walked over to the valet at the front door.

Using Liu as the interpreter, Hanna pointed out how dangerous that hole was to the well-being of the hotel guests in particular and the population in general. The valet took everything very seriously and assured Hanna through Liu that the hotel would have everything either repaired or blockaded so that no one could be hurt. It would be done today. Chop! Chop!

Having had the satisfaction of reprimanding this heathen, Hanna with Liu in tow started down the sidewalk to the street. Liu even showed Hanna her bicycle which was tied up like some old horse to what was some kind of hitching post. Hanna asked if it shouldn't be locked (it was a nice looking machine), but Liu reassured him that no one in China would ever take another person's bike. Other things maybe; bike, no. It didn't take Hanna long, with his vivid imagination to begin equating this morality to the law of the Old West. You could take anything another man owned and get away with it, but you never stole his horse unless you had a death wish.

Hanna saw the package sitting in the basket of the bike, and, out of curiosity he inquired as to what it might be.

"Sneakers, Hannasan," Liu replied. "I use to ride bike from home this morning. I change into heels when I get here."

Of course, Hanna thought. *How was she going to pedal two hours in high heels.*

They were soon immersed in each other's life and personality, talking about anything and everything. They walked the town. About one thirty, breakfast began to wear off, and they stopped along the river boardwalk at what eventually became one of the most fascinating combination tea room/restaurants Hanna had ever had the pleasure of dining in.

The food was exquisite—expertly prepared with a Westerner's palate in mind and tasty beyond description. They didn't eat facing each other; they sat next to each other so that they could rub their bodies together. Hanna had told Liu to order a table for four for two so that they could do this. The restaurant was busy so he handed her a five-hundred Yuan note (about sixty dollars) but it had the same impact as handing the maitre d' a hundred dollar bill at Twenty One in New York. Giving the maitre d' that much got them the best table in the place: comfortable, air conditioned, beautiful view of the water as if from an island in the middle of things, quiet yet very much caught up in the surrounding activity that is so much a part of a good restaurant.

They were all over each other's bodies in between bites of food to the horror of all who happened to notice; however, it didn't seem to bother Liu and Hanna sure wasn't going to let it bother him.

All of a sudden, Liu turned serious.

"Hannasan, I am applying for a passport. It will be necessary when I begin traveling to America and other places outside of China. I have a problem, however, since I don't have any English first names, which the government insists everyone have."

It was true. Hanna had noticed that every time he filled out the customs form on entering China that for all Chinese nationals the government requested their names both in the English format they had adopted for international travel as well as their birth names in Chinese characters.

"Hannasan," Liu said, "You told me that you have granddaughters. What are their names? I would like to get ideas from all my friends on what names they think would be good for me to have."

Hanna pondered this one for a few moments but eventually he said to himself, *what the hell.* Liu would probably be required by some ancient tradition to adopt the suggestions of her parents or their guru.

Hanna said, "My granddaughters all have several names. I suggest you just consider the first one of each"

"What are they, Hannasan?" Liu asked.

"They are Anne, Lady, and Mary," Hanna replied.

"Those are beautiful names," Liu said. "I think I will adopt the English given name as Lady Anne Mary. That is pretty—Lady Anne Mary Liu. I like it very much."

"Nah," Hanna said quietly to himself. "It'll never happen."

Twelve
And You Think Bhopal Was a Tragedy

After lunch, they returned to being tourists. At least Hanna did, and Liu was there to show him everything and explain what it all meant.

Hanna bought some souvenir stuff and arranged to have it delivered to his room for an extra ten Yuan (about a dime). His wife had once had three dresses sewn for her in Singapore at one of the twenty-story high rise malls with a million shops on every floor. The dresses were hanging in their suite at the Shangra La, cleaned, pressed, and ready to wear when she got back from her afternoon of shopping.

Some countries thought they knew what service was. Others truly provided it.

Chinese culture was a mess, and the warlords who had created their dynasties with a hundred concubines per male in the family approximated the lifestyle of the Saudi Sheiks with their harems. The problem in China was that there were so many of them that they ate everything the land contained. A deer was mythology in China. Hanna had seen wire statues overgrown with the local ivy and trimmed to look like the animal one time in Northern China, but when he asked the local Chinamen where the deer lived in the countryside, which was almost completely devoid of forest land, the man said he had never seen one. Furthermore, although he didn't know for sure, he didn't think there were any.

Hanna was disinclined to be concerned. The people had made their bed, so let them lie in it. Besides, Liu just kept looking more beautiful as the afternoon became early evening.

"What do you think, Liu? Should we think about heading back to the hotel? We can have something to eat and then go up to the room. On the other hand, if you want, we can go straight to the room and have room service," Hanna said.

"I like room service better, Hannasan," Liu said with an impish smile.

She probably had some clothes and makeup inside the bag she was carrying, Hanna thought. It was obvious she had no intention of going home tonight.

Hanna could hardly wait.

Liu had made him the center of her universe today, and the evening was about to begin with a young, beautiful woman who exercised by riding a bicycle for two hours every day.

Hanna couldn't help but laugh to himself: the coroner for the city would have a difficult time identifying his remains in the morning after Liu was finished with him.

They were almost back to the hotel, coming up the drive to the portico. For some reason, Hanna was turned around looking back up the street from where they had come, when he heard the first shriek. Hanna's hand was left limp and alone as Liu took off down the street and up the drive. It was almost dark, but when he looked up he glimpsed a bicycle with a man on it about to start down the far side of the portico. There was a package in the basket. Liu was running after him screaming something in Chinese. The valet had just started to do something about the abuse of this Chinese woman's bike, when a second scream came belting out of Liu's mouth.

Liu had run up the sidewalk alongside the hotel's entrance way. Hanna had a sinking feeling before he could really see her. His body sagged as he did. Liu was lying on the ground, gripping her ankle and writhing in pain, next to that goddamned hole the local meat heads had left open.

He raced over to the valet, and after screaming a dozen profanities at him in English, told him to get the hotel doctor. Chinese was flying everywhere. Guests coming and going from the hotel were trying to comfort Liu. She was in agony.

After about fifteen minutes, the doctor appeared with his bag. He took one look at Liu, grabbed her leg, and wiggled her ankle immediately causing a scream the likes of which Hanna hadn't heard since the birth of his second son. It took thirty-six hours for his second son to be born.

He sat down on the curb while the doctor worked on Liu.

The next thirty minutes played out in slow motion. Liu was eventually carried into the hotel medical emergency center, which every five-star hotel had at this point. She was treated with injections for pain. Her father had been called and in time appeared in a beat-up old truck a friend was driving. Liu now had some kind of bandage on the leg that applied tension to the break. Everyone stood around talking in Chinese. Hanna was the last person to be in the loop.

Hanna offered Liu his hand and she squeezed it, but it was obvious that the drugs were beginning to take effect. Her eyes were beginning to droop. Her father, through someone in the room, thanked Hanna for being so helpful in assisting his daughter through this crisis. He said it was no longer necessary for Hanna to remain as he and his friend would get her home safely.

"Jesus Christ," Hanna said to himself. He couldn't believe what had just happened. He would have leaned over and told Liu he would replace her bike, but she was already asleep.

Ten minutes later, everyone was gone.

Two minutes after that, Hanna was sitting in the lobby of a five-star hotel on a Saturday night all by himself. He still looked great, dressed to nines in expensive European attire as he was, the only problem was there wasn't anything left to do but engage in self pity at his incredible bad luck. By this point, the neurons in his body were so excited from the day's activities and the anticipation of the evening about to begin, they were screaming for release all on their own giving him the beginnings of a headache.

Hanna headed for the bar. If he was going to have a headache in the morning, he damn sure was going to have an excuse for it.

Rule Four For Avoiding Infidelity While Away From Home On Extended Business Travel

While abroad, the business traveler should live in conditions where manmade hazards have a reasonable chance of ruining any expectations one may have for ending the day naked in the lotus position with their guest seated on their lap.

Morality

The Chinese are a very moral people and feel a compelling obligation to insure that foreign visitors to their country are not exposed to the decadent ways of western society. To this end, the hotel regulations for the city of Shanghai firmly state "no guest is allowed to up [sic] anyone for the night or let anyone use his/her own bed in the hotel." Guests to Shanghai hotels are therefore on notice that if they are going to "up" anyone, it had better only be for part of the night. To ensure that no guests feel slighted, however, the Westin Shanghai "invites all guests to take full advantage of the chambermaids." The Cherry Blossom Hotel in Dandong, in a similar effort to be accommodating, states "Please don't let your visitors stay in your room for a whole night." The obvious assumption is that it is okay for visitors to spend part of the night without any problem.

Unpublished works by William B. Hanna circa 1996

Thirteen
There Is Someone for Everyone

The bar was an adventure in life all unto itself. This was the middle of China, but this bar transported the patron to some other part of the world. The walls were paneled from the floor to the ceiling, which was at least two floors up. Whoever designed it had perfected the acoustics so that the piano and bass over in the corner off the edge of the dance floor could be heard as though there was a Bose CD player parked up against one's ear.

Bar stools, extra large and tall, ranged completely around the horseshoe-shaped bar. There were four attendants, so that no patron had to wait more than five seconds before being served. Everything was solid hardwood. Behind the bar, the back wall was mirrored at least two-thirds of the distance to the ceiling and had to contain every conceivable form of liquor ever distilled by man. To one side, there was a glass-enclosed room, chilled, Hanna figured, to a precise temperature that housed at least two-thousand bottles of wine. It went as far up the wall as the liquor shelves, and there was a ladder on wheels like one would see in an old library that the waiters would climb to pull the bottles beyond their reach. The ladder's base rode on a brass rail as the top end glided along a similar rail at the top.

Hanna figured there had to be a million dollars worth of divinely aged grape in that room at the retail prices he saw out of the corner of his eye on a small standing menu sitting near him on the bar. Beyond the bar, if you were not seated at it, there were sofas, coffee tables, and chairs that almost disappeared from sight at the far end of the dimly lit room, and finally, there was a dance floor that was obviously built to ballroom standards. The place was nearly packed, and Hanna got the last seat at the bar. It was perfectly located on the corner so that Hanna had an unobstructed view of almost everyone seated at the bar.

He could tell that most of the people were foreign, not only from the way they looked but also from the languages they were speaking. Russian, English, German, French, and Spanish were all around him, sometimes being spoken simultaneously within the same group. To his chagrin, Hanna's stool, the lone one left at the bar, was located right next to three very inebriated males. The guy in the middle couldn't have been more than thirty, but he was so smashed that he was literally rolling on his stool. It was only a matter of time, Hanna thought. His buddies would be carrying him up to his room soon if they were still capable of doing that. In the meantime, he was loudly setting forth all the reasons why Toronto was a better place to live than New York. One more example of the Canadian inferiority complex brought on by living on the wrong side of the tracks. The biggest problem was that it was very difficult to understand what he was saying.

On the other side of him there was a couple, probably in their forties, Hanna guessed, arguing very loudly in hushed tones, if that was possible. The woman, blond and packed into a very well-presented hard body, was positioned facing Hanna. She was throwing daggers with her eyes at the slightly pot bellied and balding man she was sitting next to. It was difficult to make out the conversation between them because of loudness of the continuing conversation among the three guys sitting on the other side of him; however, the conversation, from what Hanna could gather seemed to be about the guy getting to their room really late last night, with lipstick on his collar, and standing her up for dinner.

Nice crowd here, Hanna thought. He was glad the local Chinese constabulary made everyone toss their guns before they came through customs. Why couldn't he have found a seat next to people speaking Hindu?

One of the bartenders spoke immediately to Hanna. He was dressed in the hotel's de rigueur uniform, but you could tell that he was a part of the newly emerging Chinese middle class, which was defined by the money they earned working in the proximity of foreigners. Any informed foreigner tipped these people with cash. The cash went straight into the Chinese workers' pockets. If you added the tip to your tab, it would be split at the end of the month with every other employee on the payroll in the place. Slipping the waiter a couple of bucks when you sat down was usually enough to signal that there would be more coming when you got up to leave. The first thing you noticed when you sat down was how immaculately they maintained the bar. This was China, but you could have eaten off it—it was that cleaned and polished. The bartender was tall and handsome: qualities almost unknown in describing the male of the species in this part of the world.

"Good evening sir. What would you care to drink this evening?" he said. His English was impeccable, spoken completely without an accent.

"Chivas Regal," Hanna replied. "No, make that a martini, gin, and for old time's sake, shaken not stirred." He wished he had worn his tuxedo.

He was so discouraged at the events of the day that nothing made any difference. "Relax," he said to himself and let the day wash over him in waves of self pity. After all, the primary reason for being here was to drink until all brain function ceased. Liu had broken her leg. Sheu was completely on her ass with some goddamn female problem, and he had run out of people to be with.

Just as he was about to begin whimpering, the threesome sitting next to him got up and left, to immediately be replaced by a Texan. The huge hat, boots, silver belt buckle on jeans, and overriding gut he might have been able to get away with, but when he opened his mouth and said "Howdy y'all" the cat was out of the bag. The bartender was immediately at his position.

"Good evening sir, and what would you care to have to drink?" the guy said.

"Hey, Chinaman," the butt head retorted, "I'll have three fingers of bourbon and a Dos Equis for a chaser."

Hanna cringed.

"Coming right up, sir" was the bartender's response. Good Chinese bars could fill any order any person in the world desired.

The guy, weighing in at about three hundred pounds with a six foot five frame, turned and looked at Hanna while he lit up a Marlboro.

"Hey buddy, you speak English?"

Hanna hesitated then reluctantly nodded. *Oh God,* he thought. *And the night was so young.*

"The early show hasn't ended yet, has it?" He asked.

Hanna didn't even realize there was an early show, which implied there was a late show. At the moment, there was just music being piped into the room: soft, romantic, lusty music, Hanna thought.

"Jest so's you know, there's a little woman playing that pieaner, and last night I told her I'd buy her dinner tonight if we could watch movies in my room afterwards. She's hot, man, and tonight's the night."

Hanna agreed as how that was great. Asking the bartender, he determined on the Texan's behalf that the next show would start in about ten minutes and last about forty. Hanna couldn't take this guy for that long. He thought he saw a couple at a table right up next to the piano making plans to leave. He quickly excused himself, told the bartender to guard his drink, and walked to the entrance as though he were going to the bathroom. There was a hostess there he had noticed on his way in.

Hanna was beginning to wonder if he actually was in China. The hostess at the door had two of the twenty-seven boobs in the entire country. (During the last census one woman in a traveling circus had admitted to having three.) She was tall, standing at least five foot eleven. Of course, she was wearing three-and-one-half-inch stiletto shoes. Her waist couldn't have been more than his two hands could grip it around. She was wearing a dress, low cut in the front, but more than that, the slit on the side of it revealed absolutely perfect Miss America legs. She was obviously being taken care of by someone. She had on a beautiful necklace and matching earrings and at least a three-carat diamond on her right middle finger that smacked of anything but the environment espoused by the People's Republic of China.

Hanna stood for a moment in admiration. It was an act not lost on the girl. She looked at him and smiled broadly, revealing gorgeous white teeth worthy of any Colgate commercial.

"Nah," Hanna said to himself. He'd pushed the envelope twice in the last twenty-four hours. He couldn't afford another failure. His loins would never forgive him if it didn't work. In addition, he had another purpose. He walked directly up to the hostess who stood her ground like a mother bear guarding her cubs.

Hanna said softly, "Miss, a small favor, if you can possibly help me. I am sure you have noticed the loudmouth boor that sat down next to me at the bar. He likes the piano player. She is supposed to begin singing in ten minutes. There is a table that a couple is about to leave right in front of where she will be singing. Could you please encourage him to be reseated at that table?" Hanna held five one-hundred dollar bills that he slowly nudged into her hand.

"If you could do that for me as a favor, I would appreciate it."

The girl looked down at what Hanna had pushed into her hand, and despite the opulent appearance she exuded, her eyes opened wide and she touched his arm.

"I will take care of it for you, Mr. Hanna," she said and turned to get it done.

Hanna thanked her for her help and walked on to the head. *Might as well hit the thing while he was up*, he thought. Then it occurred to him. "How in the hell did she know my name?" he muttered to himself.

Fourteen
You Don't Have To Be Rich To Be Famous

When Hanna returned from the washroom, everything had been taken care of. As he walked by the hostess at the entrance to the bar, she smiled and said, "I hope you will be happy with the arrangements I have made. I will talk with you later."

The bar was still packed. Hanna turned the corner, and there in front of the piano in a front row seat was Big Mouth, drooling out of each side of it, with a bottle of bourbon and three Dos Equis sitting in an iced tray on the table. *The sonofabitch was getting loud, stupid, and horny all at the same time. Hell,* Hanna thought, *he shouldn't be critical of the butt head. He'd done it himself in another life.*

But that wasn't the only thing that had changed. He couldn't believe it, but now sitting on the bar stool next to Hanna's seat was the manicurist from the spa. She beckoned for him to join her.

He sat down as she greeted him. "Good evening, Hannasan," she said. "I am Hong. I manicurist in the spa. I wave at you every morning when you walk across lobby from restaurant on way to your car. You must be very important. Biggest company in town send car for you every day."

Hanna couldn't believe what was happening. He was being set up again. He finished his martini, ordered another, and marveled at how cruel the world could be.

While talking in one direction to Hong, Hanna had the other eye on the piano player who Tex was planning to lay. It wasn't a pretty scene. The woman was in her late forties or early fifties. She had one tooth missing in the front, which you saw constantly since she never stopped smiling because of the constant complementing by Tex. He didn't do it softly either. By this point, everyone in the bar who spoke English, regardless of whether they cared or not, knew that he was planning on laying this woman before the night was over. *It wasn't her playing*, Hanna thought. As a matter of fact, she was an excellent pianist, and she sang as well. It was just the fact that she was so fricking ugly that it was obvious her father had tried to kill her at birth and failed. *Oh well*, Hanna thought, *Tex was no better when it came right down to it.* Hanna decided they deserved each other.

Tex kept putting the moves on her. *Thank God*, Hanna thought. Had she ever started to walk towards anyone else in the bar, she would have caused a panic.

After a few moments, it became obvious she was closing up for the night. She was doing a signature sign off: "One for my Baby," the famous Sinatra hit. Hanna was of two minds: remorse over the number of times he had hypothetically sung the tune himself at some unrequited love and the coupling with his lust for the spa lady seated next to him from which he was beginning to feel the heat.

The piano player wrapped it up and stepped down off the stage. Tex, staggering a little from the two quarts of booze he had consumed took her arm, and started walking her towards the door, presumably on the way to his room. Hanna didn't think he would be able to make dinner first without passing out. Besides, the piano player looked like she was ready, the reason for which, Hanna had to assume was the fact that she never got any. As Tex passed by Hanna he winked, leaned over, and said: "Pussy in diez minotos, senor."

Hanna could not pass up the chance.

"Hey, Tex," he whispered, leaning over to the guy's ear, "Just remember, no upping this woman in your room all night now."

"Whadayamean?" Tex said.

"It's the hotel rules. Didn't you read the little notice tag on your pillow when you checked in?" was Hanna's retort.

"No, I didn't. Are you kidden me?" he said.

"No, I'm not," Hanna said, "But it's okay. Tell her she has to leave early, then call room service. The hotel rules say that you can take advantage of the chambermaids for as long as you want."

The guy smiled. "I'll do it," he said, "thanks for the tip, Houston." Hanna had told Tex where he was from earlier in the conversation and was now going to live to regret it.

Hanna just shook his head. The guy was so shitfaced that he actually believed him.

The crowd had grown quiet since the piano stopped playing. It was still fairly early, probably about a quarter to nine, and Hanna was beginning to shrug off the disappointments of the day.

Sheu had crapped out late last night, and Liu had done the same thing earlier this evening. However, thanks to the hostess at the entrance to the bar, Plan C was now sitting gazing at him with pure puppy love and admiration. It was obvious that she wanted to be able to turn around to the crowd and say "He's with me."

Hanna didn't know the minimum drinking age in China, but this girl had to be pushing the envelope. She looked like she was drinking wine, and Hanna had finished his third double martini, shaken not stirred, so he was beginning to feel inspired.

He assessed the situation.

Both the hostess and the manicurist were beautiful. The hostess a little more mature, and the manicurist (Hong) indicated just about everything was new to her but she was willing to try it on for size. Plus, she was really impressed with Hanna. The poise, the good looks, and the power he obviously wielded with the pillars of the community made him a conquest to brag about. Hanna could probably lay back and relax with the hostess. Hong, he would probably have to teach. God only knew when the hostess would get off work for the evening. Hong gave every indication of being unattached and open to anything the evening might have to offer.

No contest, Hanna thought. Go with the sure thing.

"Have you had dinner, Hong?" Hanna asked. "I'm getting hungry, and these martinis are starting to get to me. What do you say to joining me for a little food?"

Hong was all over him like stink on a skunk.

"Oh, Hannasan, I would be honored to be your guest for dinner."

The Chinese were always "honored," Hanna thought.

"Why don't we try Benihana's? They have excellent Japanese food, and they are right here in the hotel."

Hong didn't want to wander too far, Hanna thought. He knew she was thinking about later, and she was determined that she was going to see the inside of his room before the night was over.

For his part, Hanna had ceded all event situations for the balance of the evening to the gods assigned to his fate. He was beginning to tire. Food sounded good, however, and he replied, "Benihana's it is then."

Hanna paid the check, and they left with Hong hanging onto his arm like an octopus. As they passed the hostess at the door, he stopped to thank her for her help earlier and was greeted with a look that had her envisioning dropping a knife from the roof of the building for him to catch. Hanna just couldn't bring himself to leave her this way, so he leaned over and quietly whispered in her ear: "Just going for a quick bite to eat, I'll be back in an hour. Alone."

The hostess smiled warmly at Hanna while glaring at the manicurist, (the bitch) hanging onto Hanna's arm. She responded quietly in Hanna's ear, "I'll see you upon your return then, Hannasan."

Hanna hated these encounters. Lying was not his strong suit, and he was always upset when he had to do it.

Nanjing. A five-star hotel. Benihana's on the second floor. A girl younger, but almost as good looking as his three granddaughters, and she wanted nothing more than to be porked by the most impressive man she had ever met, and here was Hanna not really relishing the situation. Hanna's philosophy was that, in all cases, booze was the only answer. Tonight, he was beginning to question the thought.

He had idly noted as they were taking the escalator to the second floor that the Morning Room, a gorgeous, bright room that lead out to the swimming pool and cabanas but now dark because it only served breakfast and lunch, had a small sign out front announcing that brunch could be enjoyed daily in this facility. Hanna hummed to himself that he just might try it in the morning if he was ever able to extricate his arm from the vise at his side gripping it.

Hanna couldn't believe what was going on. He should be juiced. Instead, he was just tired.

"Ah so, Hannasan, it is so much a pleasure to serve you. What can our humble restaurant do to make your evening more delightful than it already is?" The waiter was programmed.

Hanna could never tolerate this bullcrap.

Hong, sensing this reaction, got in the middle of the conversation.

"What wines are you serving this evening?" Hong asked.

The waiter brought out a wine list, but Hong ignored it.

"I'll have the Pinot Grigio," she said.

It was the same wine that Sheu had ordered back in another life (a day ago). Hanna could only attempt to glaze over the situation. Women in this country, once they were taught how to use it could sell "pussy on a stick" better than any carnie he had ever known.

Hanna ordered another martini. It was his fifth of the evening.

They ordered food: raw sushi for her and filet mignon with French fries for him. They talked small talk. She was enrolled in (as near as he could figure out) the Nanjing School of Seduction. Whatever it was, she was the perfect student.

And then it happened.

It was almost the same thing that had hit Sheu last night. Hanna's body came erect, and the voice began. It was that beautiful, sexy voice that announced arrivals and departures at the international airport in Brasilia. Hanna had almost missed a plane there one time, he got so engrossed in its tone and the elucidation (every word perfectly pronounced), and it didn't make any difference that it was in Portuguese. From the Spanish he knew, he could understand every word being spoken.

The voice began to speak inside his head.

"Caution, you are now running on reserve battery power. In order to preserve whatever gray matter and bone marrow you now possess, all bodily functions shall power down in one minute."

Crap, Hanna thought.

"Fifty nine seconds."

Goddammit.

"Fifty eight seconds."

Hanna had hit this wall before, and it wasn't good for anyone to see him after it happened.

"Hong," he said, "I forgot to tell you, but I have to make a telephone call to my company's corporate offices in five minutes. I will have to excuse myself and leave you now. Here is two hundred dollars. Please sit and enjoy dinner if you wish. I am so sorry but I must leave now."

Hong was pouting, but the money helped to ally her desire for vengeance. Hanna knew that she would never finish the meal in this place. She'd pocket everything she could and have a bowl of rice at some hole in the wall down the street. Christ this kind of money would buy her a half dozen completely new outfits. She wasn't going to waste it on food.

"Fifty one seconds remaining."

Hanna headed for the door and raced around to the far side of the interior walkway where the elevator bank was located. He pushed the "up" button and began to wait.

"Forty five seconds," the voice said.

Hanna pushed the button about five times. He had heard some

commotion downstairs over the balcony on the main floor. He was hoping it wasn't a big deal. He was quickly running out of time.

"Thirty seconds to a total and complete break down the voice said. Get your silly ass up to your room fast, butt head, or management will find your body lying in front of the elevator door in the morning."

The "going up" light lit up, and the door opened. Hanna looked in to see a little old lady in a wheel chair chatting French with some young slimy thing. *It had to be her son,* Hanna thought. They were on vacation with nothing to do and all the time in the world to do it.

Hanna pushed the forty-fourth floor button and noticed there were two other buttons lit up on the board. He turned and looked at the two of them with a "what the hell is going on" look, when the slime ball said, "My apology Monsieur, we accidentally pushed zee wrong floor when we first get on. I trust it won't inconvenience you."

"Twenty-five seconds" the little voice was saying.

Won't inconvenience him!! Hanna screamed to himself. *Jesus Christ, he was going to die in less than a minute and this pea soup was farting around like there was no tomorrow. There won't be if I don't get to my room fast,* Hanna thought.

The elevator door opened.

"Ziss es zee wrong floor, Monsieur, pardonez moi."

Hanna punched the "close door" button about five times, and they began up again.

"Twenty seconds remaining" the little voice inside him said. Hanna could feel every bone in his body starting to ache, including his head bone.

The door opened a second time, and Frenchie began some kind of little dance turning the wheel chair around (which he should have done when they got on, in preparation for getting off, but which the butt head hadn't done) and slowly began to disembark the elevator to ensure that she did not suffer any discomfort at the wheels crossing over the threshold onto their floor.

"Fifteen seconds remaining to total shutdown" came from the little voice inside of him.

Hanna couldn't stand it anymore. He grabbed the guy and shouldered him off the elevator. He then pushed the little old lady out the door. She was rolling down the hallway with her mouth wide open, trying to release a scream as the door closed and the elevator shot to his floor.

"Ten seconds to shutdown" the voice said.

Hanna raced down the hallway.

"Nine"

Hanna was holding the key in his hand.

"Eight"

He slid the key into the slot. The door opened.

"Five"

Jesus Christ, where did six and seven go? Hanna thought.

"Four"

"Three seconds to shutdown"

Hanna managed to slide his shoes off but that was all. Five double martinis and no food had finally colluded to erase his memory from the face of the earth.

As he toppled toward the bed, he envisioned the coroner making out his report in the morning.

Dateline Nanjing: The guest departed this life at precisely 9:43 last evening after three miserably failed attempts within a twenty-four hour period to pork three exquisite flowers of the mother land, representing the most beautiful of what the People's Republic of China has to offer. These supreme failures of a member of the decadent people of the Western world only enhance the purity of thought the people of China represent, justifying their higher position on the pillar of morality far above these fated people of lesser morals.

Hanna's head had turned sideways as he collapsed in a drunken stupor on the bed. His mouth was half open, and he had fallen asleep somewhere between the upright position he entered the room with and the prone position he now occupied.

Rule Five For Avoiding Infidelity While Away From Home On Extended Business Travel

Always insure that sufficient quantities of booze are available to provide mind-numbing protection for the body and all of its pieces when there is a danger that some beautiful nymphet may be in a position to defile its perfection.

Stability & Balance

If one is standing alone in the middle of a large room, a Chinaman, upon entering, will immediately proceed towards the person and run into them.

Unpublished works by William B. Hanna circa 1996

Fifteen
Oh, What a Torturous Road We Travel

Hanna's head was about to break in two. His face was falling off in his hands. His body was shaking violently. Those goddamn martinis.

Where am I? he thought.

The television was on some China Central Television channel with the mandatory severe female announcing the death of a couple of thousand men in a mine collapse somewhere. There was a noise in the hallway that Hanna assumed were the guards coming to drag him off to the torture room for another round of questioning like some American fighter jet pilot enjoying life as a prisoner at the Hanoi Hilton during the Viet Nam war.

Hanna ran screaming to the mini bar and grabbed a tomato juice and vodka, quickly mixing the two. He then grabbed four aspirin from his briefcase and downed everything in one long gulp without stopping.

Okay, he thought, *now if I can just stop the room from turning everything will get better. Momma told me so when I was little.*

There was no way to describe how badly Hanna felt. He looked out the window and seriously reconsidered his earlier idea about breaking the glass and jumping.

Hanna had to remain upright, get cleaned up, get out of this room, and do something. Anything. If he lay down, he would lose the entire day, and he would hate himself forever. It was sort of like your first bad landing when learning how to fly. If you didn't immediately get back in the cockpit and take the plane back up to prove you could do it, you'd never fly an aircraft again.

Getting around was painful but Hanna did it. It took about twice as long as usual to get himself together, but eventually he got there. He'd have to remember to pick up some more Visine. He'd used half a bottle just to get the veins in his eyes shrunk down to the point where he could see out between the lines still etched jaggedly across them.

He was working on his second Bloody Mary of the morning and trying to decide what to do. It was late morning and he still hadn't heard a word from the crew since talking to them on the phone Saturday morning. The thought crossed his mind that he might want to suggest switching maladies. His head ached so badly that the Chinese Blues were almost more appealing to him.

Sheu was still flat on her back or she would have called him.

I know what I'll do, Hanna thought. *I'll have brunch and then go out and spend the afternoon by the pool.*

He was immediately up and going. Bone crunching headache or not, he had to get out of this room and get some food into his body. He opened the door to his room, picked up *The China Daily,* the English version of the government's propaganda machine. "Glorious People's Republic to Loan North Korea Funds Needed to Help Feed Its Starving Population" the headline roared. He hung the card on the outside door handle to let the chamber maid know the room could be cleaned up and headed for the elevator.

Hanna forgot that he could get off on the second floor and went all the way down to the main lobby. It's okay, he thought. He needed a paper be it *La Monde, The Times* or the *Washington Post* to counter the Chinese garbage he was going to read. This done, he headed for the escalator up to the restaurant advertising brunch that he had spotted last night.

Even though it was Sunday morning, the hotel was busy. The shops were all open, and people were milling around the way they always do in such places. Hanna stepped onto the escalator. It was a good piece of equipment: only comfortably wide enough for one person of his size. Probably two Chinese could stand side by side, but he would crush them into the wall if they insisted on standing next to him while they were riding the unit.

The machine was long and travelled slowly. It seemed to not rise as quickly as most escalators with the ratio of lift to distance being less than one would normally expect.

Hanna opened the *Post* he had under his arm and folded it in the manner that one would read it on the New Haven line travelling into New York City from Greenwich on any given morning. New York was the only place in the world where reading a paper was done in a polite and civilized fashion. Anywhere else, the fat arse opened it up completely from side to side so that one hand was in the nose of his seatmate while the other impeded the flow of traffic walking down the aisle of the car.

The low rise in the escalator allowed the traveler to see people on the next level up much further down the circular walkway that ran entirely around the interior of the building than one would normally expect, and it was at this point that Hanna's gaze strayed from the article he was reading and out along the floor line of the upper level. Coming toward him was this very attractive set of legs, the feet of which were inserted in a very fashionable set of high-heeled shoes with at least a three-inch spike. Moving in the same direction further up the body, he could see that the object coming towards him was wearing a clean-cut suit, jacket, skirt, and pretty teddy undershirt. The one noticeable thing about the outfit this very pleasant woman was wearing was the fact that the bottom of the skirt narrowed, allowing her to only take about eight-inch steps.

The girl was married (obviously well married, judging by the size of the rock on her finger) but young, and Hanna got the uneasy feeling that this might well be her first rodeo. Women had to learn how to walk in high-heeled shoes. The thought had barely finished crossing his mind when the conclusion was confirmed.

The girl was smiling at Hanna when one ankle twisted. The shoe began to tilt, and in an effort to right herself, she rocked in the opposite direction as that shoe twisted. Hanna began to worry. His mind had calculated that the woman was on a trajectory that would intersect precisely with his position in about two point three seconds. She was trying to smile pleasantly at him, but it didn't really matter. Her body lurched forward hitting him squarely in the chest, knocking them both to the floor. Chinese ahead and behind ducked to avoid any encounter with the two of them. When the motion of their bodies finally stopped, Hanna was laying prone on his back with the girl lying perfectly positioned on top of him.

She moved to lift herself off of him, and Hanna immediately started to have thoughts. *Jesus, right here on the mezzanine floor of a busy five-star hotel,* he thought.

The thought was short lived, however, with the girl rising quickly, red as a beet and obviously embarrassed with having displayed her feelings in such an obvious fashion. For his part, Hanna didn't care. It had just been one more miniadventure in China, and the girl's body having briefly been attached to his was, to this point, the defining moment of his day.

They were finally in a vertical position, each having dusted themselves off. Hanna helped her pick up her shopping bags; she had been carrying three, which, when combined with Hanna's overwhelming magnetism, had to be what caused the incident. They both apologized profusely to each other, and in an instant, she was gone.

Well, at least his headache had disappeared, Hanna thought. *Time for brunch.*

Brunch

China is attempting to adapt to Western ways. In an effort to move more into the mainstream of modern society, the Chinese have now introduced the concept of "brunch." At the five-star China World Hotel in Beijing, one may now enjoy Sunday brunch any day of the week except Sunday.

Unpublished works by William B. Hanna circa 1996

Sixteen
Time to Put on the Old Feed Bag

Hanna got his bearings and headed toward the restaurant. Something strange was going on, Hanna thought. The doors were open, but all the lights were off and there was no one in the room. Hanna could see the pool outside, so he walked across the room and tried the door out to the pool area. It opened.

There was a bikini-clad waitress going by as he walked out.

"Good morning, sir. You like drink?"

"Not right now thank you," Hanna replied, "I would prefer to eat. Can you serve me brunch in the Morning Room?" he asked.

"Oh, no sir," the waitress twirled, "Can no serve you brunch today."

"Why not?" Hanna asked incredulously. "There is a sign outside the front door that says Sunday brunch is served in this restaurant."

"That true," this bikini-clad little thing said. "Brunch is served in this room. But restaurant is closed on Sundays. You can have brunch tomorrow if you like."

Hanna thought for a moment.

"So you're telling me then, Trainee, (Hanna had looked at the badge pinned to her bikini top that spelled out the name) that I can have Sunday brunch in this restaurant any day except Sunday."

"That is right sir," Trainee said. "You like drink?"

"Trainee," Hanna said, "if you can seat me at a good table in the shade that is set up for lunch, I will then have something to eat and drink. Also, I would like the table to be located in front of one of your cabanas, that one over there looks fine, which I would like to rent for the rest of the day."

"That be fine sir," Trainee said. "I get menu for you just as soon as you are seated."

Hanna followed behind her to the table where he seated himself. Trainee kept going to pick up and return with a menu.

"You like a drink?" Trainee asked.

Hanna's response was to grunt "a Bloody Mary," and she was gone to have it prepared.

Hanna had taken a look around the pool while Trainee was showing him his seat. It was a gorgeous swimming pool. Huge in fact and as fine as anything one would find in the best Caribbean resort. There were places to be seated and place one's lower half up to the waist in the water and what appeared to be a very popular swim-up bar. There was a deep end, down and far away from where he was going to enjoy his meal and his afternoon. For that, he was thankful since there were the mandatory three, ten-year-olds screaming and plunging into the water, disturbing everyone's reverie while the parents grinned and looked on in blissful ignorance.

"Now you kids be nice, okay. Be careful not to bother the other guests."

Of course, what the situation demanded was for someone to reach out, grab all three of these brats, and hold their heads under water for about ten minutes. Hanna sighed quietly. Unfortunately, it would never happen.

The pool was mainly occupied by overweight, middle-aged men and women, having their "elevenses," either Bloody Marys or gins and tonics. They would all be snoring in their chaise lounges within an hour and baked red before the afternoon was over despite the gallons of sun tan lotion they were lathering on their bodies.

There were a couple of pretty decent-looking women poolside but their hair, nails, tan, and jewelry attested to the fact that they were well taken care of by their husbands and were along on some sort of business trip or another to provide solace to their swains in time of need. It was obvious that everyone in the pool area was attached to someone. That was good, Hanna thought. No temptations always boded well for one's continued welfare, and Hanna had still not recovered from the events of the last thirty-six hours.

Hanna not only ordered breakfast (a large glass of grapefruit juice, Spanish omelet with extra tomatoes, toasted English muffin with plenty of orange marmalade, strong coffee, and fresh fruit with yogurt), he also ordered another Bloody Mary. Hanna was beginning to enjoy a Sunday noon time glow.

He opened *Le Monde* and got current on the news. He always enjoyed the articles critical of America, which were usually written after a fashion that demonstrated the French penis envy of the U.S.A. while having to suck on the hind teat and take a back seat to the better part of the planet. He didn't really mean it as a criticism. French women were almost always better than most, since they were to a person well turned out: slim, tall, scented, painted, and dressed. Hanna had more than one fond memory of encounters with this demographic.

Trainee came by with a check that Hanna told her to add 50 percent to, for herself, and he would sign off on it. Trainee smiled with glee.

"Trainee," Hanna said, "could you arrange to have a masseuse come by for half an hour? My body could use a little TLC." That acronym was lost on Trainee, but Hanna wasn't inclined to explain.

Hanna had just finished his second Bloody Mary, ordered a third, and taken a quick dip in the pool to cool off, when the masseuse appeared as Trainee was setting his third drink of the day on one of the small tables in his cabana.

Hanna laid face down on the chaise lounge as the guy went to work. There was nothing yet invented that could give a massage better than a Chinaman. The art, if it hadn't been invented here, it had been perfected here. Hanna had once had a haircut and wash at a hotel barber shop in Shanghai, and the lady barber had taken over thirty minutes to wash his hair and give him a brain massage before she ever got around to cutting it. There was no way to describe how his head felt when he walked out of the place. The cost was one hundred Renminbi, about eight dollars which was a very ritzy price that could only be charged foreigners. No Chinaman would ever pay that much for a haircut. Hell judging by how most of the men looked, it was pretty obvious that someone had just placed a bowl over their head and used a pair of scissors to cut off whatever hung out below it.

Hanna gave her a hundred-dollar bill and watched as her eyes grew three sizes and a wide grin appeared. Hanna was amazed at the smile—most Chinese were incapable of smiling. The girl thanked him ("ah shi shi Hannasan, shi shi, ah ah…") bowing with each thank you all the way to the door and half way down the hall to the main hotel lobby before Hanna was able to convince her that her idolization was sufficient for the moment.

God! His head had felt good.

Hanna took another draw on his Bloody Mary. The alcohol was beginning to do its work, as the masseuse continued to knead.

Suddenly, Hanna was dead to the world, and he kicked into a dream sequence back in one of his old stomping grounds: the Bahamas.

Seventeen
Sun, Sea, Sand, Surf, & Sex

The gulls were slowly passing overhead, looking for food left on unoccupied tables, since they had become too lazy to go fish for themselves. It was about eight thirty on a Sunday morning, and Hanna had just walked out to the back patio behind his house where there was an elaborate table with huge umbrella and chairs positioned next to the pool. Jemimeah, the maid, already had a pot of coffee, along with bagels, cream cheese, and juice awaiting his arrival.

Hanna loved his house. It was located on a height of land (maybe the highest point in Nassau) just east of Collins Avenue in a six-home subdivision off Third Terrace named Ascot Close. Close meaning there was only one road in or out of the place. Hanna loved the British.

The view out the back of his house beyond the pool and the banana tree with a stalk of ripening fruit on it was across the harbor where there were always several cruise ships floating at anchor, directly towards the private suspension bridge that led from the city across to Paradise Island. Here the casinos, their affiliated hotels, and some of the really well-heeled outcasts from America lived in true ostentation. For these folks several million dollar homes with fifty-foot yachts berthed behind them rocking gently to the swells of boats passing by in the harbor was normal.

At one time, the location was named Hogg Island; however, after the first casino was built, it was renamed to make it a bit more enticing to the tourists.

The private bridge had been built in a negotiated deal between one of the more notorious American millionaires in Nassau and some of his paid-off buddies in the government. Everybody said that the bridge had paid for itself in a year by means of the hefty toll paid by all who desired a crossing to the better part of town and the casinos. Otherwise, they waited for the ferry.

The reason why the poor wealthy Americans were outcasts, of course, harked back one way or another to some unlawful dalliance back home that had the IRS and the FBI awaiting their return. These folks had done it smart, however, and they had moved enough cash offshore before their nasty deeds were discovered that they could retire to the islands in luxury. All they had to do to maintain their "Bahamian Green Card" was ensure that the appropriate local officials had their palms greased periodically.

Jemimeah, his maid, was a perfect specimen of the opposite end of the spectrum. She had six kids at the age of twenty-nine, topped the scales a little over three hundred and fifty pounds, had never been married, and her standard response was "oh he no good, he fonny" if anyone suggested she might want to wed one of the fathers. She lived "over the hill," as the expression went (meaning the poor side of town), went to church Saturday evenings with all of her brood, and worked seven days a week from six am until noon without complaining.

Hanna sat in quiet, uninterrupted solace and read the *New York Times*, which hit the island newsstands about the time it was delivered to the Forty-Second street newsies back home in New York. He always read it from cover to cover to keep current on happenings back home in civilization.

The sky was absolutely blue, not a cloud in it, and since it was late November, the sun was low enough that the air was warm with a freshening breeze but not hot like July, when everyone double checked to make certain their wills were current just in case they melted into the sidewalk.

Hanna was in the banking business at the time, and the Bahamian Bank company, headquartered here for tax purposes, had most of its holdings in Central and South America, where Hanna spent most of his time. Hanna loved his job. There was no way to describe walking through the lobby of the small Ouro Verde boutique hotel across the wavy tiled street to Copacabana Beach in Rio to spend a Sunday afternoon. The women were mostly single like Hanna. Almost everyone had a carved glass figure with a deep tan, and they were all very friendly. Hanna had even taken the time to learn enough Portuguese to be able to ask them the proper questions.

It really wasn't that difficult. All you had to do was feed them at the incredibly fine restaurant located right in the hotel, and they were yours for the night for a few dollars more. Some even stayed just for the fun of it.

The question now was lunch. His "steady," although it would be difficult to classify anyone of his harem that way because there were so many, was British, and a nurse working at the main hospital in Nassau. She would have been at work at six am, having stolen away from his bed an hour earlier to clean up and make it on time. Sunday they usually reserved for themselves. She would go back to her apartment after work to gossip with her girlfriends, while Hanna would hit a bar and work on his mindset for the coming week.

Hanna decided it would be the Coral Harbor Resort on the south side of the island for lunch—brunch actually, held poolside and delicious. Not to mention all those tourists from Detroit and Cleveland covered with oil, their whitest of white skins faded by the complete lack of sunlight in the frozen wasteland they called home slowly turning red on an island Sunday.

He checked his watch. It was eleven thirty. The coffee and bagels had done their work, so he got up and headed inside to get cleaned up.

Hanna's Sunday dress seldom varied regardless of his itinerary. It was white slacks, a navy-blue cloth belt, short-sleeved golf shirt, and a blue jacket with a yachting emblem (a pair of anchors) embroidered on the breast pocket. The shoes were always white sandals worn without socks.

Hotel guests were generally on a seven-day schedule, changing over completely between Saturday morning and Sunday noon. No one ever saw Hanna more than once, and he viewed that as a good thing.

Hanna left the house about twelve thirty noontime and headed for his car, which just happened to be an Aston Martin two-seater convertible. There was one time on a short two-mile stretch of Adelaide Road he had once put the speed up to one hundred and fifty, but there really wasn't any other place around the island where one could drive faster than fifty with any assurance that they would live to see tomorrow.

He started the engine and moved smoothly out of the Close, making a left at Collins Avenue and smiling quietly to himself at the power and quiet built into the vehicle. He made a right onto Wolff Road, taking it over to Blue Hills Road, where he made a left and turned south taking it to Carmichael Road. There, he made a right and headed west towards the South Shore resort. At Coral Harbor Road he turned directly south, driving through to the arrivals main entrance of the Beach and Yacht club. It was ten miles and had taken him twenty minutes.

He had his car valet parked, giving the valet a twenty-dollar bill as he turned over the key. The valet knew Hanna well from his frequent Sunday visits, and he knew there would be another twenty dollar bill to stick in his pocket when Hanna returned to pick his car up. The valet always took special care of Hanna's car.

Hanna passed through the lobby of the upscale resort and moved out to the main pool area. Brunch was always served in the grass under the palm trees back between the pool and the beach. His favorite waitress recognized him immediately and grabbed for Hanna's favorite table—favorite because it had the best view of the extremely skimpy bikinis walking back and forth between the pool and the beach.

The waitress brought him his first mimosa of the day. Ten minutes later, she arrived with all his favorite food. The buffet contained every conceivable kind of fruit and salad vegetable. Hanna's plate had it all, along with an impeccably prepared order of eggs benedict. It took three mimosas to wash all the food down.

Hanna went up to his cabana at poolside, which his waitress had made arrangements for when he arrived. Inside, he closed the entrance with the cloth doorway and quickly changed out of his clothes into a bathing suit that he had fitted into the inside pocket of his jacket. The suit was a Speedo, which was not noticeable in the inside pocket of his jacket, unlike the overalls that men seem to prefer back in America.

Five minutes later, he was lying on a chaise lounge, soaking up the mid-afternoon sun, which just made his body look more handsome and drew unending sighs from the bikinis as they admired it while walking by. At least three bodies interrupted his afternoon revere, the first being a doll whose husband was out on the bounding main fishing for tuna and would not be back before five.

The other two were single, and he had to ask for their room numbers and promise to call them later to get them to leave him alone.

Hanna knew the exact reason for the unseemingly forwardness of these babes. They were on a time schedule. "We're only here for five days, Delores. You go that way for yours, and I'll go this way for mine."

Hanna didn't know why but for some reason he just wasn't in the mood. These gals would have to go home without ever finding out how good he was. Maybe it was because his bedmate last night had sucked all the juice out of him.

He had a couple more mimosas over the course of the afternoon and dozed for an hour and a half. About five thirty, he got up, went back to cabana, and changed back into his street clothes.

After making his way unseen back to the front entrance, Hanna had the valet bring his car around and left. He decided to turn left on Carmichael Road, which immediately turned into Adelaide Road. A little further down the road, Adelaide became SW Road, taking him north by Clifton Point. At this point, he could look straight west and into a setting sun that was generating incredible color. He continued north.

Hanna decided to drop in on an old friend just as he was coming up on Lyford Cay located on the Northwest corner of the island. His friend owned the house at the end of the road where the studio had filmed the scenes from Ian Fleming's James Bond book *Thunderball.* The biggest problem she had during the filming was that she couldn't use her pool for a week because of the sharks.

Hanna was beginning to regret not taking one of the bodies at Coral Harbor up on their offer. It was amazing how quickly the neurons regrouped when you were thirty years old. *Oh well,* Hanna thought, *his friend would be more than willing to take care of him and he even kind of liked this older woman.* It probably had something to do with the millions she had in the bank from several successive wealthy husbands that appealed to him the most.

He pulled up to the gate. The heavy entrance was hard closed, and the guard came out of his guard shack to Hanna's car.

"Could you please call Mrs. Rearguard's residence and see if she would be willing to ask me in for a drink?" Hanna asked.

There was no way anyone got beyond the gate without confirmation by the resident that the visitor was welcome and expected.

"I am very sorry, sir," the guard replied, "but Mrs. Rearguard was called back to England very unexpectedly this past Wednesday. At the moment, the only people in residence are her maid and the butler. Her lady-in-waiting returned with her to the United Kingdom."

Well, of course, Hanna thought to himself, *how in the hell would she ever get herself dressed if her lady-in-waiting were not available to help.* At the same time, he was thinking about the three seconds it took her to become completely naked and drag him into bed the first time they went at it. Mrs. Rearguard was in her early forties, but she was just about the horniest thing he had every met and there wasn't one part of her body that hadn't been nipped or tucked, which had allowed her to retain the figure of a twenty-two year old.

"Very well then," Hanna told the guard, "I shall carry on home. If you hear from her, please extend my best wishes to her."

"I shall do that," the guard replied. The guard knew Hanna from the many previous visits he had made.

Crap, Hanna thought, *now he was in real trouble.* The neurons were beginning to heat up again. His British steady wasn't going to offer to come by. The wife's husband at the club was back from fishing, and those two single broads would already be in bed with the nearest body that had a handle on it they could grab.

Hanna was headed east bound on West Bay, going faster with each passing second when he made his decision.

He had to have something to help him through the night. Charley Charley's, his refuge of last resort, was going to have to come up with an answer.

Hanna slid into downtown and again turned on to Blue Hills from the North shore side of the island. Charley Charley's was half way up the hill. He parked the car across the street and walked over to the front entrance. At least ten couples were there waiting to get in; however, the door manager waved him to the front of the line and unhooked the gate so that he could enter. Hanna virtually lived at Charley's since it was so close to the office where he worked, and Charley took care of his regulars.

Hanna walked through the front-door curtain hanging just beyond the entrance and had to stop until his eyes adjusted. There couldn't have been more than one candle power of light for each table, and the bar had about five. The only thing that you could clearly identify was the cash register on the end of the bar. Hanna had frequently wondered out loud why Charley hadn't called the place the Blackout. It was so damn dark you had to slide your shoes along the floor to make sure you didn't trip over anything. None of this bothered Charley. This wasn't the U.S. where you would get your ass sued if someone fell and broke a leg. If you did that was your fault. Charley, however, was the kind sort who would call an ambulance if you needed one.

"How you doin' tonight?" Charley asked. "There's no broad hangin' on your arm so I assume it's not well. And, knowing your tastes you prissy buggar, I can tell you there ain't anyone in this place that you would find acceptable."

"Hi, Charley," Hanna said. "You know, tonight I'm almost ready to lower my standards. Right now I'm ready to hit on anything that moves and will stand still."

Hanna had reached for his glass of Chivas Regal as he took his place at the stool with his name on it at the end of the bar. It was positioned so that he could watch the dance floor and the front entrance at the same time. Charley always had his drink waiting for him by the time he sat down.

"Well, well, you don't say," Charley replied. "In that case, there are two sittin' over at that table just off the far side of the dance floor, and they are in the process of eating you alive. I can always take a drink over to them in your name and ask them if they have a place to sleep tonight. I'm sure they would welcome the suggestion as long as I was honest and sincere."

Charley stood five-five and was seriously overweight because of his diet consisting entirely of beer. Anything on the face of the earth "animate or inanimate" had his interest as soon as he saw it. Hanna suspected Charley kept several molls in business, since he had never introduced Hanna to a girlfriend and he knew Charley didn't respond to alternative lifestyles, Hanna having watched him kick a proponent of it out of his bar one time.

Hanna looked over at the two women seated across the dance floor. Charley was right. They were both eating him alive. He quickly expressed his concerns to Charley since the first one with the hairlip and two missing front teeth would leave scars and the second one looked slightly more muscular and heavier than Hulk

Hogan. If that thing ever came over the bed post after him, he'd look worse than Beetle Bailey after a bad run in with Sarge.

"Yah see, Hanna," Charley said, "picky, picky, picky. It's no wonder you always leave here alone. Nothing is ever good enough for you."

"Boy you sure have a short memory," Hanna replied. "I walked out of here with one of the best last summer."

"I rest my case," Charley said.

Hanna finally noticed that there was a four-piece band playing a quiet meringue. He had no other way to describe it. You could hear conversation around the room while the beat pulsed thought it. In three hours, the floor would be packed, and there would be pandemonium as fifty white boys and girls tried to do the dance and completely screwed it up because they had no sense of rhythm and no understanding of the moves you made.

At the moment, there was only one couple on the floor and they were natives. They were doing a slow dance in rhythm with the beat but moving effortlessly across the floor. When the guy backed up you could see the hip muscles moving under his pants and the two of them swayed in perfect unison back and forth. "Jesus, Charley, are those two breeding out there?" Hanna asked.

"They might as well be Hanna; they might as well be," was Charley's response.

The line out front had to be moving, Hanna thought; new couples were entering as retiring patrons left to go back to their homes or hotel rooms.

And then it happened. The three stooges came through the front door. *They had to be from San Francisco*, Hanna thought.

Momma Cass in her flip flops and mu mu designed by none other than Omar himself was leading. She couldn't have been more than five six, and she had to be over three-hundred pounds. Behind her walked this five foot ten, straight-haired blond, wearing a fishnet dress, under which she appeared to be wearing the bottom half of a bikini. There was nothing up top. Hanna stopped short of salivating uncontrollably, however, since behind her walked this scraggly, skinny-legged, eighteen-year-old boy. He was obviously older than that, but Hanna figured a lot of waiters probably asked him for proof of age. His hair was twisted and knarled with a combination of sand, sea, sun, sweat, and surf. The sweat, it could be assumed, probably occurred because of his use as a boy toy by the two women.

Hanna took one look at him and immediately thought that someone ought to warn him about being careful when he lifted the blind. He was so stinking skinny Hanna thought that he could easily go up with it.

"Okay Hanna," Charley said, "go over there and make a foursome. If you're as bad off as you say you are, either of those two should be able to solve the problem."

Hanna didn't even turn to look where they had sat down over to his left.

"It's obvious the way that crowd breaks down Charley. Skinny and blonde are together, and the mu mu is available to service all truck drivers on the turnpike. Come on. I have my pride."

"Someday you're going to learn Hanna," Charley said, "Things aren't always what they seem."

"Yeh," Hanna replied, "and you have a good day to."

The waitress had served drinks to the threesome's table. Umbrella drinks for fatsy and skinny and a glass of white wine for blonde.

Man, Hanna thought, *skinny had to be having a lot of fun here with doll face. I wonder how frequently the other one was allowed to climb on?*

The band had stopped playing and was taking a quick break with a beer at the bar. Momma Cass got up with her drink and came over to the bar sitting down next to Hanna.

"Hey gorgeous, why don't you join us?"

Hanna shrunk as far into his seat as he could. The only overweight person in his entire life that he had ever called friend had been his grandmother.

"You know, Miss," He said, "I would love to join the three of you, but I've had an extremely long day and living on the island, I have to be back to work in the morning so I really must be going home as soon as I finish this drink." There wasn't a way in the world that Hanna was going to gratify the thing sitting next to him, even though by now the neurons were killing him.

Missy got up from the bar stool as the band began to play again and returned to her table with the other two. She hadn't said anything more. Hanna heaved a sigh of relief and turned back to Charley who had quietly been listening to every word from behind the bar. He was standing there with his hands on the bar leaning slightly forward.

"You silly bastard," Charley said, "Someday you're going to regret your inability to read people. You ought to turn around and take a look."

Hanna turned around.

Fatty and skinny were out on the dance floor. The half dressed blond with the hour glass figure in the fishnet dress and no bra was sitting at the table by herself.

"Charley," Hanna said, "you really are more stupid than I thought. Skinny is just taking fatso for a ride before starting to rub the real thing."

After mu mu and skinny began their third straight dance together, never having left the dance floor, Hanna couldn't stand it anymore. He got up with his drink and walked over to the table where she was sitting.

"Would you like to dance?" Hanna asked.

She looked up at him with the enthusiasm of a pit bull about to bite the head off a chicken. Hanna thought, *if she stands up, I'm going to have to run.*

"You had your chance you handsome fart. Also, you would have been invited to enjoy probably one of the best lays of your life. But you blew off my best friend, and as far as I'm concerned you can take that thing hanging between your legs and stick it up your ass."

Just as she finished her remarks, that half the room heard, a john walked up and extended his hand for her to dance. She was up and gone in a second.

Hanna slowly walked back to his seat at the bar. He put his glass down and stared at it. Charley poured him another on top of the one he already had in his glass.

"You fricking, stupid, miserable, dumb bastard," Charley said. "I knew if I stood around long enough I'd see you screw it up. Congratulations."

Hanna downed the double in one long draught and quietly left. He even forgot to pay his bill. Charley didn't worry; Hanna would pay it tomorrow.

Hanna got outside, walked to his car, got in, and started to scream.

"No, no, no!" he was hollering. "No, no, no, this can't happen! No, no, no, I won't let it happen!"

"Houston, wake up. You're having a nightmare. You've been asleep for hours. Come on, wake up."

Hanna looked up and realized he was back in China. It was Tex. "Thanks Tex," he said. "You're right, I was having a nightmare. Thanks for the wake up."

The piano player was standing next to him looking like Momma Cass's twin, the pool kimono unable to cover up the fat gut and cellulite-wrinkled legs that were her trademarks.

Rule Six For Avoiding Infidelity While Away From Home On Extended Business Travel

Medical research at the finest wellness facilities in the world has yet to determine why it is that when one is sitting on top of the Tower of Arrogance he loses all sense of depth perception. As a result, one wrong move sends him sliding over the edge. The result is a precipitous fall into an abyss of blackness, which renders him unable to recognize either the train wreck he has just caused or the opportunity to achieve a new conquest he has just forfeited. Becoming stupid drunk is the only known antidote to rectify this situation; thus, the business traveler must ensure that his medical insurance premiums are up to date at all times so that he will not have to declare bankruptcy while undergoing detoxification.

Eighteen
Truths Hidden in the Cosmos

Sometimes, gems turn up in strange places: like a muddy dollar bill half hidden in the gutter; or a golden nugget lying for centuries at the base of a tree out in forty-niner country, walked over time and again without being noticed; or a two-carat, uncut diamond at last revealing its location with the sun's rays being bent by its crystalline surface after being covered for the millennia at the bottom of Crater Canyon in Arkansas.

It was Monday morning, and after the frustrations of the weekend, Hanna's life was in dire need of some form of injection to renew bodily function and calm down all those neurons that had been disturbed numerous times in an almost criminal fashion over the course of the last forty-eight hours.

The day had started as usual: wakeup call at six; breakfast at seven; van ignition at eight; lift off at eight thirty to the halls of negotiation, where, as usual, Zhang asked after their health and expressed his hope that they had all enjoyed a relaxing weekend playing tourist in his fair city. He didn't need to ask. He had already read the report that detailed every movement Hanna's group had made since they all departed the dance floor Friday evening. This preliminary bullcrap that occurred every morning before serious talks began always brought Hanna near to tears. The only way he avoided a total breakdown was to smile quietly at the cute little female chick from the kitchens that bent over next to him pouring his first cup of steaming hot coffee, served with copious quantities of cream and sugar and little dried fruit cookies. She occasionally leaned right on to his shoulder if no one was looking.

As remarkable as it sounded, the coffee was good. It was strong and rich, like he had often been served in South America in places like Columbia, Brazil, and Argentina, using a tiny demitasse for the service. Every time Hanna ever accepted an offer of this sort his initial reaction was to shrink at the liquid being poured from the long-handled utensil designed for this purpose. This so-called coffee had the consistency of Formula One motor oil, yet it was tasty with an aroma out of this world and no hint of having been burned in the pot since last night, which is what it looked like. It also had the uncanny ability to snap Hanna's brain back into place and, on occasion, when conditions were appropriate, standing his manhood on end to gaze around and see if it had missed anybody. Why couldn't America with all its power produce a coffee that tasted like this?

It was at this point that Hanna began that trip into the universe that would forever change his life, turning one of those unanswered question of the ages into an epiphany that all human kind would be forever grateful to him for having the insight to identify, quantify, and publicize to the masses.

It started off simply enough. Hanna leaned over to Sheu and asked her a question to pass on to the Chinese delegation, which was seated across the oblong table with plastic green things parked in the middle of it that were supposed to look like some form of vegetation. The question was truly innocuous (or at least Hanna thought so) and required nothing more than a simple "yes" or "no" response. To his amazement, it took Sheu at least ten minutes to translate the question to the other side—so long that Hanna got up from his seat and moved to one of the several windowsills looking out to the plaza below.

Then, the translator for the Chinese got up, leaning with his hands placed against the table, and two other people on the team also stood. Everyone lit up, and the room hung heavy with smoke. It occurred to Hanna that he would have to pack away today's attire until he had it all cleaned back home. He could feel the stench seeping into every fiber of his clothing. The Chinese didn't smoke ordinary cigarettes. What they stuck in their mouths was something between a roll-your-own Bull Durham and an unfiltered Galois that the French loved so dearly. Sheu concluded presenting the question, and the Chinese immediately went into executive session. They all gathered around in a circle, screaming loudly at each other.

It was the classic fire drill. Zhang was the only one still seated, but he had rotated in his seat and was in the middle of the melee. Sheu tried to interrupt to no avail. Hanna inquired as to why she would try to do that, since these guys appeared to almost be ready to kill one another. Sheu's response was that everyone was screaming so loud it was hard to catch all the conversation, but she thought they might have misinterpreted the question she had asked. *Oh, God,* Hanna thought. Well, it was too late now. They would just have to wait until this ad hoc meeting came to order.

Hanna expected a declaration of war within seconds.

He moved to the end of the room where the old 1950s hot plate with its worn electrical cord plugged into the wall kept the coffee warm. He poured himself another cup. Chinese was whirling everywhere, and Hanna heard his name (Hannasan) mentioned innumerable times.

By this time, Hanna had again sat down at the table to muse over the fact that he needed a good manicure from that exquisitely formed piece of Barbie doll from the hotel spa whose miniskirted frame and fully made-up face with lips painted ruby red had so enamored him Saturday evening. She always beckoned to him to come over every time he came or went through the lobby. He had begun to dwell on how much she would be willing to give up for even a mention of the possibility that one might be able to sponsor her emigration to the good old U.S.A. Many would have considered this a vile game to play with an unsuspecting young thing; however,

Hanna was always able to marvel to himself at how easy it was to do this, once you got beyond the moral issues involved.

Hanna picked up a digital camera he always carried in his briefcase and walked back over to the window. The company they were negotiating with was one of the larger ones in town, a pillar within the community so to speak, supplying good-paying jobs to thousands and therefore justifying its office location at one of the prime central areas of city, where the peons teemed below and the views of the mighty Yangtze were spectacular.

He took several pictures of the plaza and the thousands milling around looking as though that was all they had to do. No one seemed to be going anywhere or doing anything. It was a bit like the chaos that ensued when one kicked the top of an anthill. He then took several more shots of the river. All this behind him, he sat back down in his chair at the negotiating table. *They'd been at it for an hour,* Hanna thought.

Just as he sat down in his chair, the conversation died around the room, and the Chinese delegation team all took their seats. They all smiled and lit up cigarettes. Sheu turned to him. She was still standing.

"Hannasan," she said, "the answer to your question is no."

Hanna sat quietly for a moment. He then arose without speaking and walked over to the window to look out one more time at the teeming masses below. He then returned to his chair, picked up his Mont Blanc, and wrote the epiphany of the ages:

"POPULATION: The reason China is overrun with people is simple. By the time the woman has had a chance to say 'no' the act of copulation has already occurred."

It was better than Einstein's theory of relativity.

Hanna began to work on his acceptance speech after being awarded a Nobel Prize.

Nineteen
Time to Get out of Dodge

When it comes time to leave, the anticipation grows, and any male begins to think of what he left behind and what he will be returning to. As the second week moved along, time began to slow as Hanna's anticipation grew. It was always that way, but Hanna knew what it was and tried to ignore it as best he could. He was a lot better off than his cohorts, who were chaffing at the bit to get home. Two-week trips were always tough, but you didn't fly half way around the world for three days the way you would fly out to L.A. for lunch and back home for evening dinner. Even Hanna's boss (Diamond Jim as he called him) for all his money didn't permit this kind of luxury.

Negotiations continued apace, and Hanna, with his knowledge of the Chinese, generally viewed the current round as moving successfully toward some form of deal. It would take time and many more visits, but the goal could be accomplished. Hanna also knew that the Chinese would not be pushed. They would move at their own pace, and consensus was always necessary among them before any deal was inked. Chinese people did not think of accomplishment in the same way as the Western world and Americans in particular. Moving towards a goal showed progress and that satisfied their need. Infinity was their horizon, and when they came to a point where they felt their successor could carry on, they believed they had achieved their objective. Americans were trying to get a mile down the road, and the other side had yet to take a step forward.

It was the very reason why the Chinese were regarded as tough negotiators. "Inscrutable" was the word most often used by the other side of the table to describe these people when they sat down to negotiate a deal with them. It was also the reason why Americans, Hanna in particular, frequently returned to the hotel at the end of the day extremely frustrated with seemingly no progress made. As far as the Chinese were concerned, if no agreement could be reached on today's agenda, it just got tabled until the next meeting. Of course, they expected Hanna and his crew to return next month for more of the same, and after five or six trips to oriental heaven, Hanna as usual found himself with a month's worth of negotiation on tabled items being pushed along in front of him with no apparent way to break the deadlock.

"Ah, Hannasan," the interpreter for the Chinese negotiating team said. "You and your team are excellent negotiators. We are all trusting that you will come back with alternative proposals that we can debate and agree to."

"Hong," Hanna replied, "Our company must have written assurance from your banks and financing institutions that they will accept a deferral of all repayments as long as our company has debt in your company that must be repaid. We must come first until our financing is repaid in exchange for our technology transfer to the joint venture."

The Chinese partner owed various local banks and other investment vehicles in the city over $250 million, and Hanna was not going to take any chances that this jar head with the buck teeth and the soup-bowl haircut was going to sucker his company in to repaying their debt for them. The company needed technology desperately, but Hanna was not going to agree to any transfer of technology or expertise without assurances that it would be repaid first and that included any salary increases to the ten thousand people on their payroll. His company accomplished the same results back home with about fifteen-hundred employees.

"Hannasan," Hong replied, "not only do you bring assets to the negotiating table. We do as well. As you know, we are prepared to place all our factories and employees into the joint venture. You must agree that this gesture is at least equivalent to if not greater than your company's transfer of technology."

"Hong," Hanna said, "Technology is the life blood of industry. If you don't have technology, you don't have a product. You have some good features on your production lines, Hong, but they add very little to the value of your company, which has to advance to the twenty-first century before it will be competitive. Our company can do this for you, and both you and I know how valuable our technology is, considering the fact that we have the largest market share for our product in North America. Our technology is so advanced that I am not prepared to sign anything until I have the agreement of your company's executive committee and your bankers that we will be paid first out of the joint venture's earnings before any of their debt is repaid."

"Hannasan, you and your company are very wealthy. On the other hand, we and our company are not. We look to you for help for our people and to bring our company, as you say, into the twenty-first century. How can you step away from this opportunity to become the first joint venture in our field of expertise in China? You must view it as a great honor, Hannasan."

"Hong, what we are having a difficult time with here is your company's lack of understanding of the profit motive that drives American business. The welfare of the people comes only once the business is profitable and indicates that it is self sustaining. If business is good, the employees will benefit. If it is not, the employee must wait. I cannot go back to my executive management without being able to tell them that I have your agreement that our loans and the value of our technology will be repaid before anything else is."

"Hannasan, I am sure that you, in your wisdom, will come up

with a solution to this small problem. Meanwhile we will await new thinking from your side. We know you can do it, Hannasan."

Hanna shook his head as he turned away to leave.

Just one more example of Chinese bullshit, Hanna thought. They were going to sit on their asses until the Americans gave up and acceded to their position.

Not this time, Hanna thought.

There were only two things Hanna could do to retain his composure when this situation developed. He either had to grab a bottle or grab a body. As Waylon Jennings wrote: "He'd always been crazy but it kept him from going insane." Hanna usually felt the same upon returning home from the negotiating table.

Today was Thursday and they were headed home Saturday morning: only two more nights left to go with one more banquet. Hanna looked forward to the next thirty-six hours with a combination of elation and dread. There was nothing better than getting on the road, but to get there they had to get by one more "Thank God It's Friday" night.

All the foregoing having been said, Hanna sat over dinner with the others with an uneasy feeling. The only person in the world who had better instincts than he did was his wife, and in some way, her spirit was telling him to gird his loins and take a deep breath.

It was about eleven pm when the crew finished dinner. They hadn't gone anywhere this evening, having decided to eat in the hotel. Everyone was slowly returning to normal from the previous Friday night's debacle. The only telling fact of the damage it had inflicted on the men because of food improperly ingested was the occasional quick "excuse me" as someone had to retire to the bathroom.

It was at this point, two double martinis in the bar, three glasses of merlot with dinner, and an after dinner café amoretto that it happened. They were just rising from the dinner table when the waiter approached Hanna.

"Ah so, Mista Hanna. There is telephone call for you."

As usual, Hanna was always completely overwhelmed when

this happened. *How in the hell did the Chinese know where he was and know his name? You couldn't move in this country without every footstep being mapped and documented.*

"Where is it coming from?" Hanna asked the maitre d'.

"From America," was the instant response.

"I'll take the call in my room then. Please advise the caller to hold until I am there. It shouldn't take more than a minute or two."

Screw it, Hanna thought. The call was either from his wife, which would be virtually unheard of at this time of day since his beloved would be standing in the middle of Neiman Marcus with one of her VBF's discussing whether they should lunch there or go down to Sak's. *Nah, it had to be the office.*

He entered his room to the sound of the phone ringing.

"Hanna speaking," was his response as he lifted the receiver.

It was Mindy, the receptionist at their Houston offices.

Mindy was one of those good-time gals: blonde haired and blue eyed, dresses hemmed just slightly below the crotch, and dumber than a post. Her horizon never got beyond who was going to feed her dinner this evening in exchange for a good lay.

"Ah, well," Hanna sighed to himself, "you didn't want someone who was over qualified for the job."

"Just tell me real fast what I can do for you when I get back to Houston Mindy then let me go to bed. I'm tired."

"Is that a promise William or just another one of your miserable lies?" Mindy replied. "Someday I'm going to hold you to your word."

"Mindy, how long have you known me?" Hanna asked. "Have I not always been as good as my word?"

"You've never been as good as your word, William, but don't worry, I'm laying in wait for one of your vulnerabilities to appear and then I am going to dance on your naked body."

"Put me through to whoever is calling me Mindy. I'm tired and it's bed time in China."

Houston was exactly the opposite time as China. Noon in

Houston was midnight in Nanjing. Actually, in China the eastern third of the country was all one time zone so that on the eastern side daybreak occurred at five am, while on the western side the sun rose at seven am. The sun rose at six am in Beijing.

Besides, Hanna had given up trying to best Mindy with this banter. She had absolutely no concept of what sexual harassment was, and she was in the game as though she had just cornered some seventeen-year-old male virgin who was about to excuse himself and go to the bathroom for a few minutes.

"It's the boss himself, William. Hold on a second while I put you through," she said. "Love and kisses till we meet again."

Crap, Hanna thought. He could sense a change of plans coming. The boss never called when you were this far away from home without a reason.

That old expression came to mind: you never call an airplane in the air unless what you have to say will make the people on board turn the thing around.

"Mr. Hartfield-Llewellyn's office," the sweet voice offered.

"Good morning, Mrs. Goldwin," Hanna responded. You never got to the boss without prescreening, and the only title Rebecca would respond to was "Mrs." "Bill Hanna here. I understand the boss wants to talk to me."

"Yes, he does, and you are simply going to love the news. As you have always said, 'travel is its own reward' and to that end, Mr. Hartfield-Llewellyn has fascinating plans for you."

Jesus Christ, Hanna thought, he was headed somewhere but it sure as hell wasn't home. *Goddammit, how could that butt head do this to him? He had already served his time, and now this sonofabitch was about to lengthen his sentence.*

"Jason here," the voice boomed into the phone. "How are things going in China, William?"

His voice could have been recorded for use by the Air Force to launch missiles, it was so commanding, Hanna thought.

"Very well, Jason," Hanna responded. "We're making great headway. I would anticipate us inking a deal over the course of the next three or four visits. By the way, I want to thank you for providing me with the use of the three men that you had tag along with me on this trip. They have been invaluable to our mission." Might as well make a plug for the heathens Hanna thought, even though they had run at about 35 percent efficiency since last Friday.

"I told you they would be of use, William. Never turn down a gift horse. By the way, I hope you're making full use of the local opportunities. The last time I was over there Zhang had some really good stuff put at my disposal. As a matter of fact, truly amazing stuff. And don't worry about putting it on the old expense report. You're my best man you know, and I want you to always have the very best."

Oh God, Hanna thought, *here it comes.*

"By the way, William, I would like you to consider a change of plans."

Consider, Hanna thought, *he'd just been given an order.*

Jason went blithely on, unaware that Hanna had just stuck his middle finger straight up in the air and cursed silently at the ceiling.

"You know our friend in Singapore who wants to invest a $100 million in our China plans but got cold feet the last time we talked? Well, he called me this morning and indicated he was back on plan and wanted to finalize an agreement with us. Of course, I mentioned to him that you were already in China and would be delighted to change your plans to accommodate him. I have Rebecca working on air travel and hotel rooms, and she has you scheduled to fly out of Nanjing to Hong Kong Saturday morning and then on to Singapore later in the day."

"But that's not the good part," Jason said. "My plans call for me to attend the world championship backgammon playoffs in Malaga the following weekend, and you're invited to join me and a few of my friends and relatives for a weekend of fun in the sun. We'll have a great time. Rebecca has made plans for you to meet us Friday in Marbella and then fly out to Paris and home to Houston on Sunday after Mrs. Llewellyn arrives late Saturday evening. I know you're going to be in pretty tough shape before you get back to that beautiful wife of yours but find something to appease the problem, if you know what I mean."

Hanna knew what he meant. If nothing else, his boss excelled as a womanizer. Even his wife knew but opted to do nothing. Life was too good for her to toss a fit over a few out-of-town dalliances.

Hanna rolled the pros and cons through his mind. On one hand, he was fighting to overcome an excruciating desire to kill the bastard. On the other side, the boss paid him about a million a year in salary, and his bonus had always been one hundred percent of that amount. His family lacked for nothing, and happiness prevailed around him. What to do?

"I would very much enjoy meeting Chou next week and finalizing the deal Jason. I assume Rebecca will have my itinerary and tickets delivered to the hotel here in Nanjing by morning."

"That's the plan," Jason said and hung up.

Hanna sat in the overstuffed chair looking at the receiver for a good minute. He was assessing his immediate situation. It was midnight on a Thursday; there would be a full working day tomorrow beginning at six am; and any decent female body had retired for the night. The only answer was booze.

Hanna went over to the minibar. Two hours and three Chivas Regals later, he fell asleep in the big chair still wearing his clothes.

Twenty
You Can Always Make a Friday

The standing wake-up phone call from reception came at precisely six am. Hanna couldn't stand it. He felt as bad as he had felt last Sunday morning. This morning, however, he would have to fix the head with aspirins alone. The Bloody Mary cure would have to wait until nightfall.

There was silence at breakfast. The boys all knew when Hanna was hurting, and this morning he even looked the part. Nevertheless, he had to be nice to their host, and as breakfast began to go down (two fried eggs over medium, Canadian ham, hash brown potatoes, raisin toast, a large glass of grapefruit juice, and a gallon of coffee) his body started to come around.

The table was so quiet that Sheu had begun to talk to the Chinese host in Chinese without bothering to translate. She had assumed, rightly so, that none of the Americans were interested in Nanjing's progress in building a museum for the people that would house artifacts and film honoring the heroic efforts of their elders when the Japanese invaded their homeland prior to the start of World War II. The "Rape of Nanjing" as they referred to that era. Thousands died from a bullet in the back of the head.

The museum depicted conditions in and around Nanjing prior to the start of World War II. The Japanese had invaded China long before the start of the war, and they really weren't very nice.

As a matter of fact, their tactics bordered on the macabre. They treated the Chinese the way the Germans treated the Jews. The Americans tried to help the Chinese in those days, since they were allies against a common enemy; however, the resources simply were not available to mount any effective response to the massacre being perpetrated.

It was the Chinese Pearl Harbor.

The day passed with reasonable speed for which Hanna was truly grateful. Since it was their last day, lunch was about a half hour longer, providing extra time for karaoke and, believe it or not, a local beer with the meal. Beer in China was good, just like their coffee. Hanna relished the treat and made a point of thanking Zhang.

With the drink, his hangover finally disappeared.

The afternoon was filled mainly with plans for the evening's banquet. Tonight's affair would not be held at the company's entertainment facilities, rather they were to meet at a "better" restaurant known locally for its "upscale Chinese cuisine," truly a contradiction in terms but heralded by the natives as being the finest in Nanjing.

Amazing as it seemed, there was some business discussed. An assessment was made of progress to date. The Chinese were ecstatic. From an agreement that would ultimately contain fifty to sixty clauses and run a hundred pages or more, the negotiating group had agreed on four. That made eleven accomplished to date. Seven others had been tabled to be readdressed at a later date. That status had now been awarded to a total of fifteen. Everyone around the table agreed to re-examine their current positions on those items tabled so as to be able to return to the negotiating table at the next set of meetings with new and fresh ideas to overcome the disillusionment that hung over these issues at the moment.

Negotiating with the Chinese could be as depressing as your girlfriend announcing to you over dinner that since you were not willing to divorce your wife to marry her, she was going to ditch you for some hot new Romeo that would. Contracts in China were no different than any other part of the world except for the fact that they had about double the number of issues that had to be discussed and agreed to and the contract had to be written in both English and Chinese. Who was going to pay for this, who for that? How was the need for insurance going to be addressed? In what bank would the money be placed to close the deal? What was the price going to be when the Chinese wanted twenty times earnings and the Americans figured the deal was worth about three?

Hanna loved the phrase "re-examine their current position." He knew that when his team returned the Chinese would still be sitting there with the same demands and expecting the other side to have agreed to their position.

It got to the point where Hanna almost gave up. Some of the Chinese positions were simply not acceptable.

Fat chance, Hanna thought. He would be retired before these butt heads backed off of their position, and if they did, the clause that addressed the issue in the final contract would never be honored. The reason for this was simple. The contract had to be written in both English and Chinese, and guess what would happen when some event occurred that triggered the clause? The Chinese contract would say something completely different than the English version. This would allow the natives to continue on with absolutely no concern, doing what they always had done. On the other hand the idiot Americans, who thought they had an airtight deal would be left holding the bag, wondering if they shouldn't just set their contract on fire and put their Hong Kong attorneys on a BBQ spit.

Hanna knew how these deals worked. Whenever he was in Beijing for the event, he would attend the evening business meeting at the U.S. embassy held the second Tuesday of every month. You checked your guns (cell phones, tape recorders, and all other electronic devices) with the Marine standing guard at the entrance to the meeting room. No briefcases or note pads were allowed inside, either. The ambassador always made a short statement before turning the meeting over to the business attaché, who would make pointed reference to the fact that the meeting was to be regarded as a meeting among Americans far from home, whose goal was to accomplish some financial endeavor with a Chinese counterpart within the country, and everyone was to regard the forum as very open. Attendees were free to discuss their problems and listen to their counterparts discuss theirs. Finally, everything said in the room was to be regarded as confidential and to be discussed only with others who had been in the room. This was a very gallant rule Hanna always thought considering that half the people in attendance were obviously of Chinese heritage even though they might be American citizens.

Hanna always took the opportunity to buy dinner for a couple of long timers in country who were searching for any opportunity to tee off with some countryman in English. The men of just about every Fortune 1000 company in America all had tales to tell that made Hanna's blood run cold. A contract with the Chinese was meaningless.

All of the guys Hanna ever met at these meetings appeared young, intense, and handpicked by their respective companies for the job they were doing on the far side of the globe. They were all well spoken, educated at one Ivy League school or another, and exuded an air of confidence. At the same time, they all appeared tired. The position all of them held as the senior executive in their company's venture in China appeared to be taking its toll, and they looked and talked like all they wanted to do was throw in the towel and go home.

One evening after the Tuesday meeting, Hanna had invited three guys back to the China World Hotel and complex, taking them up to the roof top restaurant to dine formally while enjoying a view of Beijing. Before the first drinks arrived, Hanna was into a tirade about how impossible it was to negotiate with the Chinese. At first, the guys were reluctant to talk in specifics, but after the drinks loosened them up, one of the fellows began to recount the problems their company had encountered.

They had agreed on a joint venture to build some kind of

widget in a plant about thirty kilometers outside of Beijing. Of course, you had to have a Chinese partner who had at least a 50 percent interest in the venture if not more. It was guaranteed that the venture would fail if the Chinese did not participate at least equally in it. Secondly, you, the American partner, put up most of the money, technology, and other resources for the project and your Chinese partner whiled away his time selling and advertising the product locally to the masses.

In this case, the Chinese partner was to maintain the facility out of his investment in the venture. The first winter all the water lines broke, and the Chinese partner began arguing that it was not his responsibility to repair them even though it was. The American partner ended up paying for all repairs, which were in the millions. If they hadn't, the whole venture would have gone belly up. The Chinese partner would have simply walked.

Hanna had come to realize it some time back that contracts with the Chinese were worthless.

If you ever had a disagreement with your Chinese partners, you could rest assured that the case could be appealed to the World Court in The Hague after ten years in and out of the kangaroo courts in China where no one ever won except the Chinese. You invested in China at your peril.

He ought to be taken off the negotiating team, Hanna thought to himself. His broad experience, longevity with these people, and the realities of earlier experiences all told him what he could expect.

"Screw it," he said under his breath. Progress had been made, and he was going to take credit for that in his report upon his return to the corporate offices in Houston. Plus, the boys would need a little credit just so that they wouldn't feel they had been used.

Back at the negotiating table in Nanjing, it was finally time to call it a day, a week, and a visit. They all cleared the table, closed up their briefcases, and Hanna and his team headed for their car.

It was five o'clock on the nose. They would be picked up at seven for the banquet.

Two hours to relax before again returning to battle, Hanna thought. He planned to spend at least thirty minutes in the shower. For some reason he felt particularly dirty today.

Twenty One
The Closing Banquet

Hanna went down to the lobby about twenty minutes after six. He wanted to pick up his revised itinerary and tickets, which he knew were waiting at the front desk because of the message that had been flashing on his phone when he first entered his room. It was less than eighteen hours to "wheels up" and he still didn't know how he was getting to Singapore or where he would be staying.

Everything was waiting for him, bound tightly in a thick envelope. Hanna figured it had to be four-inches wide. His only thought was to ask himself what in the hell had Rebecca done?

Sheu had joined him as he plunked into an overstuffed chair in the lobby, and she ordered him his favorite, a Chivas Regal, while she asked for tea. Sheu was still looking peaked but that was not the reason for the tea. She had to translate all the evening's conversation, and she needed all her wits about her to do it in a professional manner.

Ah, what the hell, Hanna thought, *he'd try to get her in bed the next time he was in town. There sure wasn't going to be any action tonight.* Hanna was amazed at how quickly he had forgotten about this monthly inconvenience young women had to schedule their sex lives around. His darling wife had been in menopause for two years, and he was only now appreciating how much more blissful life had become once they no longer had to work around the consistently untimely intervention of this affliction. Hanna loved his wife deeply, and the end of this monthly event had only made life much better for both of them.

Hanna opened the envelope as the rest of the troop joined him and Sheu. They all needed a drink before heading out to the banquet.

Everyone looked up as the air being sucked into Hanna's lungs became audible to all of them.

Lying on top of all the paperwork was a brief note from Rebecca.

William:

> *Mr. Llewellyn had lunch with Mr. Putnam of Putnam Petroleum at the Petroleum Club today, and during their conversations, they discovered they both had teams in China working on new ventures. Moreover, Putnam Petroleum has a leased G-V that is now sitting at the Nanjing airport, which a couple on their negotiating team is using to fly out to Tokyo first thing tomorrow. To make a long story short, they arranged for you and our team to join them on the flight. Their aircraft is doing a turnaround taking new employees back into China, however, so you will have to pick up commercial service from there on to Singapore while the other members of our team continue on to Stateside. Since it only takes an extra hour or two to fly from Tokyo to Singapore rather than going directly through Hong Kong, I thought you would enjoy the opportunity to sit with a few of your countrymen for a while before once again becoming immersed in the fog that is the Far East.*
>
> *Since the Putnam Petroleum employees are coming in from the field on a bus to catch the flight in the morning, you will have to make your own introductions when you board the aircraft.*
>
> *Rebecca*

The note went on to name who the other people on the flight would be as well as the names of the pilots. There was no mention made of the names of the cabin flight attendants, nevertheless, knowing Jason, his boss, and Putnam, their associate from the petroleum company, both of whom bragged loudly and often about how many times they had each had the pleasure of joining the mile-high club, it could be assumed that the women were hot as a pistol.

Of course, Hanna always got pissed at the way Rebecca dismissed distances overseas. She assumed every flight was like taking a hop from Houston to Vegas, a trip she made at least once every three months, or whenever her husband was out of town, to have a tryst with a friend forever to remain anonymous. All this having been said, Hanna had just had an elongated flight from Hong Kong to Singapore turned into a Tokyo-Singapore run, which was akin to flying non-stop from Houston to Paris. Hanna had made that trip any number of times while commuting to Bucharest during an earlier life.

Hanna knew Putnam personally and had also had the pleasure of having had lunch with him at the Petroleum Club. The lunch and dinner club occupied the top two floors of the Exxon tower located in downtown Houston, and it was the unofficial home of the oil barons whenever they were forced out of the River Oaks Country Club to go downtown to work. It was huge, and everything exuded money—vast amounts of money. You couldn't afford to join the place if you had to ask what the fee was. There wasn't a menu or any document in the place that had a price listed, and a haircut and shine was a hundred dollars before the tip. The place was over sixty years old, having been founded in 1946, and it was as tradition bound as Texas.

One thing that always fascinated Hanna was that it was not uncommon to sit and have a drink with a multimillionaire as pleasant and well mannered as any Wall Street broker, and yet they didn't have a high-school education. They had come by their money by the accident of birth, which was provided by their fathers in the form of land that eventually became an oil field.

Hanna always walked down the hallways with care. *You had to watch,* Hanna thought, tongue in cheek. *The floors were all slippery with the oil the members dragged in on their shoes.*

Behind Rebecca's note were new itineraries and flight tickets for everyone. The old itineraries had been cancelled. The boys would fly out of Tokyo for San Francisco, then on to Houston tomorrow afternoon about four pm. Hanna would leave for Singapore about an hour later and arrive in the early hours of Sunday morning. *It's not fair,* Hanna thought. Here he was giving his crew tickets home to their family and friends, morning commutes to the offices, Friday night dining at La Griglia in Highland Village two blocks east of the Inwood Street entry to River Oaks, home of Houston's royalty, while he was migrating to nowhere. *Yes,* he thought, *death was the only option for his boss.*

They were on their way home. Hanna was on his way to oblivion. As a final testament to her efficiency Rebecca had arranged for a car to take them to the airport in the morning.

At least Rebecca had reserved a suite for him at the Shangra La in Singapore. It had consistently ranked among the top ten hotels in the world for thirty years.

Sheu was gently touching his arm.

"Time to go, Mr. Hanna. It's 6:59 pm." She had already paid the bill.

Hanna got up to go. He hadn't touched his drink.

They started towards the door as the van pulled up into the porte cochere. It was exactly seven.

They drove for five minutes and were at the restaurant. *They could have walked,* Hanna thought, but the Chinese would never have allowed them to do that. It would have been an insult to have a guest walk to dinner.

Despite the fact that it had to be within a mile of their hotel, no one had ever taken the time to mention this place. You knew you were at Nanjing's finest when a white-uniformed doorman in tails and white gloves opened the door for you. It was obvious the main open-dining room was straight ahead through fifteen-foot double doorways from which a lot of noise was emanating. A double-curved staircase either to the left or to the right led to a second floor, which obviously was reserved for larger groups wanting privacy. Carved ivory, despite the fact that it was illegal even in China, and huge floor-standing porcelain vases and jade figurines decorated the lobby. It was the typical rich folk being above the law. Most of the diners in the place probably had more carved ivory at home that only close friends and relatives ever got to see. "Oh, this acquired before law banned it" would be the answer if anyone questioned its presence. Flowers adorned everything. All the males were dressed in tuxedos and all the waitresses in floor-length dresses with neck-tight high collars and one side of the skirt slit to just below the hip.

Not the best example of the definition of the Communist ideal. Still, the restaurant was teeming with people dressed to the nines.

Zhang was standing in the middle of the foyer. He came forward as soon as they entered and greeted each of them with a warm handshake. Following in suit behind Zhang was every member of the negotiating team, including a couple of tough old broads who, from time to time, had been in and out of the negotiations. They both looked like the South American female wrestlers from Bolivia that Hanna had once had the pleasure of reading up on in some weekly gossip magazine back home. Of course, the article came with the usual pictures which conjured up an image of terror as Hanna wondered what he could possibly do to defend himself if one ever started to become amorous with him and put him in a bear hug. On more than one occasion, Hanna had wondered quietly if they would infect him with typhoid if they bit him.

Zhang took Hanna's arm and began guiding him up the staircase, talking a blue streak with obvious warmth even though Hanna understood nothing of what he was saying. His mannerisms and tone of voice evidenced his fondness for Hanna. Sheu could hardly keep up translating as he mouthed homilies while they climbed to the second floor.

The tuxedos took over at the top of the stairs. Everyone bowed low to Zhang. *He had to be a regular*, Hanna thought, as they ushered the two of them into a large private room. There were three large circular tables inside. At least a dozen waitresses stood alongside the doors exiting to the kitchen with their hands behind their backs. They could only be described as gorgeous, and it immediately brought to the surface a long-standing conflict in Hanna's mind.

In China, there didn't seem to be a middle road when it came to appearances. The women were either beautiful or they were ugly. There was no in between. Hanna actually wondered for a second if these servers had not all been born out of the same litter. To a person, they were tall, wore their long hair in either a bun, pony tail, or a French roll, and all were dressed in what was obviously the restaurant's uniform.

Uniform conjures up the wrong image, Hanna thought. Their apparel was 100 percent pure silk, which Hanna recognized from the time the local dignitaries had arranged a tour for his team through a silk factory. The dresses were all black and white, buttoned up to the neck and slit up one side to just below mid hip. All wore a pearl necklace on the outside of the black high-buttoned collar, and they were all in three-inch black heels.

At one point, Hanna had a fleeting vision of his caravan pulling up to the oasis for the evening, the camel jockeys erecting the huge Bedouin tent with rugs covering the entire sand under the roof, and then returning to their filthy quarters while these twelve nymphets dressed in see-through pajamas fed Hanna grapes and poured him wine, while he laid on the pillows in the middle of his bed.

Zhang and Sheu quickly brought him back to reality.

The table in the center was slightly larger than the other two. Zhang took the seat of high authority at the best spot for viewing everyone in the room and waved to Hanna to be seated next to him on his right. This Hanna did, after which Sheu sat down next to him so that she could translate into Hanna's right ear as Zhang talked Chinese into his left. Clifford, the senior executive in the team after Hanna, sat on Zhang's left with his counterpart from the local company seated next to him. Cliff was smooth, and he carried off his secondary role with handsome good looks and a "clothes make the man" attitude. Actually, Cliff was in better luck than the others, since his man spoke half decent English.

Rudolf sat to the left of Cliff's counterpart with his own. All Hanna could say was that the two of them looked, acted, and thought exactly the same. They probably would have both been offended by being compared to the other if they had known what Hanna was thinking.

To Hanna's right beyond Sheu sat Jaime with Pong the "economist." Jaime hated Pong. He commented frequently on how dumb and greasy the guy was. Beyond Pong, on the far side of the circular table was the Chinese company's interpreter. He was a short little shrew, and as near as Hanna could figure, he had worn the same outfit every day the team had been in town. After the center table was seated, the outer two tables filled up with the also rans.

All the shot glasses had been filled to their one-ounce brims with the local gasoline, and Zhang stood to welcome everyone with a toast. Sheu stood alongside of him translating for the Americans. The toast was warm, well thought out, and sincere. Everyone drank the entire shot. Rudolf and Jaime grimaced, while Clifford threw it back with quiet aplomb. Hanna figured they would all be polluted by the time they hit the hotel since tonight was the last night the locals would have a chance to booze it up until the next time Hanna's troop hit town. With that thought in mind Hanna figured each of them would have to "gambi" with at least five of the locals to accept one toast from each. Of course, there were always the drunken few who put their careers at risk by coming over and doing a toast with each of Hanna's troop.

Hanna had never gotten through one of these banquets with

less than ten gambis under his belt. The effect calculated out to about ten extra-dry double martinis Hanna figured.

They all raised their glasses to drink to Zhang's toast and the first ounce of booze hit the stomach.

The glasses were refilled before they had a chance to sit down.

Hanna responded in kind, and a second ounce of booze hit the stomach.

Food, Hanna thought, *I need some food fast.*

It didn't take long before two dozen different courses were placed on the table by the super efficient serving staff. As is the custom in China, Zhang served Hanna his first course. Since it was cold and appeared at one point to move a bit, Hanna quietly pushed it to one side and reached for some steaming rice and hot meat, which looked like beef or pork. All he could assume was that the dish was some form of sushi or, again, those damn shrimp, which were an ugly white before they were cooked. It was often difficult in China to determine what the food was. It was always laid out on huge lazy susans that could be rotated so that each diner had access to everything. Hanna always kept looking for things that appeared to be well cooked.

There were all kinds of salad vegetables and fruit placed strategically around the table, which Hanna avoided like the plague since he assumed that they were at least partially responsible for E-coli-based food poisoning and other gruesome diseases that regularly surfaced around the country. It didn't make any difference how food was prepared in China, its handling and cleaning were never guaranteed and China had more diseases than Africa.

Hanna thought idly to himself about the time he had gone out for BBQ with his hosts in Taiwan. It was unbearably hot and high noon. The hole in the wall they went to was cooled to about ninety degrees and the humidity was 100 percent. The cooks were wearing old dirty knit shirts of the type that had two straps going over the shoulders and left their chests half bare. The Taiwanese stood in a line next to the stove that looked more like an old barrel while the cook, sweating profusely and gushing it all over the meat cooking on the open grill, served up the meal with a spatula and a toothless grin.

Hanna ate all the rice he had been served and begged off eating the BBQ pleading a lack of appetite. Actually, he was starving but he was not going to admit it.

At the banquet in Nanjing, Zhang and all the locals stood and began clapping loudly. The chef had just entered the room with a steaming tray held high. Several of the waitresses had cleared a large spot in the middle of their table, and one of the waiters had grabbed one end of the large tray to assist the cook in positioning it in the space that had been cleared. It was a large fish, at least twenty-five pounds, and despite the fact that it appeared cooked to at least a rare temperature, it was still moving. One of the locals who had had more than his share of booze and had already migrated from cigarettes to a cigar that was making Hanna nauseous stood up and placed the thing in the fish's mouth, which began to puff it, bringing a roar of laughter from everyone who had gathered around the center table.

Hanna's stomach was starting to turn. He asked Sheu to excuse him to the table while he went to the bathroom. Even that would be a breath of fresh air compared to this place. And if you had ever visited a Chinese bathroom outside the five-star hotels built to house American travelers, you knew that was saying a lot.

When he returned, a skeleton was all that was left of the animal, and he was able to beg off eating the piece that had been placed on his plate by quietly complaining to Sheu that it had gone cold in his absence.

The Chinese loved these opulent displays, since it could be justified because of the presence of the Americans. It also gave them an excuse to get absolutely bombed with the local booze as they took turns walking up to their guests between courses and toasting their health. Of course, the guests ended up flat on their asses at the end of the evening, staring at a massive headache in the morning.

Hanna had now toasted four more times in addition to the first two he had downed when dinner began. Fortunately, Hanna had a lot of experience in handling these bloodless ambushes and could usually tolerate the onslaught with aplomb. Looking around the table, he figured the rest of his men would not be as lucky. They were being toasted as much as he was, and their tolerance for the local antifreeze did not match his own.

Screw it, he thought. They were all grown men, and they could always spill half the shot glass's contents on the tablecloth like he did to slow the process of ingestion. To the contrary, they were all laughing and joking loudly with the hosts, which sealed their fate.

Hanna turned to Sheu and asked her to translate a profound thank you to Zhang and to thank him for serving the extremely delicious entrée that they had just finished enjoying.

Hanna was about three quarters the way through his polite speech when Zhang threw up his hands to Sheu. The Chinese flew for a good minute before Sheu turned around to Hanna.

"Hannasan," Sheu said, " Zhang says that was only one more of the exquisitely prepared appetizers. He said that he feels most warmly about the fact that you participated with everyone in its enjoyment, but the entrée is yet to come."

Hanna was about to apologize for his misinterpretation of the facts when, once again, all the Chinese rose, roaring in unison and applauding loudly as the chef once again entered the room holding a tray high over his head. Unnoticed to Hanna, the fish skeleton had been quietly removed to make space for the new tray. Once again a waiter helped the chef place the tray in the middle of the table. The meat was well cooked and the steam once again rose from the meat. Well cooked apples and other vegetables were positioned judiciously around the serving to provide color and whet the participant's appetites.

Once again Hanna almost puked. It was half a dog, drawn from end to end.

Sheu recognized Hanna's discomfort and immediately

requested a Chivas Regal scotch (double) from one of the waiters. If the drink did not help, she was in trouble since she did not have a Plan B to solve his problem.

It worked.

Slowly the scotch brought Hanna around. He ate the cooked vegetables that had been placed on his plate by one of the waitresses and studiously avoided the dog.

"Hannasan," Zhang said, "You have eaten very little. You must eat, otherwise you will fall ill."

Through the interpreter, Hanna, while apologizing profusely for appearing not to enjoy the meal, responded that his small appetite was the reason why he only carried 195 pounds on a six foot one inch frame, and he really wanted to stay that way.

Zhang accepted the apology and excuse with grace.

The evening was quickly coming to a close. There was no entertainment room for them to reconvene to for dancing since the facility did not have one. Moreover, it was getting close to nine o'clock and Zhang's affairs always ended at nine.

Hanna responded to three more gasoline toasts and topped them off by finishing his scotch. He had to do it to wash the taste out of his mouth and settle his stomach.

To Hanna's everlasting delight the evening ended quickly. Promises were made all around to reconvene the negotiations quickly: hopefully within the next month. Hanna did not want to take the wind out of anyone's sails, so he kept his thoughts to himself, but there was no way that he was returning to this place within the next month.

It was a quick trip back to the hotel.

Twenty-Two
Help

Everyone decided on a nightcap in the lobby. The boys were verging on being stupidly smashed, but Hanna figured that all they would suffer in the morning would be a huge, splitting headache. He had noted that none of them had participated in the banquet tonight the way they had last Friday night.

Nobody's heart was in the spirit of the evening, however: they still had to pack and everyone had to be up at six am. They were all beginning to look as though they were regretting all the toasting this evening and they were slurring their words.

Sheu would meet them for an early breakfast in the morning and get them into their limo for the ride to the airport. After that, she had mentioned that she was going to visit friends and take the train back to Shanghai on Sunday. Monday, she would be back in the class room at Shanghai University teaching English to a bunch of China's finest, who would then be accepted into Harvard and Yale to study business, economics, and medicine before joining their colleagues back home in taking over the world while America kept looking around wondering what had happened.

As Dylan had once said in a song: "Well you know something is happening here but you don't know what it is, do you Mr. Jones?"

Hanna paid the check, left a 50 percent tip, and got up. All the others followed suit. Hanna motioned to Sheu to follow him up to his room. The entourage all figured Hanna was going to take one last one for himself before leaving. Actually his purpose was quite different.

The boys slid off the elevator on their successive floors, each hitting at least one side of the door as they did so. The good-night salutations were perfunctory. Everyone had to pack, and they all needed at least a couple of hours of sleep.

Hanna got off on his floor, Sheu in tow. They quickly walked the hallway to his room and went inside.

"Let me see, Sheu," Hanna said once they were inside. "Ten days work; you were ill all last weekend; ten hours per day at $300 per hour. That is $3,000 per day or $30,000 for the trip. Correct?"

"That is what I calculated as well Hannasan," Sheu said.

Hanna reached into the personal safe, an amenity provided by the hotel, where the cash had resided since he had arrived in China. He pulled three wrapped packs of brand-new, hundred dollar bills out of it and handed them to Sheu in exchange for which she handed him a receipt on which she had just filled in the amount and signed her name. The Chinese did not bill you for their services and wait to be paid forty-five days later from halfway around the world. They demanded their money immediately. From here on out, Hanna thought, the security of this cash was her responsibility, thank God. Sheu didn't blink an eye at the idea. Actually, Hanna was carrying another ten thousand dollar pack but Sheu was sick all the previous weekend and, at the price he was paying for her translation services he wasn't paying her a dime more than he had to. Americans, just like the Chinese, could also become very businesslike when the situation demanded it.

Sheu thanked him politely and gave him a firm handshake. Her "goodnight" was perfunctory, and in a flash she was gone.

When it gets down to the nutcutting, Hanna thought, *the Chinese were all business.*

Hanna locked the door behind her, poured himself a Chivas Regal, and packed his things for the trip out. He prided himself that, after a lifetime of travel, he had perfected the art of packing in such a way that he was always able to unpack at the next stop without a wrinkle in any piece of clothing. Not that it mattered. At the Shangra La in Singapore you called room service, and everything hanging in your closet was cleaned, ironed, stuffed with paper to hold its shape, and back in your closet within an hour.

It was two thirty when Hanna's head finally hit the pillow. He took four aspirins before lights out in the hope that they might somehow mitigate the awful way he was going to feel in the morning.

Twenty Three
A Day Late and a Dollar Short

The phone rang with perfect timing at precisely six in the morning.

Hanna showered, dressed in expensive casual clothing, and was waiting for the bellhop when he arrived at 6:40 to escort him and his bags down to the front desk to check out.

Sheu was already there, waiting, but no one else was.

"Hannasan," Sheu said, "Should I call your colleagues rooms since they have not yet arrived at the agreed time?"

"Nah," Hanna replied, "Get me checked out first and if they are not down by then, you can call them."

He could tell that the instructions upset Sheu. *How could anyone ever possibly be late?* he could see her thinking.

His bill paid, Hanna turned around to see Rudolf and Clifford standing behind him in the line to settle accounts. They both looked as though they were hurting. Jaime was just stumbling off the elevator holding his head. *That poor thing,* Hanna thought. He made a mental note to start spending more time with Jaime, teaching him how to drink. Hanna liked Jaime.

Hanna went over to the newsstand and bought a *China Daily* while the others finished up. There would be a selection of five good newspapers on the plane when they boarded. Sheu was at the side of each of them to ensure that the hotel didn't slide extra charges onto their bills and to make sure they paid the correct amounts. He was sitting in an overstuffed lobby chair with Cliff and Rudolf while Jaime settled up when he heard the scream.

"Hannasan! Hannasan! Hannasan!" the voice was calling.

It was Liu, being pushed in the front door by her Olympic training wrestler "friend" in a wheel chair. She was waving wildly at him.

She reached up her hand and took Hanna's in a firm handshake, which he had taught her to do earlier in a proper moment. The Chinese didn't show affection in public.

"Oh, Hannasan, I thought I would miss you. I was told you were leaving this morning, and I just had to come by and tell you the news before you left."

"Liu, good morning," Hanna replied, "It was really fortunate that you arrived when you did. Five more minutes and we would have been gone. Tell me, what is the news?"

Liu reached up and motioned him to come closer. When he did, she pulled his ear up to her lips and whispered, "I no longer virgin, Hannasan."

Hanna swallowed hard to keep his composure. "How did it happen Liu?" he asked.

Liu was grinning ear-to-ear. "Last Sunday, Hannasan," she replied. "Parents gone. We do often. All week: Many times. It fun Hannasan."

It didn't make any difference that Liu was twenty-six years old. Unmarried daughters lived at home with their parents until they were married.

Hanna looked at Mr. Olympic. Liu had told him the Saturday they spent together that the butt head didn't understand a word of English. He was standing there like some frozen Buddha. Hanna did notice a bit of smugness in his demeanor, however, the sonofabitch.

"I hope you're protecting yourself Liu. It is very easy to become pregnant when you're young like you are."

"Oh, don't worry Hannasan. I went on pill the first day I saw you at the train station. So sorry that last weekend did not work out, since I now have other lover. I was yours until I broke my ankle Hannasan, but I couldn't wait any longer," Liu said.

Virginity didn't seem to have much appeal, Hanna thought.

Hanna couldn't believe it. Here he was standing in the lobby of a five-star hotel in China, checked out and ready to fly out of country to continue, now, on a round the world trip, a young chick sitting in a wheel chair in front of him, one leg parked on a leg extender to keep it straight in its cast, and, he was being told that he could have nailed this gorgeous thing anytime he wanted until Mr. Olympic showed up.

Hanna looked up at the guy from his bent over position in front of Liu and extended his hand to acknowledge goodbye to the fat boy. He smiled as he said, "You dirty rotten plick, defiling this flower of the Republic this way. If I ever meet up with you again, I'll kill yah."

The wrestler smiled and bowed.

Hanna had turned away from Liu so that she couldn't hear him, and everyone else had gone out to the porte cochere to supervise the loading of their luggage into the limo in anticipation of being under way as soon as Hanna got his crap together.

Hanna turned back to Liu. "I wish you a very long and happy life Liu. Please keep in touch." How she could do that, Hanna left to her to figure out. He sure wasn't going to give her his home telephone number.

"Don't go just yet," Liu said. "I have more news for you."

What in the hell more could this one-week-ago, perfect virgin have as news that he could possibly be interested in? Hanna thought.

As pleasantly as he could, Hanna asked, "And what else do you have for me, Liu? I hope we can discuss it quickly. My car is waiting now to take me to the airport to catch a flight directly to Tokyo within the hour."

Liu was ecstatic: Beside herself as she handed him a small

booklet. "I got my passport, Hannasan. Look at my new English name."

Hanna opened the passport and looked.

There it was: Lady Anne Mary Liu.

The blood drained from Hanna's face but he kept some modicum of composure. "How very nice, Liu. The names go together perfectly."

Liu was smiling from ear to ear. "I think so too, Hannasan. Thank you for this legacy."

"I must go Liu," Hanna said. "All the best to you and Mr. Olympic. I'm sure you will have many beautiful children together."

"Maybe, maybe not, Hannasan," Liu said. "I still want you to take me to America with you. I see you next time you in town."

She'd obviously picked up that line from some western TV show, Hanna thought, as he turned and walked to the car.

Hanna's brain kicked into gear.

One point two billion people in China.

Half of them women.

Knock off a hundred million due to the fact that all Chinese parents, in an effort to always have a first born male son had led to a fratricide rate that would result in a country with an all male population within two generations.

That left five hundred million females in the country.

Three hundred million people in the U.S.A.

Half of them women.

That totaled up to six hundred and fifty million females between the two countries.

Hanna calculated that his wife and three granddaughters would have the news of Liu's naming in about four hours and twenty-three minutes.

Better have a response before he hit the ground in Tokyo, Hanna thought. Bad news always traveled fast.

Just Because You're Anonymous It Doesn't Mean You're Flying Under The Radar

If nothing else, one must always observe the three most sacred rules of life, the most important of which is, never waste anything.

Anonymous

Twenty Four
On The Road Again

They got underway. The limo streaked towards the airport, horn howling violently as the car swept through a sea of humanity teetering on bicycles that should have long since been junked. It was as though each Chinaman was awarded a bicycle when they came of age, and they had to ride it until the day they died. The one saving grace in this whole mess was that as one looked out at the oncoming sea of bike traffic, all those young female riders with their skirts cut about two inches below the you-know-what, displayed an unprecedented view of certain parts that otherwise would have gone unnoticed. And they loved the new fashion statements like thongs. What amazed Hanna was that most Chinese males appeared to be oblivious to the display. Either that or the culture of the country frowned upon men who openly lusted after the view. Whatever the answer was, Hanna never figured it out.

Once at the airport, they were directed to the private terminal set aside for travelers with personal aircraft at their disposal. It was a small, unimpressive building. There weren't many Chinese who had G-V's at their disposal.

The chief pilot immediately came over and introduced himself and his copilot. "Everyone else is already on board," he said. "You guys all headed back to Houston today?" he asked.

"Everyone except me," Hanna said, the disappointment showing in his voice.

"Sorry to hear that sir," came the reply. "If you're staying over in Tokyo tonight maybe my buddy and I can show you a good time."

Hanna thanked him but then mentioned how his plans would be taking him on to Singapore before nightfall.

"How much longer are you guys going to be over here?" Hanna asked.

"We have one more turnaround, and then we're home to Hobby airport," the pilot said. "Sounds as though we're going to make it back before you do, sir"

In twenty minutes, they had cleared customs and the bags were loaded on board. Hanna waited until everything was there before he headed for the aircraft. The guys were walking ahead of him, all of them holding their heads. It was at this point that Hanna looked up and saw the angels standing at the doorway of the plane.

All Hanna could do was stand there and marvel. *Where do we find these people?* Hanna thought. They looked better than Liu.

"Life's a bitch Mr. Hanna," the pilot said. "Com'on and I'll introduce them to you."

Hanna couldn't believe it. It had taken an hour, and Liu had been nearly forgotten. Hanna hoped that they were paid for. He didn't have enough cash on him to buy one of these for the amount of time he would need.

"And they're paid for," the pilot said, reading his mind. "Go ahead, enjoy."

Just Hanna and the pilot were still outside the aircraft at this point. Everyone else had boarded and the copilot had the starboard engine running.

Hanna climbed the stairs and entered the harem room. Everyone was being served Bloody Marys that included tall celery stalks and cold lobster with red sauce and fresh horseradish. There was a choice. The girls had large dipping bowls containing beluga caviar with crackers (American by the way) and chilled vodka to wash everything down. If you wished, there was even coffee and Danish with marmalade.

Hanna looked down the length of the plane. There were eight huge seats, six facing forward and two facing back. There was a table between the two seats in the center on each side. All of the seats folded out into a full size single bed, and Hanna would have bet his last dollar that there was bedding on board to service every seat comfortably. The two seats in the front were occupied by the two guys from Putnam Petroleum. It was obvious their last evening in wherever they had come from was about the same as Hanna's group. They appeared to be holding their heads and groaning as they took the first sips on their drinks. Both of them had accepted one of everything being served.

Should be lots of fun here in about an hour, Hanna thought, *and it was a four hour and fifty minute flight out to Tokyo.*

It wouldn't make any difference if they lost cabin pressure on this flight at thirty-nine thousand feet, Hanna thought to himself. Everyone had so much booze in their veins that they could survive several hours at a temperature of minus fifty degrees, and a complete lack of oxygen wouldn't harm anyone.

Hanna's troops had occupied three of the four center chairs that surrounded the tables, two facing forward that Cliff and Rudolf had commandeered while Jaime, the runt of the group and the youngest officer in the company, was delegated to accepting the seat facing rearward. Both Cliff and Rudolf got up to offer him one of the preferred seats facing forward, but Hanna waved them off.

He sat down in one of the two seats facing forward in the very rear of the plane. For some reason Hanna wanted to be alone.

One of the flight attendants was instantly at his side offering him sustenance from both trays. Hanna elected to have the coffee and Danish with marmalade. He was starting a twenty-four hour day, a lot of which he was going to be spending on his own while flying ten thousand miles, and he really couldn't afford to screw up before he got to a point where he could expect a few hours of peace and quiet. That wouldn't happen until he was on his way from Tokyo to Singapore.

The door had been closed and locked. The second engine started, and they were taxiing out for takeoff. One of the girls came around and checked to make sure they all had their seat belts fastened. Nobody was asked to put their seat backs up and no one picked up the food or drinks.

Ahh, the luxury of being able to make your own rules and thumb your nose at the FAA, Hanna thought.

A minute later, they were airborne and climbing to their cruising altitude as fast as those MIGs parked idly in disrepair on the grass at the edge of the runway ever could.

Hanna looked forward to see how everyone was doing. All the cabin lights were out except the one above his seat, and the fellows on the flight with him were succumbing to the land of nod at about thirty-second intervals. He was going to be the only one left awake in about two minutes. Not only that, the girls had covered them all with blankets and offered each a pillow. One drink and all of them were out. Hanna figured they would all be gone for the entire flight. He could feel himself slowly going. The only thing that was keeping his eyes from closing was the coffee he had ordered but that wasn't going to last long.

One of the flight attendants saw him looking around and was immediately at his side asking if there was anything else he might wish. Hanna sensed from the way she said "anything else" that it could be taken in the broadest possible context. Hanna sensed immediately that her home had to be Miami Beach because of a desire to be where the boys were. It was obvious that she knew what the question meant, and she was prepared to respond to any request that Hanna might have.

"Anything else," Hanna asked, "do you mean that there are other services on this aircraft that I am not aware of?"

"Mister Hanna," the flight attendant replied, "when I was advised that we would be carrying you and your delegation on this flight, I immediately called your office in Houston as we are instructed to do, to ascertain what your particular desires might be and was advised that as a world traveler you usually requested everything. Consequently, my question, 'is there anything else you might wish'?"

As his eyes were beginning to close despite all his efforts to stay awake, Hanna asked, "So who did you talk to in our office?"

The flight attendant's response was instant. "Mister Hanna, if I recall correctly she said her name was Mindy."

God damn Mindy, Hanna said to himself, as he thought about it for a second, and then declined everything, wishing only for a blanket and pillow like the others.

What the hell, Hanna thought. He'd joined the mile-high club with his darling many years ago on an almost empty flight between Hawaii and San Francisco.

No female would ever top what she had done with him that night.

Hanna hated to digress, but sometimes his mind just took control and his body was swept along for the ride. Right now he was getting very sleepy, and he was too weak to fight off the memory beginning to materialize.

In the good old days, if you wanted to ride on an empty commercial airline flight, Hanna though, *catch a ten pm flight eastbound on New Year's Eve.* It was so long ago that Hanna could not remember why the two of them were flying that evening, but for some reason they were and their seat assignment was in the rear coach section of the aircraft. Hanna counted two people flying alone in the middle section of the plane, and he thought he had seen about five people step into first class while they were in the boarding process. At this point in his career, Hanna was only allowed to fly steerage. First class was still a dream.

It was a wide-bodied jet with a coach seating configuration of three seats on each side next to the windows and five seats in the middle. The flight attendant came on the PA and, after wishing everyone a Happy New Year, she announced that all drinks would be on the house this evening. There wasn't a sound in the plane.

Obviously, the other seven people on board were already asleep. Being the only two people awake on the flight, after it lifted off they were asked by the flight attendant what they would enjoy. His darling's response was instantaneous. Blankets and pillows, a bottle of champagne, two glasses, turning off all lights except those required by the FAA to be left on at all times, and a request to not be bothered for the rest of the flight.

The flight attendant thanked her profusely saying quietly that this was the first time in her life that she would be able to sleep in the New Year on a flight. She also indicated that if no one was looking, and Hanna couldn't figure out who might be, she might just have a glass of champagne herself at midnight.

Hanna's darling had selected a center row that had the five seats. The champagne arrived. The blankets arrived. She poured a glass for each of them. She had placed about two dozen pillows along the row of seats. She then lay down, placed a blanket over herself, and invited him under the covers with her. In two minutes she had Hanna almost completely naked, and Hanna had done the same for her. As she invited him in, Hanna once again marveled, as he always did, why he had been the lucky one in her life when she could have had anyone she wanted. They were asleep that way when the lights came on announcing their descent into SFO. The flight attendant was kind enough to give them five minutes to dress before she appeared, walking towards them down the aisle.

The flight was as smooth as silk, and the champagne was untouched still sitting on the floor between the two glasses where Hanna had originally placed it. His darling skipped down the aisle to freshen up before landing.

Hanna was exhausted.

Headed out now for Tokyo, Hanna had just finished his coffee and Danish, when he looked over and noticed that one of the two flight attendants had plunked down in the seat across from him, placed the seat completely back to form a bed, pulled a blanket up over herself, smiled gently at him, and was sawing a log before he could smile back.

Sure must be nice, Hanna thought to himself, *when you are paid do all that is required of you in thirty minutes and can then retire on a flight out of the country to complete your day's work activity.*

Hanna was just about to drift into unconsciousness himself when it occurred to him: *where in the hell was the other flight attendant?*

He shouldn't have asked, even if it was only a thought. The cabin light above his head had just been turned off, and with all the cabin's window blinds drawn, the interior of the aircraft was almost completely dark disturbed only by the snores of a half dozen people who had had too little sleep and too much to drink the night before.

The only conscious motion remaining on the aircraft was the body that appeared in the aisle to his left. He looked up and realized most of the uniform had disappeared. The jacket was off, the blouse was gone, the cap had been laid away somewhere and the girl had unfolded her hair so that it dropped below her shoulders. Before Hanna could gasp, the body had crawled in under the blanket beside him and, with a supple, ballet-like move grasped his hand and pulled it in between her legs at which point he realized she had removed her panties as well.

Things were really beginning to look up, Hanna thought. The only problem was that he was beginning to get really tired: so tired that his hand (the one that the flight attendant had placed strategically on her body) had stopped moving. The problem was that a hand had reached over and grabbed his crotch and he realized that there was still one part of him that was capable of reacting to stimuli.

Hanna fell asleep drugged by a night of over doing everything and the concept of having a day off where he could do nothing.

"Mr. Hanna, Mr. Hanna," the voice was saying, as a hand gently shook his body. He looked up to see his erstwhile sleep mate looking absolutely prim and proper—hair drawn back into a bun, makeup perfectly applied, fully dressed in the uniform he remembered, and acting with absolutely dispassionate professionalism. "I thought you might wish to get refreshed before the others are awakened," she said.

Hanna woke and opened his eyes to look across the aisle. The other flight attendant was just beginning to stir. All the guys were still out.

Thank God that what had happened was all a dream even though it was a pretty good one, he thought. He got up and headed for the ornate head located in the rear of the plane. He had used it once just after they had become airborne, and it even had a shower in it.

I'll be quick, Hanna thought to himself. It's going to take half an hour for everyone to clean up and by then they would be on final approach into the airport.

Obviously, there's a certain order to things, Hanna observed. Use the bathroom before washing hands and splashing water on face to give the appearance of being awake.

Hanna reached down. His fly was undone, and he noticed a certain dampness that he had almost forgotten existed. Sonofabitch he thought.

Dream or something better he thought, *it didn't make any difference. He'd slept completely through it.*

Rule Seven for Avoiding Infidelity While away from Home on Extended Business Travel

Forcing people to allow you to inflict yourself upon them is one of most detestable of crimes, frequently having an extremely debilitating effect on the victim, if not now, at some point in the future. Therefore, the business traveler should always ensure that the body is so close to passing out from neglect, abuse, and over-indulgence that nothing is capable of stimulating its nerve endings, thereby, allowing it to avoid any recollection of the ordeal to which it has been subjected.

Twenty Five
When You Come to the "Y" In the Road…

Four hours and thirty minutes after they had taken off, they were on a glide path into Narita, a few miles outside of Tokyo. Once on the ground, they cleared customs and then headed off for the in-transit lounge at the main terminal. Hanna had been coming through this Heathrow of the Far East for twenty years. When originally conceived and built, it was regarded as ahead of its time and a refuge for the tired passenger. Now, if you weren't in first class, it was a cattle drive.

Hanna could think of so many of these deteriorating airports it was constantly upsetting him. Dallas had quit Love Field for DFW, and now that facility was overrun. Houston had built Intercontinental to replace Hobby, and the same thing happened there. Philadelphia was a wreck as was Minneapolis, LAX, SFA, Chicago, and every airport up in the Northeast including La Guardia, Newark, JFK, and Boston. Denver had finally built a new one to replace Stapleton, and it was already a failure. The facility didn't lose your luggage, it ate it. For the rest of them, finding your luggage after your flight arrived was a crap shoot.

None of the other airports, however, were willing to allow Denver to take home the award for bad service. This was one competition in which everyone wanted to excel. Having to change a flight put you in a line that was longer than the one at the unemployment office. And no one was allowing some also-ran in the Rockies to beat them. Service from any airport was nonexistent; getting a seat at any bar for a quick drink before boarding one's flight was no longer possible; and finding a seat on the aircraft without two overweight people sitting on either side of you was out of the question.

Narita exemplified everything that was wrong with airports all around the world. The problem was that it was designed to accommodate people who weighed a hundred pounds less and stood a foot shorter than Americans. The place had come to be as inhospitable as Antarctica in the middle of winter.

Thankfully, Hanna was in first class.

Hanna signed into the first-class lounge with his troops who had slept off some of last night's ordeal on the G-V flight in. Cliff mentioned how a little chicken soup for dinner on the flight home sounded good. Unfortunately, the other two who had only semi-recovered were not so lucky. It would take several days for them to be able to stand once again on their own.

For Hanna's part, the flight attendant on their inbound flight at least had the civility to thank him for his presence and to express her desire for his speedy return.

People do learn, Hanna thought. The boys were in much better shape today than they were a week ago. It just takes a little time and a swat with a two by four upside the head now and again. Hanna had absolutely no sympathy for their predicament and expressed none. Let the bastards suffer was his motto.

He poured three fingers of his favorite scotch at the unattended lounge bar. What the hell, they had left Nanjing at eight this morning, landed in Narita at one, and were in the terminal around two thirty after an interminable taxi to their ramp at the private-aircraft concourse. Of course, after that came the bus ride to the terminal proper and then the Alpine climb to the first-class lounge on the third floor. They were all so tired and weak from the accumulation of the last week's events that they decided to take the elevator.

Taking the elevator at the international-departures terminal at Narita was an adventure unto itself. In the first place, there was only one, and it looked more like a closet than an elevator. About four Japanese with luggage in tow could fit into it. Finally, it was hydraulic, so it moved at a snail's pace, and it stopped on every floor. The reason it stopped on every floor was a simple one that Hanna realized on his first trip through the terminal years ago. It all became clear when he saw a man get on going down, and then, when the door opened going up, there he was going up. At this point, Hanna realized you got on the damn thing if there was room regardless of which way it was travelling, otherwise, it took an hour to get to the floor you were going to.

Hanna explained this to the guys, then told them they were on their own after he grabbed the first open space that turned up. Actually, since they were getting on at the lowest floor they caught a break. There were only two people on the thing going up, so Hanna and Cliff made the first trip together. The other two passengers that rode the elevator and did not get off when they had stepped on went all the way to the top floor with them. As the door opened on each floor, a hoard of people tried to squeeze on.

Hanna didn't think it was possible for anyone to do this; however, one shapely, thin, young thing that Hanna later realized worked at the bar in the first-class lounge did manage it. There was no room to turn or breath after that, and since she had backed up right into his crotch, Hanna had some difficulty getting off on the top floor due to the bulge in his pants.

The other two guys made it up over the course of the next ten minutes or so. They arrived on separate elevator runs.

They were now able to take refuge from the great unwashed down in the main in-transit lounge.

"Okay boys," Hanna said, "you have an hour and fifteen minutes before you have to head back down into the morass to board your flight for San Francisco. You'll have to be at the boarding gate an hour ahead of time just in case customs singles you out for a second check. If that happens, you're in trouble. Call me, and I'll see what

I can do. If you can't raise me, you're just out of luck. You'll never make it back to the U.S.A."

Hanna relished it as all three went white as a sheet. Cliff and Rudolf both recovered pretty quickly, once they realized Hanna was pulling their chain but Jaime just continued to get whiter. He was looking like he had a heart-lung machine hooked up to one foot that was drawing all the blood from his body without replacing any of it.

"Jesus Christ, Hanna," Jaime said, "you mean there is the chance that they won't let us board our flight?"

"It's possible Jaime," Hanna replied, "but you can avoid any problems if you have a hundred-dollar bill ready to hand the customs guy when he picks you out of the boarding line for questioning."

"Good luck getting home, men." Hanna said. "I wish you all a safe and uneventful return to the motherland."

As he moved away, Hanna turned slightly and said over his shoulder, "By the way Jaime, you can't put that payment on your expense report. American laws against bribery of officials overseas and all that stuff you know."

Hanna went over and began watching CNN news. Despite the fact that he couldn't handle the network's left-wing views, it was the only place where one could listen to an American on this side of the world.

The time went by quickly. It seemed like no time until the lounge hostess came over and advised the guys they should head downstairs to catch their flight. Hanna could see they were all still upset by his remarks on a second search at the gate, but as he shook their hands goodbye and wished them well on their flight home, he decided against alleviating their concerns over his remarks.

An hour after the boys left for home, Hanna headed downstairs for the overnight flight to Singapore.

YOU CAN SAY THAT AGAIN

The best argument against a democratically elected congress is a five-minute conversation with the average voter.

Winston Churchill

Twenty Six
The City of the Lion's Gate

Hanna had been to Singapore any number of times previously, but the first sight of the city always brought him to a state of awe. They approached the island nation shortly after dawn, and to Hanna, it always seemed like the pilot's approach on their Singapore Airlines flight had a glide path completely around the city as a local Chamber of Commerce ploy to impress everyone as to the mystique of the place.

There were few single homes left on the island. Only the filthy rich could afford one. Most had all long since been replaced by fascinating high rises of every shape and size and containing every level of luxury. Flying over the straits separating Singapore and Indonesia, one was amazed by the seemingly endless line of ocean-going ships moving back and forth through the channel— thousands every day. It was obvious why the British had claimed the island as their own hundreds of years ago. No ship could pass through these waters without the permission of the people holding the high ground, and Britain always held the high ground.

Above and beyond all that, the people were fascinating. They had taken on the appearance of all the nations that had overrun the island since the beginning of time. Many had an oriental look about them, but many did not. Everyone was taught English from the moment they entered school and most had been exposed to the language since birth, which gave them a distinct advantage when it came to any aspect of life. Their manners were to be admired by all who came into contact with them, and their demeanor was absolutely professional. *It was almost like being in England,* Hanna thought, *the land of please and thank you.* Hanna loved Singapore.

Singapore was not that big a place (less than three-hundred square miles, which was about half the size of the city of Houston that Hanna called home) or that populous (4.6 million people), but foreigners always got a little tipsy when they first got off their flights and stepped onto ground at Changi International Airport. It was a bit like being on a ship at sea with long swells causing a slight pitch and roll. Actually what the unknowing did not realize was the fact that Singapore was not built on land.

Singapore was built on money.

Lee Kuan Yew, the first prime minister after the island's breakaway from Britain in the early 1960s, was the most benevolent of dictators, even though the country insisted it was an elected democracy. He kept most of the power for himself and his peers. In exchange, he made the country an example of the pinnacle of achievement for anyone who knew their history.

Lee was a believer that everyone should be able to retire in dignity after thirty years of work for their employer. To that end, early on he had parliament enact legislation to provide for everyone's retirement on the island by decreeing that, henceforth, all natives and their employers would each contribute 15 percent of the worker's pay each week to an account placed in local bank's savings certificates in the individual's name where it would gather interest for thirty years. After that, the individual was allowed to retire. In the meantime, no one was allowed to touch the account for any reason. If the worker died before he could retire, the account passed on to his heirs.

It was a somewhat better system than what Hanna's country had. Hanna often fanaticized over what the U.S.A. would be like today if the peasantry had been required to do the same as the Singaporeans. *Let me see now, people collectively earn $2 trillion* *dollars a year in the U.S.A. Fifteen percent that is $300 billion. Match that with an even contribution by the employer: $600 billion a year. Multiply that by thirty years. Yes, America would be in a lot different position if it had that kind of foresight. Problem was, politicians in a democratic republic could never think beyond their own pocketbook and their reelection.*

Lee had figured it out.

Lee also decreed that everyone would have a job. As a result, the island was landscaped and manicured from one end to the other. The terrain was absolutely beautiful, done by the least fortunate of all: those who had no education or training or who otherwise were incapable of performing work requiring some skill. And, they were paid as well for their work as a welder was in the shipbuilding yards of Jurong Town located as far away from the center of Singapore's commercial district downtown as possible. Singapore was always trying to promote itself as a high-tech financial center with green living conditions. Old nuts and bolts industries didn't fit this picture; thus the relegation of the shipbuilding and repair industry to the end of the island that no one ever visited.

Lee also eradicated malaria from the island by throwing anyone in jail who allowed standing water on their property that allowed mosquitoes to breed. He then eradicated drug usage by jailing users for twenty years and putting dealers who were caught plying the trade in jail for the rest of their lives after having them sit naked on a block of ice until it melted. All this, if he didn't decree a worse fate for them.

If only we could appreciate the sanity of these moves, Hanna thought. Unfortunately, it would never happen because the liberals always won the argument that, somehow, we could rehabilitate these assholes.

Besides all the other adjectives, Singapore was incredibly efficient. Everything was well oiled; nothing squeaked. Hanna passed through customs with an absolute minimum of inconvenience and with a maximum of speed. It had taken thirty minutes to walk the concourse from the plane, have a redcap retrieve his luggage, and pass through customs.

It was early Sunday morning.

"Shall I call you a car, sir?" the redcap asked.

"Thank you, but I believe I will be met," Hanna replied.

It took no more than walking to the curb outside when a driver approached and asked, "Mr. Hanna? My name is Tan, and I will be transporting you to your hotel today."

The guy obviously had my picture in the limousine, Hanna thought. He'd never seen the man before in his life.

"It is my privilege to welcome you to Singapore in the name of Mr. Chou," Tan continued, "He is unfortunately detained by pressing business matters; however, he intends to keep his appointments with you in the coming days to consummate the ventures that yours and his companies wish to join to accomplish." The limo driver's English was so perfect and without accent that Hanna figured he had to be teaching the subject in his spare time.

Obviously, Chou was on his yacht dallying with some sweet young thing, Hanna thought. The only thing that could keep him from working to double his already incredible net worth was the prospect of a good lay: And a good lay did not include his wife.

Easterners were able to document their lineage for about five thousand years, if not longer, while the English had settled the U.S.A. only a few hundred years ago. The Easterners had perfected the art of concubines and extra wives, while Western males were still wondering why they had opted for only one woman and were required by the courts to pay all ex-wives until they died, if the ex-husband decided he wanted more wives.

Life wasn't fair, Hanna thought.

"If you have the opportunity to see Mr. Chou between now and when we meet tomorrow, tell him that I will await his call on a time to meet," Hanna said.

This arrangement suited Hanna's demeanor to a T. Chou was older, smoked and drank too much, and worked harder at getting laid by twenty-two year olds than most. He knew he wouldn't hear from Chou before lunch.

For Hanna that was perfect. He needed a day of rest, a good night's sleep, some time to play the small three-hole golf course at the hotel in the morning, have breakfast by the pool, and admire the female bodies that frequented the chaise lounges poolside. All of the above while sipping on a Mai Tai. The Singaporeans were so civilized he thought: they weren't concerned about someone having a drink before lunch.

The car came to a stop under the huge drive that marked the entrance to the Hotel Shangra La. It was just as beautiful to behold as Hanna remembered from his past visits. The growth was lush everywhere, the architecture defied description, and the interior of the building was as ornate as any Hanna had ever been in.

"Mr. Hanna," Tan said, "the hotel staff will attend to your needs from here on. I shall leave now and return in the morning at such time as you and Mr. Chou agree to meet. Until then, I bid you adieux."

Hanna shook Tan's hand while handing him a hundred dollar bill. "Thank you, Tan. I will look forward to seeing you tomorrow then."

The sonofabitch had learned to speak Dicksonian English to impress his riders and collect those hundred-dollar bills, Hanna thought. Not that this was all bad. Hanna loved the sound of what he described to himself as High English. Besides, everyone had to make a living. This character had just figured out a way to do it better. Of course Hanna realized that in Singapore, this guy's main target was not the foreigners: no, most Singaporeans were wealthier and tipped better than foreigners.

The bellhop placed his luggage in security as he entered the hotel. Hanna rewarded him with a hundred-dollar bill after being handed IDs for each piece of luggage they were holding at the entrance reception area and headed for check in.

At reception, Hanna only had to sign his name. All documentation supporting his stay at the hotel had already been prepared and ready for his arrival. His passport number was on file, and all they did at check in was look at his current document to ensure that the number had not changed.

China thought it had five-star hotels, Hanna thought. *The Shangra La in Singapore was a five-star hotel and there was no comparison.*

"Is Mrs. Hanna not travelling with you on this trip, Mr. Hanna?" The check-in clerk asked. "We enjoyed her presence so much during your last trip. She kept all our staff busy with her shopping trips and daily lunch-time meals with a Mai Tai poolside."

Hanna had to laugh at the thought. His darling had made a confession to him one evening over a thousand-dollar dinner for the two of them (caused mainly by Hanna ordering two bottles of Chateau Lafite Rothschild) at the rooftop restaurant on the fiftieth floor of the hotel when she traveled to Singapore with him the last time. The dining room was actually a cabaret, having a stage that slid out from underneath the bandstand for the singer's nightly performance.

She admitted that during the daily thunderstorm that day she had retreated under an umbrella while the lightning flashed and boomed. She had laid her head down and slept off the morning's Mai Tais over the course of the next three hours. When she woke up, the imprint of the table top was deep on her cheek and everyone else was back frolicking in the pool. Everyone was staring at her wondering what her problem was. The funniest part was that a poolside waitress was immediately at her side saying "Mai Tai?"

Mrs. Hanna loved this kind of scene. While she was no lush (she had never allowed drugs or booze to compromise her well-being), the thought of the pool waitress calling her Mai Tai instead of Mrs. Hanna was very funny to her.

While a dog is dragged down the street on its leash believing its name is "Come on," Mrs. Hanna had begun to think that her name was "Mai Tai."

"No, Ling," Hanna responded with a grin, "This trip came up very unexpectedly and unfortunately, Mrs. Hanna was unable to join me." Right now, Hanna mused, he was prepared to fly her over first class for the sole purpose of wreaking havoc on her body. Quite frankly he thought, she was probably in the same mood.

Oh well, Hanna thought. *His darling's love was capable of carrying her through such trying times, and his bad luck kept him true to the vows they had made to each other many years ago. Hell, it wasn't bad luck. He already had the best.*

Like everything else in this city-state, the hotel was as efficient at checking him in as customs at the airport was at moving him through. Within five minutes, the receptionist had him registered, waved for a bellhop to carry his bags to his room, and wished him a pleasant stay until his departure the coming Thursday.

It was a quiet Sunday morning with only a few people stirring. The place would be a beehive of activity by noon, Hanna thought. This hotel was always 100 percent occupied, despite the fact that the rooms started at nine-hundred dollars a night and a suite like his was triple that.

Any foreigner, especially Americans, who thought other countries did not think big had not visited the Shangra La in Singapore. Every suite was twice as large as it needed to be. The bedroom contained a king-sized bed and had two full closets with a safe for valuables located inside of one. Two overstuffed chairs with a coffee table between them were placed in front of floor-to-ceiling windows looking out onto the grounds. There was access to the marbled, Hollywood-style bathroom from the bedroom, which also had a door providing access to it from the outer area as you walked into the suite.

Both entryways to the bathroom had their own sink and cabinets for linens. From either direction when you walked through the door, you were greeted by a large shower, Jacuzzi, "Bidet por Madam," and a regular water closet. Of course, the front door was for guests to use since you didn't want them walking through the boudoir!

There was a fully functioning kitchen, which Hanna doubted if any guest had ever used. He had always just assumed that it was for your personal cook/waiter to keep things warm when you dined in with company. Hanna had never used the thing, except for the minibar located in it, since he had not even yet visited all the restaurants located in the hotel.

The main seating area was very large. It had a sofa and chairs surrounding a large coffee table. Beyond that, there was a circular table with four chairs to dine at if you wished.

But, the pièce de résistance was the outside patio and the exit through the floor-to-ceiling French doors. Hanna was on the main floor, and there was a trellis that swam in color because of all the flowers and plants. Beyond the color was the scent. You felt like you were walking into a perfume factory when you stepped out onto it to read the morning paper and get a bit of sun before the heat became unbearable.

Hanna had concluded sarcastically to himself one time that the reason the suites were so expensive was that there were not enough to meet the demands of the patrons. After all, he had once heard there were only about 350. "Let me see," Hanna said to himself, "that would only represent about a million a night in revenues and of course did not count the forty-nine story tower that formed the main center of the operation." Regardless of the cost, it was worth every penny, Hanna thought.

Hanna couldn't remember how many pools there were in the hotel. He did recall that room service always took about two-thirds of the time that one would normally expect it to take, and it was always white-linen impeccable. You placed your shoes in a cabinet in the wall adjacent to the entry door before retiring for the night, and they were sitting there glowing at you when you went to put them on in the morning. Room service could be called when one entered the shower, and all the attire one planned to wear that day would be pressed, freshened, and hanging back in your closet before you had dried off.

It was as though there was a personal-service crew standing outside your door at all times, waiting for you to ask for something. As Hanna had observed earlier, the Singaporeans were far ahead of their Asian counterparts, which endeared them to the western traveler.

The bellhop opened the door to Hanna's room and motioned for him to enter. There were at least a half-dozen vases full of flowers positioned throughout the rooms that he could see, and he could only assume that there would be many more in the bedroom and the bathroom as well. The bellhop immediately opened up the double doors to the terrace that held an ornate table and chairs for two. The early morning perfumed scent of all the jasmine and hibiscus that landscaped the area immediately beyond the patio and wound around trellises attached to the outer walls of the terrace would make someone who was allergic swoon. Fortunately, Hanna wasn't.

The bellhop laid his two fine-leather luggage pieces on their stand, placed the third large bag on the luggage rack provided, then turned to ask him if there was anything he needed. Hanna flipped him a hundred dollars but declined.

"Breakfast is coming." Hanna said "I'll be fine."

The waiter was standing at the door with breakfast as the bellhop opened it.

The waiter rolled the cart in and proceeded to the terrace. Starched white linen tablecloth and napkins immediately appeared, followed by silverware. The first course of grapefruit juice and coffee was immediately poured, and the waiter produced copies of the *New York Times, Washington Post,* and the *London Financial Times.* Hanna took the opportunity to retire to the bathroom where he donned a swim suit and a hotel kimono. The waiter stepped back from the table and hid himself at the corner of the terrace. Hanna returned from the bathroom dressed for the pool and sat down.

It was a glorious Sunday morning in Singapore. There was a slight breeze, and the temperature was eighty-two degrees with 90 percent humidity. By noon it would be ninety-eight degrees with 75 percent humidity and a thunder shower imminent. Singapore was very predictable.

The first cup of coffee went down in a flash. He had read the waiter's name off his tag on his left collar and began, "Tan, you may serve breakfast now, I am actually quite hungry."

Tan leapt to the serving station trolley to produce poached eggs, Canadian bacon, warmed spinach with English muffins, and marmalade. Without any hesitation or questioning of Hanna, he reached into the serving tray and removed a Bloody Mary from the freezer, placing it in front of Hanna. He then returned to the freezer, extracted a bottle of champagne, poured half a glass of orange juice and created a mimosa.

The Shangra La noted all patrons' likes and dislikes and was prepared to serve exactly what most guests had previously enjoyed on every morning they had ever stayed at the hotel. Hanna would not bet against the fact that tomorrow morning the serving group would be there with exactly what he wanted to be served on Monday mornings. All you had to tell room service was that you wanted breakfast served at a certain time. They already knew exactly what you wanted.

At the Shangra La, there was nothing that humankind could do to beat the service. The management had a system that recorded every nuance of the traveler, and they provided it before you asked.

Hanna loved Singapore.

He read all three papers.

How they were delivered in Singapore on the same day they were published halfway around the world didn't concern Hanna. Two weeks' worth of the *China Daily* made him absolutely fixated on how lucky he was to be able to read a newspaper produced by a free press.

Hanna began to reflect. Two weeks in China, the complete change in his itinerary, the flight out of country, his uneventful flight to Singapore, the opportunity to put together a deal that would add one-hundred-million dollars to his company's impending investment in China—all were reasons to think that things were moving forward. He quietly reflected on how fortunate he was.

Hanna got up from his chair and walked across the manicured lawn to the pool. You didn't have to worry about someone rifling your room while you were away. Everyone in this hotel had been vetted so well the guests had no reason to worry.

Afternoon by the pool was a beautiful diversion. Hanna sipped on a couple of Mai Tais as the time passed, ducked back onto his terrace when the afternoon thundershower hit, and spent a lot of time in the water. The crowd was friendly and hailed from every corner of the world from Germany to Chile. He made small talk but kept it to that.

Hanna did not want to overdo anything. The next three days were important to his company.

He dressed for dinner about seven after a long shower and took the elevator to the fiftieth floor to enjoy the piano bar, have a quick Philly Cheese Steak with a couple of glasses of wine, and admire the city from the perfect vantage point. He only requested two songs from the piano player: "Autumn in New York" and "A New York State of Mind," his favorite Billy Joel number, which, if you closed your eyes, Billy was playing.

His sandwich was prepared to perfection. No street-corner vendor in Philadelphia could have done it better.

He left after signing his check with an added 50 percent for the waiter and a hundred-dollar bill dropped in the glass vase for the piano player.

Hanna was in bed, sound asleep, by ten thirty.

Twenty Seven
Not Even an Oilman Could
Have Done It Better

Hanna was up Monday morning with the dawn. He'd left the patio doors ajar overnight and turned the air conditioning down to compensate for the ever-intense humidity. He quickly changed into a new, dry bathing suit, threw on a lightweight Nehru jacket, and headed for the pool.

He and about five other people enjoyed the huge kidney-shaped pool for the next hour, doing laps and stopping occasionally to enjoy a sip of coffee set next to where they had dropped their outer wear at poolside.

Hanna headed back to his room at seven thirty just in time to watch room service setting his table with the breakfast he had ordered before retiring. His coffee had been poured and he was able to sit down with the *New York Times* in one movement without missing a beat.

The waiter retired to hide in the shadows until such time as Hanna dismissed him, which he did after reading the headlines and having been served the main course. For as long as Hanna had been coming to Singapore, he never stopped marveling at the early morning smell of all the flowers, including the orchids for which the island nation was famous.

The call came about ten am from Chou's secretary.

"Good morning, Mr. Hanna," the voice trilled in perfect English without accent. "Mr. Chou asked me to call and see if you could join him for lunch at twelve noon."

Hanna acknowledged as how that would be perfect timing and thanked the voice profusely.

The voice responded, "Then our driver will be there at eleven thirty. Mr. Chou usually dines at Raffles for lunch, and it will take you about thirty minutes at that time of day to get from the hotel to the club. Should you need anything, please do not hesitate to call and ask for me. My name is Tan."

"Thank you Tan," Hanna replied. "I doubt that I will need further information after your explicit instructions, nevertheless, I appreciate your offer."

Hanna loved Singapore. If you couldn't remember a person's name on this island, call them Tan, and you would be right 25 percent of the time: That much of the population had that last name. It was the Smith of Singapore.

Hanna showered and shaved after breakfast and dressed in his finest "tourist chic." He put on a light-blue jacket to complement his light-tan slacks and shoes. Few people wore a tie in Singapore. It was just too hot. *It was hot all year round,* he thought. The temperature range day to night, winter to summer was about fifteen degrees. The humidity dropped to 75 percent during the day and climbed to 100 percent by midnight. Not really, but, it sure felt that way. Whatever it rose to, every window in the country was "sweating" before dawn. *Oh well,* Hanna thought, *when you were a hundred miles from the equator at sea level there was nothing else you could expect.*

He left his room for the hotel lobby and entrance way at 11:25. When you lived in a suite at the Shangra La, you didn't have to take the elevator. He walked out front to the livery area at 11:28 to see Chou's limousine pulling into the porte cochere. Before Tan could come around to his side to open the door for him, a valet had opened it and ushered him inside. Tan slipped the car into gear and they moved off. They arrived at Raffles promptly at twelve noon.

Raffles was one of the oldest original buildings and the oldest hotel in Singapore as near as Hanna could discern. Before the arrival of the British, the only things the island was famous for were malaria-infected mosquitoes and deadly snakes. Raffles was named after the man who began the renaissance of the island in the early nineteenth century. The hotel itself was built in the late 1800s, and the building and grounds were magnificent. The hotel had become a jewel in Singapore's crown, and it was renowned for its unsurpassed service, having been named the best hotel in Asia many times. The only things that Hanna had to compare the place to were the Greenbrier and Homestead Hotels in the Virginias, The Beverly Hills in Los Angeles, The Peninsula in Hong Kong, or the Charles V in Paris. Raffles had everything all these hotels had and was better than all of them.

The cost of entering the front lobby of Raffles was more expensive than the Shangra La with its five-star extra charge.

Tan brought the car to a halt at the entrance, and a club valet opened the door for Hanna. Chou was standing in the middle of the lobby as he entered.

" William, it is so good to see you again. How is Mr. Llewellyn? I trust he and his family are all in fine health as I hope yours is as well," Chou said.

"It is good to see you as well," Hanna responded.

Chou was the typical Singaporean. He stood about five foot five inches and he looked a lot like Goldfinger's henchman in the James Bond movie. While he was at least a hundred pounds overweight, he had a well-exercised body and he was light on his feet if that were possible. Hanna knew that he had an indoor handball court in his home and a workout gym located next to it. He had the stereotypical moonface, one of the most distinctive Asian features. But above all else he was wealthy beyond anyone's imagining, and he was always in a good mood that Hanna felt was a reflection of the life he could afford to live because of that wealth. He wanted for nothing.

Hanna had learned of Chou's wealth and far-flung business empire early on in their relationship. After learning that Hanna's company was negotiating with the Chinese to close a very large automotive deal in China that Chou himself had been quietly investigating, he asked them to consider him coming in as a partner with them. Before Hanna agreed to anything, he made a confidential investigation of Chou, his jaw dropping when he was finally made aware of how vast the man's holdings were.

Hanna recalled that Somerset Maugham once described Raffles as "all the fables of the Exotic East." He was right. Maugham wrote his first book of short stories here and had a suite named after him. Every kind of luxury was available here for the traveler. There were over a dozen bars and restaurants on site and, for those staying there, a personal butler from the time one arrived until the time one left. It was finer than the Shangra La.

Chou liked the billiard room and bar with its hundred-year-old snooker tables. Hanna had wasted most of his youth playing pool, and he loved the game. In any case, Hanna didn't argue. Wherever they went at Raffles was fine with him.

After a two-hour lunch consisting of a jumbo shrimp salad, bread rolls with butter, two medium-dark Guinness ales, and a lot of small talk, they finally agreed to move back to Chou's offices where a battery of assistants and attorneys awaited their arrival.

It was difficult to refer to Chou's business center as "offices." A gourmet restaurant open to the public occupied the top floor of the building. The next floor down housed the offices of Chou and his executive management. All the administrative personnel that oversaw and reported on the far-flung empire of Chou were located on the three floors below that. Two high-speed private elevators ran directly from street level about sixty floors below to the Group's private floors.

The ceilings were fourteen feet high, and everything was constructed from the finest woods to be found anywhere in the world. One would have expected this to make the floor dark and depressing; however, indirect and direct lighting made all the working areas surprisingly bright and warm. Another hydraulic elevator made the last one story trip to the dinner club on the top floor.

Chou's personal office consumed at least half, if not more, of the twenty-thousand square feet on the floor. What was left was assigned to about five trusted advisors and their executive assistants. You saw this if you got off the elevator and walked straight forward. The paths to each of the offices radiated out from this point after one passed through a penthouse-like outer waiting area. A central receptionist relayed your arrival to the appropriate executive whose assistant came out to escort you back to her bosses' personal suite.

If you walked around to the rear of the elevator, you encountered another large waiting area with a receptionist's desk, behind which sat two fine Miss World candidates, neither of which would ever enjoy the title, because Chou paid them a lot more to adorn the floor with their orchid-like beauty. The hallway behind the reception desk flowed straight to Chou's principal office. The hallway was twice as wide as it would otherwise be so that a dozen original oils, none of which would have auctioned for less than $10 million were hung for the private viewing of the fortunate few that made it this far.

Hanna spotted two artists immediately. A Vincent Van Gogh with the yellow glow of a restaurant at night with its lighting backed by a late evening deep-blue starlit sky and a Claude Monet with a view of a garden in his home town of Giverny portraying a festival of pinks, purples, and other blended hues that completely overwhelmed the viewer. As Hanna moved down the hallway he also spotted a Cezanne and a Renoir. There were other artists that Hanna didn't recognize, but that didn't distract from the sheer beauty of their work.

Hanna had always figured Chou's main office as containing somewhere in the neighborhood of two-thousand square feet with more artwork displayed around the several seating areas and an elaborate yet unpretentious desk from which he worked. Bookcases filled with classics lined one wall and a fireplace another. Doors lead from both sides to outer offices, one set aside for intimate discussions, the other to a formal meeting room set for twelve with another ornate table and high-backed leather chairs. Chou didn't need a board room: He was the only shareholder of the realm and reported to no one but himself. One wall of this room contained a sixty-inch screen with video-conferencing equipment from which Chou directed the operations of his far-flung empire. Behind this room was a spa with sauna, marbled executive bathrooms, lockers, and showers.

A doorway lead from the other side of the room for quiet negotiations to a dining area after one again passed by an elaborate array of executive washroom facilities. Two dining tables in this room could seat sixteen people comfortably. The dining room had complete kitchen facilities; however, they were rarely used since a dumbwaiter ran between this room and the kitchen of the dinner club located on the floor above, and most meals were catered from that location. From the reception areas and the offices located on this floor no one would ever suspect that there was a dining room located here, since a slight negative pressure gradient in these rooms evacuated all food smells directly to the outside.

At this point, as far as Hanna could assess the situation, Chou regarded him as royalty. Hanna could see that Chou really wanted a piece of the action in China that Hanna was negotiating, and he was going to make certain that Hanna received the treatment appropriate to someone with the capability to allow him to achieve that goal.

Hanna knew that all the agreements had been drafted previously before Chou had gotten cold feet and backed out of the original deal. After Chou and Hanna spent a few final moments in Chou's office, they both moved over to the board room, which contained six attorneys, three for each group of interests. Houston had made arrangements over the weekend for Hanna's aides, and they were fully up to speed on what was left to consummate the deal. After two hours of serious but affable discussions, an updated draft was ready for review and distribution to the Houston offices, where they would be reviewed by the bank of attorneys that Llewellyn paid to keep him out of trouble.

Within moments, with Hanna standing behind the bank of attorneys carefully watching the process, the new draft was in e-mail format and on its way to the U.S.A.

With nothing further to do, everyone made a few moments of small talk and headed for the elevators. Chou begged everyone's indulgence, stating that he had domestic duties to attend to. *Chou's current love interest must be really hot,* Hanna thought. You could see the guy's mind drifting off into nirvana as he excused himself and headed out on his own. Hanna's attorneys had already suggested dinner with him, and off they went.

As could be expected, dinner was excellent, the service superb, the evening filled with small talk after a few business details were hashed out, and the outrageous bill paid graciously by one of Hanna's hosts. Of course, Hanna realized that it would appear on the firm's invoice for this contract work with a 25 percent markup to cover their overhead.

Hanna didn't care.

He was back at the hotel in bed and drifting off to sleep by eleven pm after a quick dip in the blue, illuminated pool and a nightcap on his patio.

Twenty Eight
Closing on a Positive Note

Everyone was met in the office Tuesday morning by a string of e-mails containing amended drafts. *Thanks a lot*, Hanna thought. Attorneys could not leave a document alone. The six local attorneys would have to negotiate further and reach a final compromise. Given Chou's desire to close the deal, however, this was not too great a challenge, and by late afternoon, a new draft was ready and e-mailed to Houston.

Wednesday morning, when they reconvened, an approved draft had been initialed by Houston, and everyone in Singapore was authorized to move forward with closing.

By late afternoon, Hanna was able to confirm that $100 million had been transferred to his company's bank account in Houston, and the contract was inked in duplicate with Chou signing for his Group and Hanna signing on behalf of his company.

Hanna sat back quietly in total amazement. A half a dozen trips to China had drawn agreement on about fifteen clauses of what would eventually be a minimum sixty-clause agreement, which had already wasted months of time for everyone involved. Seventy-two hours in Singapore was all it had taken for $100 million to pass from a new participant to a deal to those already involved in the negotiations.

It all harked back to private enterprise and capitalism versus collective responsibility and socialism. (And that was only possible if China could demonstrate it had moved on from Communism to the new socialism it aspired to.)

Over in the quiet negotiations office after signing the deal, the kitchen staff served champagne and canapés to everyone to celebrate the successful conclusion of the deal. Thirty minutes later, everyone had said their goodbyes and left. Hanna and Chou were alone in the room.

The butler suggested they have something a little stronger for a private toast. Hanna ordered a martini; Chou bourbon and water. They sat down in resplendent comfort with their drinks and an incredibly fine cigar that had been offered from Chou's humidor.

Having clinked their glasses in a toast, the two of them slid back into their well-cushioned chairs to relax. Floor to ceiling windows provided a spectacular view of the city. They were going to have dinner together this evening to celebrate the signing of the deal, but Hanna was beginning to sense that Chou was bothered by something.

"So, William, how was your visit to China? Was anything accomplished, or did you just continue to banter with the politburo and waste time?"

"Well, Chou," Hanna replied, "it was, as usual, a frustrating experience. Nevertheless, I think that we will reach some agreement, given the time. However, I don't want to lead you on. It could be another two years before we get there, and that would require my being over here talking to them every other month between now and then."

"I have every faith that you will accomplish our goal, William. The government has ordered them to go out and get technology at any cost. The problem is, they don't know how to negotiate, therefore, they are always asking for everything with the intent of giving up nothing. I have a good negotiator on staff, William, and he is fluent in Mandarin. If you wish, let me know when you are planning to return to Nanjing, and I will have him meet you in country to assist."

"I'll take you up on that offer, Chou," Hanna said. "Obviously, there is no time to meet him now. The hour is late and I leave Singapore tomorrow. Why don't you have him come through Houston on his next trip to the United States, and I'll buy him dinner at Vic and Antony's in downtown Houston and send him home with a ten-gallon cowboy hat."

"He is scheduled to be in the United States next month, William. I will have him add Houston to his itinerary," Chou said. "He will be pleased with the cowboy hat, and you can advise him of your plans for returning to China."

Hanna leaned forward in his chair so that he was no taller than Chou and quietly spoke. "Chou, it appears that something is upsetting you. Is there anything I can do?" Hanna knew it wouldn't take long for him to blurt it out. Chou was too strong a personality to let something he was concerned about lie secretly hidden in the back of his mind.

"William," Chou asked, "how long is it since you have been at your home in Houston?"

Hanna was not particularly taken aback by the question. Contrary to their Chinese counterparts from whom most of them drew their heritage, Singaporeans had come to be direct just like Westerners.

Hanna took a sip of his martini and a long draw on the cigar he had lit up. "Well Chou," Hanna replied, "I left Houston two weeks ago last Friday afternoon. It is just a little bit short of three weeks since I had the comfort of my home and family."

"Oh, William, that is far, far too long for one to be away from one's family, especially one's wife," Chou responded. "Far, far too long. We are having dinner this evening to celebrate our agreement. Let me see what I can do."

Chou did not elaborate further and Hanna didn't ask. He was afraid to.

It was turning late afternoon. Both of them had to be on their way to clean up and dress for dinner. They finished their cigars and drinks chatting amicably about the world in general and a little about their respective companies and their operations. Hanna tried to keep up with Chou as he talked adding up an estimated value of everything he controlled. As best as Hanna could figure, Chou had to be worth several billion dollars.

Hanna quietly smiled to himself. *It was the reason why Chou was able to write a check for $100 million and have it transferred to Hanna's company on about twenty-four hours notice,* Hanna thought. The thing about it all was that Chou did not appear on anyone's list of the wealthiest people in the world. Even though Chou held the fate of thousands of employees in his hands and made decisions daily that had hundreds of millions of dollars involved, he flew completely under the radar.

Hanna figured there were many more just like Chou. They didn't have to deal with a *Forbes* which would plaster their names all over the cover of the nation's magazines after researching their SEC filings. No, Hanna thought, *these people quietly amassed fortunes worth billions, built or destroyed political systems within and beyond their shores, substituting others into positions of influence that aided their personal success, and lived a life of quiet luxury while gaining the complete admiration and loyalty of their inner circle of employees because of their benevolence.*

"I wonder if Chou would let me play with his toys," Hanna said to himself as he hit the marble halls of the executive washrooms one last time before heading back to the hotel to dress for dinner.

Chou and Hanna left together. Almost everyone had left for the day; however, the two heavenly angels had now been replaced by two guards at the reception area. They both wore pistols, and there were probably loaded Uzis with the safeties off, lying quietly on the desk top next to them. Anyone who had ever been on this floor would quickly realize they could get ten million or more by fencing the art work for 10 percent of its value. These guys were so big and obviously well trained that Hanna figured any erstwhile thief had about one chance in a million of making it out alive if he was stupid enough to convince himself that he could do it.

The guards rose bowing deeply as they did so, and smiled their good evenings to both Hanna and their boss as the two walked across the reception area towards the elevator. Hanna marveled how they both looked like Goldfinger's chauffeur as he quietly crushed a golf ball in his hand at St. Andrew's after Bond had caught his boss cheating in their golf match and consequently having to forfeit the game.

Chou pushed the button for the first floor of the garage located beneath the building. They were there in a flash, not having to stop anywhere in route to pick up or disgorge other workers in the building.

The door opened, and Hanna immediately saw two limousines awaiting their arrival. Another driver with a three-carat diamond on his pinky was holding the door open for Chou. Tan was doing the same for Hanna.

"I will pick you up with my car in two hours, William," Chou said. "Tan will leave after he returns you to your hotel."

Twenty Nine
Don't Cry for Me, Argentina

Back in his room, Hanna poured himself a drink. He then walked over to his laptop, and despite all of the traffic back and forth between Singapore and Houston over the course of the last three days, he e-mailed a two-word message to Llewellyn.

"Mission accomplished."

He hit the send button. Hanna didn't want anyone else taking any credit for this deal. It was his deal, and his alone.

By now, Hanna was standing in front of the full-length mirror in the bathroom, fully erect but about to remove his silk jockeys. He admired all 195 pounds of muscled good looks staring back at him.

"Congratulations, you handsome bastard," he said aloud. "For your unflinching focus on your personal responsibilities plus your uncanny ability to move beyond your normally assigned duties to have a man give you a $100 million we shall attempt to award you with a piece of exotica from the local talent pool before the evening is over."

Hanna stepped into the shower. Possibly he would be able to locate something in the lobby after dinner with Chou was over. As Chou had said earlier this afternoon, it had been far, far too long for Hanna. His body was primed for dessert. It was beginning to insist that he partake of some before he headed for Malaga tomorrow afternoon. Besides, he had noticed a couple of potential candidates in the lobby the last two nights who, he figured, could be convinced that for some monetary consideration their presence at a command performance in his room was a viable suggestion.

Tonight, Hanna thought, *we're dressing for the kill.* The clothes he had laid out for the valet to press, as usual, were hanging on the bar of the closet door, looking immaculate as he stepped out of the shower to dry himself off. He then put on fresh silk jockeys and continued with a button-down, long-sleeved, white, silk shirt of which he left two buttons at the collar undone. He closed the sleeves with a fifteen-hundred dollar pair of cufflinks. He then slid on his very favorite pair of slacks after slipping into silk socks; finally adding a belt with matching shoes.

As a final action, Hanna quickly blow-dried his hair, sprayed it down, and dabbed a bit of Givenchy Gentleman on his freshly shaven face and the upper part of his chest. He then slid into a very lightweight dinner jacket and turned once again to check himself out in the mirror.

He decided he was going to have to audition for the male stud on TV's next session of "The Bachelor." No woman should be deprived of the opportunity to win some time with this godlike form. It would be best to stop keeping it a secret, and all it would take is getting his beautiful, darling wife to agree. The only problem in all of this was that she was so self-confident she probably would let him do it.

Hanna had about ten minutes before he had to leave. He sat down on the sofa, drink in hand, and let himself relax. The flowers around the room had been replaced, as they were every morning. The sound he had turned on very low when he first entered the suite earlier this evening was playing some of the very finest music Hanna could ever recall.

Life was good, Hanna thought to himself again. *It was just that sometimes it was better than others. This moment was better than most.*

Hanna finished off what was left of his drink, got up, took one final look at the Adonis staring back at him from the mirror, and headed for the door. Two minutes later, he was standing out at the livery stand waiting for Chou to arrive.

Chou's limo pulled up thirty seconds later. Hanna looked at his watch. It was seven thirty.

God, Hanna thought. *Asians were uncanny when it came to time.*

The limo was even bigger than the standard stretch that could seat six.

Before Hanna could step off the curb, the valet had opened the door, and Chou stepped out. "William, I feel so good about our seeing each other once again and for having the opportunity to dine and visit with you one last time before you continue your journey on around the world," Chou said. He grabbed Hanna's hand and arm with both his hands and shook it firmly several times.

Chou then leaned over and asked for Hanna's ear. Hanna, who was quite a bit taller, leaned over so that Chou could speak directly into it. Chou lowered his voice and said, "William, please forgive me if I have overstepped my place, but I hope that you will give me the opportunity to introduce a couple of lady friends of mine whom I have invited to have dinner with us this evening. Would you be adverse to such a suggestion? If you would like for just you and me to spend the evening together, I will have the ladies take a taxi home so that we can do that. My thought, however, is that we could both use a little relaxation after the events of the last three days, and as I said earlier this afternoon: you have been away from your wife far too long. What are your feelings about my proposal?"

Hanna had to suppress his ecstatic elation over Chou's suggestion. He wouldn't even have to cruise the lobby tonight when he returned to the hotel. The body was coming gift wrapped from Chou.

"Well, Chou," Hanna began, "while it is a little unusual, and I'm sure my wife would be very upset if she ever became aware of this, I think I can at least agree to the suggestion for dinner.

After that, I would have to further consider anything untoward. Nevertheless, Chou, inviting the two of them to dinner is certainly agreeable to me. Let's get the evening started."

"Excellent," Chou said, "We will begin our evening then. Let me enter the car first, and then you can step inside as I introduce you properly."

"After you, Chou," Hanna said. To himself he just hoped that the girl wasn't an obvious hooker. Thinking about it though, Hanna thought, Chou was good to him, and this was exactly in character, so what the hell, he'd gamble a couple of hours of his time and give it a shot.

Chou reentered the limo. Hanna gave him a moment to turn around and seat himself then he entered behind him.

"William," Chou said, "this is Sui. She is a very close friend of mine, and we try to get together at least twice a month to keep abreast of each other's comings and goings."

Sui extended her hand. "Mr. Hanna, it is such a pleasure to meet you. Chou talks about you constantly in such glowing terms that I expected a god. Frankly, you don't miss the mark by much."

Sui couldn't have been more than twenty-five, and she was absolutely stunning. Not only that, her English was formal and without accent. Obviously, her higher education had been in some English-speaking country.

"It is a distinct pleasure to meet you, Sui," Hanna said, "Chou has spoken often and with much warmness about you, and it is so good that we are finally able to meet each other."

Actually, Chou had never mentioned the woman but he was smiling broadly, so Hanna could only assume that he had clinched Chou's late-night bedtime activities for him.

To this point, the conversation had been between Chou, his date, and Hanna. Hanna was aware of another presence in the car, but he had not yet turned to look at her.

Chou said, "And now, William, I would like to introduce you

to a very close friend of Sui. This is Renee; Renee, please meet Mr. Hanna."

For the second time on this trip Hanna lost his ability to communicate. Renee had to be about seven-eight's Caucasian and the balance Asian. Most people would read her as having American parentage. She was taller than most, probably five-foot seven without her shoes on. But that was not what caught Hanna's eye the most. She was wearing an Yves St. Laurent two-piece suit that looked like what a new bride would change into to begin her honeymoon after the wedding was over. The hemline on the skirt was about an inch above her knee. The jacket probably should have been worn with a teddy underneath, but it was missing and with good reason. The décolleté was undone one button more than would have been appropriate, and it gave those sitting near her viewing rights to an extraordinary promise of things yet to come. Hanna had only rarely been witness to a body this priceless. Jimmy Chou shoes graced her feet, and her skin was exquisitely soft and smooth with a slight olive tone and the hint of Cristobel perfume. To top everything off, she was painted by what must have been the best makeup artist in all Singapore. Together, everything complemented her unblemished olive-skin complexion perfectly.

"Mr. Hanna, it is so wonderful to meet you. Chou has told me so much about you, but he was much too conservative with his remarks. You are far beyond the highest expectations that I had for this evening. I can't wait to begin."

Neither can I, Hanna thought. Cristobel was a rope tied to his soul.

Hanna had to control himself. He held his breath to slow his heartbeat, and he turned around to Chou before replying to the woman.

He could see that everyone was waiting in anticipation of his response.

After a moment of colossal awe, Hanna finally got to the point where he felt he could respond without his voice cracking with school boy angst.

"Renee," Hanna replied, "It is such a pleasure to meet you. As Chou was with you, so he was with me, but I now realize why. No one could have done justice in describing your beauty and demeanor. I also look forward to this evening with great anticipation."

Renee gave him a smile that would have melted six inches of protective armor on a Sherman tank.

"Before we move, William, could I interest you in a drink? A martini perhaps?" Chou asked.

Hanna replied in the affirmative, after which Chou poured wine for the women and prepared himself a Bourbon and water.

"Sit back and relax, William. It will take about forty-five minutes to get to dinner," Chou said.

He then instructed his driver to move off, as he raised the soundproof, smoked-black window that separated the driver's seat from the cabin. For a moment, Hanna was concerned because Chou had filled his martini glass so full. He didn't want to spill some of it on his pants and make him look and smell like some Kentucky moonshiner the rest of the evening.

His concerns quickly dissipated.

This vehicle must have been borrowed from the president's fleet in Washington, D.C., Hanna thought.

No matter how the car moved or what it hit, the cabin remained straight and level. The weight had to be five or six tons and resistant to missile attack. Hanna had a vision of twin twelve-hundred horse power engines under the hood that could accelerate the vehicle from 30 to 412 miles per hour in about four seconds flat. So much for American drag-strip racing.

Chou began to discuss a little business, not the personal kind but more in the nature of investments in general and how the Dow Jones average had been moving recently. Hanna kept Chou from asking him about his opinion on future market swings by responding to all his comments with a question, thus keeping Chou as the person doing all the talking.

How could I respond to an investment question from this guy? Hanna thought. Chou made millions of dollars in net income each month, while Hanna still wrestled with a monthly payment on a $3 million home with a fifteen-year mortgage that was a significant drain on his cash flow.

At a lull in the conversation between the two men, Renee spoke up. She discussed her personal portfolio and asked for some guidance on what she might expect in the short to medium term.

Hanna's jaw dropped. This girl was gorgeous, educated, and wealthy. Chou must have made a mistake about her shacking up with him for the night. She couldn't be a hooker. Nothing in her movements indicated this social status. She never put her hand on his leg to stroke it. She adjusted her skirt every time it began to creep up and except for an occasional light touch on his arm when she was trying to make a point everything she did was absolutely proper and could be expected of a lady who had turned her life over to Jesus. Hanna began to wonder if she wasn't a missionary sent to bring Christianity to the heathens of the Far East.

Hanna was just draining the last sip from his martini when the limo came to a halt. Chou had opened the moon roof on the vehicle a few moments before, and Hanna noticed the hint of salt air carried on a slight breeze.

"So where are we dining this evening Chou?" Hanna asked. "Is there some spectacular view of Malaysia across the harbor or what has that devilish mind of yours cooked up?"

The driver had come around to the rear of the limo and opened the door. Chou had motioned to Hanna to step out, and he did so. He stopped immediately. There, thirty feet from him on the other side of the berth, was a yacht, with the gangway down, so large that he had a difficult time seeing both ends of the thing if he looked straight forward at it. The engines were running.

"Come, William," Chou said as the girls squealed with delight behind them. He led Hanna up the gangway with the girls following. It only took a moment for them to all be on board. The gangway was lifted, and the ship immediately put out to sea.

A maitre d' motioned them over to a large circular table set for four on the middeck located slightly under an overhang where fans rotated slowly to provide just the correct amount of cooling breeze. Hanna, knowing what he had paid for each piece of silverware in his darling's set estimated that each piece in this set rang in at about a thousand. There was no way one could possibly describe the ship. It must have cost thirty million, if it cost a dollar.

The ship showed three floors above the water line. Someone had once described this behemoth to Hanna, but looking at it now he stood in awe of its immense size. The boat had been built in the late 1980s. There were nine staterooms with the owner's master quarters at least twice the size of the master bedroom in Hanna's home. It was a party boat that was rarely used for parties. The eight lesser staterooms probably sat there collecting dust from non-use most of the time. Of course that was completely nonfactual. The onboard crew kept the vessel immaculate.

There were three dining areas on the ship: a formal dining room set for sixteen inside, just in case there was bad weather; one on the upper deck that was there to ply those lucky enough to be invited on board with booze from the bar while sitting on high-backed swivel bar stools and hors d'ouvers as they toasted themselves in the boiling sun that, to their chagrin, would prune their skins before they turned forty. This, of course, began the inevitable trips to the plastic surgeon who would, for a massive fee, treat their malady, renewing on roughly a biannual basis the look of youth they once possessed.

On the lower deck was a third dining area designed for entertaining. It was a huge area, considering they were on a yacht, that contained a dining table and opulent chairs that could be set for any group from two to ten people. The upper deck with the bar and chaise lounges for tanning extended out over, and formed the ceiling of the intimate dining area below it. Even though the two outside areas were completely open to the fresh salt air, ceiling fans in the lower dining area kept a steady flow of cooling air wafting over those assembled.

A piano, normally hidden from view, could glide out

electronically on an elevated stage to provide entertainment and a site for sultry dancing if one was so inclined.

The floors and rails came from solid teak and were so polished that not one fingerprint could be seen anywhere. There was art hung on the interior walls that was as fine as that hung on the executive floor of Chou's offices downtown. It took a permanent crew of twelve working around the clock to keep this toy in shape to sail on an hour's notice. Everything was immaculate.

All one could do was enjoy the hospitality. Reciprocation was impossible.

They had no sooner sat down when they were offered drinks— chilled Champagne, the finest wines (white or red), or any type of liquor drink one's little heart might desire.

There had been music playing as they moved away from the dock and out to sea, but it quickly faded to nothingness as a circular floor, much like the one in the top of the Shangra La, slid out over the deck and a pianist began to play "A New York State of Mind."

"Chou," Hanna asked, "How could you have possibly known?"

All Chou would say was, "We have our ways, William, we have our ways."

Hanna couldn't stand it any longer. The deck they were on was huge by any standard and polished to perfection.

"Chou," Hanna asked, "Would it upset you if Renee and I had a dance? Of course, that is only if Renee is willing to stumble around the floor with someone who has two left feet."

Everyone laughed at that, and Chou only emphasized what this evening was all about by encouraging them to get out there.

It was a half hour before Hanna decided they had to return to the table. Renee had melted into his arms, giving him the biggest hard-on he had ever experienced. *It's amazing how distance and time will do that to someone*, Hanna thought.

The meal was exquisite. Chou said he had two cooks from the Cordon Bleu on board, one to work on the first four courses, another to handle the last four. Hanna tried a little of everything, but he concentrated on the sushi and the entrée of Kobe beef and asparagus. The bread pudding served was so soaked in brandy that one didn't have to have anything else to be on a high, and that was topped by coffee of any sort imaginable served with the guest's favorite liquor. Hanna selected cappuccino, and his favorite after dinner drink, an amaretto.

After dinner, Chou took them up to the forward deck where they could all catch the breeze and glimpse Indonesia off to the south across the straits. As Chou and his friend walked aft, Renee slowly moved her hand up to Hanna's chest, looked up, and waited to be kissed.

It was Liu all over again. *Jesus Christ,* Hanna thought, *where did his business associates find these women?*

They mauled each other for a couple of minutes, but Renee was good. She knew they were not going to be invited to spend the night on board, plus her swain was leaving for Europe tomorrow, which meant he had to be back in his room to pack tonight. As a result, she kept things under control, and when Hanna began to cop a feel she gently grabbed his hand and whispered "later" in his ear.

Hanna was beside himself, but he decided he had no option but to go along with it. This was one lay nobody was going to screw him out of. From what Hanna had experienced so far, Chou was paying somewhere in the neighborhood of twenty-five-thousand dollars for Renee's affections for the night. Not even Spitzer, New York's ex-governor, could have afforded this one. This was no hooker he was with, Hanna realized. This was a high-end escort, who was amenable to anything the buyer might suggest.

Thirty
Time to Go It Alone

The yacht slowly slid back into its berth about eleven thirty pm. Hanna had discussed returning to the hotel rather than staying, and Chou understood Hanna's agenda, agreeing on his return to the hotel without protest. Once docked, Hanna and Chou walked down the gangway together with their escorts for the evening stepping down behind them.

"William," Chou said, "it gives me great honor that you accepted my invitation to dine together this evening. I look to you as being, how do you Americans say, the point man in our future negotiations with the Chinese. In time, you will achieve our goal of partnering with our Chinese counterparts to create a joint venture with huge prospects for the future. I have Mr. Llewellyn's word on it."

"Chou," Hanna replied, "you are placing immense confidence in me, which I appreciate. However, I will feel much more confident returning to China with the assistance of your representative. Your confidence in him and his knowledge of Mandarin tells me that he will very quickly become indispensible, and for that, I want to thank you for your willingness to help in our negotiations in such a positive manner."

"William," Chou replied, "you will accomplish all the goals you have set for yourself. I know you realize that my man is only along to protect my investment. You will never notice that he is in the room. But, all this is a conversation for the next time we meet. Please give my fondest regards to your wife when you get back to Houston. She is a very wonderful lady. Meanwhile, tonight you must take some time for yourself. Renee is a very close friend of mine. I have told her to attend to your every need. Enjoy it, William, and be sure to get home safely. You are an indispensible part of our team."

Hanna thanked Chou warmly for the evening. They even gave each other a hug, which was rare in this part of the world. Then, after a warm handshake and a wave, Hanna and Renee headed down the gangway to the limo, which was waiting with the driver holding the door open for them to enter.

After the limo with Hanna and Renee moved away from the yacht, Hanna could no longer control his hands. The two of them came together briefly, but then Renee pulled back.

"William," she said, "let's wait until we get back to your room. I don't want to walk through the lobby looking all disheveled, and I bet you don't either. How about a nightcap? You're not going to have time for one after we get back."

Hanna had to agree.

"You're always right Renee. I'll have a Chivas and water."

Renee poured the drinks, and the two of them sat back for the hour-long ride back to the hotel. It would take them quite a bit longer to return to the hotel than it had taken them earlier to drive out to the yacht club. Singapore came alive at night, and at midnight, the streets were jammed.

Hanna had to do something to get his mind off the events to come. If he didn't, it was going to be the shortest lovemaking session in the history of the world.

"So, Renee, your given English first name is a little unusual. I guess the reason is that it is French rather than English."

"Mais oui, Monsieur," Renee said in perfect, unaccented French. "You see, my mother is one-quarter Vietnamese and three-quarters

French. She was educated in a French school, and she graduated just as the war was beginning. She and my father, who is also part Vietnamese and part French fled to Thailand to escape the war. They had no children for twenty years—then I came along. Mother had always loved the name, and I became her Renee."

"I went to French schools, just like mother. We didn't speak Vietnamese at home; we spoke French. When I was fifteen, I was sent to live with friends of my mother and dad in London, where I learned my English.

"Everything was fine until I received the telephone call."

"What was the call?" Hanna asked. He could see tears welling up in Renee's eyes.

"I received a call that my parents had been in a terrible car accident. My father had been killed and my mother was paralyzed. I had to return home to take care of her. Taking care of my mother and our home cost a lot of money. Much more money than I could make. Plus, I had no formal training to take a job where I could make enough."

So this is why she's in the escort business, Hanna thought. She was beautiful enough to command the very best prices in the industry. And, in this part of the world, her business was an industry.

Renee read his mind. "Yes, William, I became an escort to support my mother, myself, and our way of life. Bangkok was my town, and in a short period of time I was having my way. Then, three years ago, I met Chou in Bangkok, and he offered to move me to Singapore. He said I could make much more money here, and he would take care of me. Mother had recently passed away so I took him up on his offer. Thailand no longer held any allure for me.

"Even though I still go back to Bangkok at least once a month to take care of certain old friends and special customers, I am now officially a Singaporean."

Hanna's antenna had begun to go up. He had to know.

"Well, Renee, I presume you take precautions. There are very serious diseases around these days, and Thailand is one of those countries that have a serious problem, one that is worse than most countries. Actually in your business, and I am not criticizing you at all considering everything you have been through in your short life, I assume you are taking precautions wherever you are," Hanna responded.

Renee was completely candid, Hanna thought, surprisingly so, but Hanna had begun to realize that she viewed her line of work as business and she was willing to discuss it openly.

"Oh, William, I take precautions with all American and European clients," Renee said, "I will do so with you as well, even though I am sure that were you infected with anything, you would tell me."

"That is very responsible, Renee. I assume you do the same with your clients in Thailand and Singapore," Hanna said.

"Oh no, Hannasan, there is no need to. HIV and AIDS are American problems. We do not have this disease in our part of the world. Our people are very clean and very cautious. Oh no, it is your people who are spreading the disease. We do not have it over here among our native peoples. No, I don't have any problem being an escort with my people; it's just your people that I must be careful with."

Hanna could not believe what he was hearing. This opinion was not coming out of the mouth of a babe. It was being spoken by a beautiful, well educated, wealthy person. Hanna had read about this phenomenon. She was obviously in complete denial regarding her own people.

More importantly, Hanna's erection that had previously impaired his ability to sit comfortably in the car had disappeared. All Hanna's mind was concerned with now was how to plan as painless an exit from this beautiful woman as he could. Bedding her had just become a nonviable option.

Hanna did not realize it, but they had just pulled into the porte cochere at the hotel. The driver had stopped the car, and the hotel valet was instantly at the limo door opening it. Hanna reached into his breast pocket for his wallet. He pulled out eleven one-hundred dollar bills. He handed ten of them to Renee.

"Look Renee," Hanna said, "I am developing an upset stomach. It must have been something I ate. I want you to take this money and just go home. All I feel like doing right now is going to sleep. Thank you for a wonderful evening, and I hope we will meet again the next time I'm in Singapore."

"But, William, are you sure? I am yours for as long as you want me—at least until tomorrow."

"I know Renee," Hanna said, "it is not your fault, and I have thoroughly enjoyed the evening with you."

Hanna leaned over and kissed her on the cheek. He was almost fatherly as he did it. In a few hours, he had come to like Renee and to enjoy her company even though her sole purpose in being with him this evening was to gratify his male sexual urges. *Oh, well,* Hanna thought, *the urges would have to wait.* The only thing he wanted to take home from this part of the world was money.

"Driver, please take Renee home," Hanna said through the limo window to the driver's cabin. He handed him the other hundred-dollar bill.

"Yes sir, Mr. Hanna. I will. Good evening then."

Hanna backed out of the car, waved goodbye, then turned around and walked into the hotel lobby. He didn't look back. It would have been too painful.

Rule Eight for Avoiding Infidelity While away from Home on Extended Business Travel

STDs represent a global scourge, at the moment defying all attempts to develop a cure. It is therefore, incumbent upon the business traveler to avoid developing any relationship with ladies of dubious credentials and to wash one's hands frequently in an effort to avoid inadvertently contacting any viruses such as the H1-N1 swine flu virus.

Thirty One
The Luxury of Time Alone

Hanna was distraught—here was a gorgeous woman with everything going for her, yet she took the locals straight up while making the Americans and Europeans dress before partaking of her delights.

Life wasn't fair. As a matter of fact it was so unfair on Hanna's last night in the City of Lions that he walked straight through the lobby and went to his room.

He poured himself a drink as soon as he entered. Chivas and water. *Booze was the only answer*, Hanna thought. This thought, born of accumulated wisdom over the years, had never failed.

The next thirty-six hours were going to be relaxing. No wake-up call, a leisurely breakfast, pack bags, checkout around two, then off to the airport to catch the overnight Alitalia flight to Rome. He would be early getting there. The flight didn't leave until seven in the evening, but he could pick up a couple of souvenirs, read a paper, have a drink, and people watch. Then again, he could always sit in the hotel lobby and do the same thing.

There was no need to debate with himself; he could do that tomorrow.

He put on his swimming trunks, poured his drink into a plastic cup, and headed for the pool. There seemed to be a lot of activity around the pool tonight and a dip would be refreshing before lights out.

Thirty Two
One More Stop and We're Headed for Home

It was two thirty, Thursday afternoon, and Hanna had just checked out of the hotel. In a moment or two, the Shangra La would just be a reflection in the rearview mirror, and another successful visit to the island nation (well, almost completely successful) would come to an end.

Hanna decided to head for the airport. He needed some new scenery.

Until now, Hanna hadn't even looked at his reservations. Rebecca was very efficient at such things, and Hanna had had a lot on his mind over the past few days, especially last night with Renee. He now pulled his ticket out and sighed deeply as he began to read it. Rebecca loved to fly, and she loved the take offs and landings. Therefore, she just assumed that everyone else did as well. Hanna was on an Alitalia flight with stops in New Delhi and Athens. *Jesus, Rebecca, why do you do these things to me?* Hanna thought.

If he had opened the ticket twenty four hours ago, he could have changed it for a nonstop flight. At this point, however, the nonstop would be completely full, at least the first-class section, and Hanna was not going to down grade on a twelve-hour overnight flight to anywhere. The problem was that he would spend the next five hours rubbing shoulders with the Muslims, spreading out their carpets to kneel and pray to Allah in Mecca in the aisles of the aircraft. Then, from New Delhi on, he'd be sandwiched among loud, drunken Greeks trying to act like Zorba.

Hanna couldn't contemplate the thought. Once again, he turned to the only form of solace he had over the years, found to be an answer to this problem.

Booze.

If you can't lick 'em, join 'em, he thought.

An hour later, he was checked in on his flight to Rome, with stops in New Delhi and Athens and onward connections to Malaga, through customs and passport control, and sitting in the first-class lounge. Over the course of the next two hours, he had three martinis, helped himself to a tray of hors d'ouvers, and watched the Italians who were preparing to support their flagship airline while getting on with their lives. Hanna loved Italians. They were expressive, friendly, and always had a smile on their faces. In addition, the Italian woman was simply beyond description. Hanna had long since decided that the words "sex" and "voluptuousness" were English derivatives of the Italian language.

The flight was announced at six, and half the people in the room headed for the gate to be personally ushered onto the plane by a gate agent assigned to do nothing else. It was a 747, and the first-class lounge upstairs had not as yet been converted into additional seating. The other half of the people in the lounge would be on the nonstop to Rome, which would leave an hour and a half later and arrive an hour and a half before Hanna's flight.

As usual, Hanna had one of the two seats in the middle of the first-class cabin just ahead of the stairs that led to the bar upstairs. A middle-aged German with a receding hairline and smelly breath became his seatmate.

What the hell, Hanna thought. *If the guy played true to his ethnic origin, he'd be full of borsch and beer and sound asleep thirty minutes after takeoff.*

The flight attendant asked Hanna if he wanted a drink, and he responded with a "yes," ordering another martini. He wanted a guarantee that he would be able to sleep undisturbed at least as far as New Delhi.

Hanna was standing in the aisle in advance of being ordered to fasten his seat belt so they could start the engines. That would be at least thirty minutes from now, only after the great unwashed got seated in steerage.

"Your martini, Mr. Hanna," the flight attendant said.

"Thank you very much," was Hanna's response as he accepted the glass. "Are you going to be my keeper through to Rome?" he asked.

The flight attendant was very nice and very pleasant, but for some reason, Hanna was not particularly attracted to her. Hanna knew why. He had made just such an observation to his extremely beautiful and confident wife one time very long ago, and the response was instantaneous: "She's very pretty darling; she's just not sexy," after which she put one leg forward and one leg to the rear of his and wiggled a bit.

His wife was always right, Hanna thought. More than that, she was the smartest, most intuitive person he had ever known. *Thank god she had married him.*

"Oh, no, Mr. Hanna," the flight attendant replied. "There will be a crew change in New Delhi. This crew only does turnaround flights between there and Singapore. My husband works in Singapore, and this schedule is just perfect for me. Would you like to see a picture of him?" she asked, as she pulled one out of her jacket pocket. "We have been married a year now."

Hanna looked at the countenance of a Singaporean Adonis, although that was probably a contradiction in terms. Hanna acknowledged the guy was pretty good looking. The flight attendant's job was probably perfect for him as well, Hanna mused. He probably had a half dozen butterflies hanging off his body all the time his wife was out of town.

What the hell, Hanna thought, *there was someone for everyone in this world, and most people got exactly what they deserved. Far be it from him to intervene with fate.*

"My goodness," Hanna said back to the flight attendant, "he certainly is a handsome catch. I only wish I looked like him."

"Isn't he though?" The flight attendant gushed.

Hanna figured the comment had just won him outstanding service for the rest of the flight.

He turned and looked at his seatmate. He was downing a beer.

"I hope you not vish to read this evening, Herr Hanna. I have difficulty sleepink when the overhead lights are on."

It was more of a demand than a request, Hanna thought. Politeness just wasn't the German long suit, although they never realized it: their language was just that way.

"Don't worry, Herr Helmut," Hanna replied, "I intend to spend the flight asleep myself."

They both knew each other's names because the cabin crew had not yet removed the small name tags from each seat after passengers had been escorted to them.

Ten minutes later, they were seated, and fifteen minutes after that they were airborne.

In a flash, "his" flight attendant was by his side.

"Would you care to have another drink before dinner?" she asked.

Hanna nodded in the affirmative.

A minute later, he was sitting there with another martini in hand. *Memo to self,* he thought. *This is my sixth since noon today. I'm beginning to become tired. No more hard stuff tonight.*

"Have you had the opportunity to read the menu, Mr. Hanna?" the flight attendant asked.

"Yes," Hanna replied, "I really don't want to overeat this evening so I believe that I will just have a portion of the light side of the menu. How about a wedge lettuce salad with Roquefort sprinkles and a blue-cheese dressing, the shrimp appetizer, and the green grapes and cheese with chilled vodka? I believe I'll pass on the entrée this evening. You can serve all that with a fine Chablis, and you'll make me very happy."

"I'll bring your salad in a moment," she replied.

Hanna looked over at his seatmate. He hadn't even been asked for a drink order as yet, and he looked like he was really pissed. *Memo to self,* Hanna thought. *Teach this Kraut how to be nice the next time he was in this part of the world.*

With his doting attendant anticipating his every move, Hanna was finished dinner in forty five minutes. He moved his seat to a sleeping position and was gone two minutes later. Just before drifting off to oblivion, he looked over to his seatmate. He was just starting to slug down his well-done filet mignon. *He'd be lucky to be asleep within in the next hour if he had ordered every course,* Hanna thought. The only thing that kept him acceptable in polite company was the fact that the flight attendant kept refilling his glass with beer, and he appeared to be a happy drunk.

Once you are wheels up at Singapore, regardless of whether it is day or night, there was absolutely no reason to look out the window. There was nothing to see between there and New Delhi, once you were in the air. Despite all the modern-day electronics aircraft were now outfitted with, pilots still needed a turn and bank indicator just to confirm that they were flying straight and level. There was no horizon at night.

"Mr. Hanna, Mr. Hanna. I am so sorry to wake you, but we are on final approach to New Delhi. I must ask you to raise your seat to its full upright position even though you were sleeping very soundly. I apologize for that but it is for your safety. I will say goodbye after we land."

Hanna did as he was told and in a half-dazed manner looked over at his seat mate. The attendant was telling him the same thing.

The landing sounded like a controlled crash. The aircraft hit so hard that Hanna thought the wings would fall off after they drove the wheels through the engine nacelles. Fortunately, that thought dissipated as the behemoth they were in slowly rolled to a crawl. Not that the first crushing bang was the last. The bumpy landing went on for twenty seconds before the flight deck seemed to get things under control.

The German seatmate turned to him and said his first civil words since boarding in Singapore. "You can alvays determine the intellect and wealth of a nation by the quality of its airports."

Hanna had to agree.

As the aircraft slowed to taxi speed, he put his seat back down to form a bed and was once again almost instantly asleep. His only conscious recall was the German saying, "It was a pleasure flying with you this evening Mr. Hanna. I hope that we have the opportunity to fly together again at some point in the future."

Whatever, Hanna thought to himself.

Thirty Three
Fate Is the Hunter

They slowly taxied towards the terminal. Hanna noticed little. The booze, the food, and the soft rush of air over the airliner's wings had all colluded to put his body into a soporific state. These inputs were better than any sleeping pill yet developed by the medical profession. The doors opened to let in the 100 percent humidity at one in the morning with the temperature still hovering around the eighty-eight degree level that signified one was on the ground in India. People came and people went. The German left; others left.

At one point, he awakened to a quiet shuffling and sweeping motion sound only to open one eye and see someone hunched down beside him sweeping the carpet with a whisk. No one could crouch like an Indian laborer down on his haunches with his ass almost dragging the floor sweeping up dirt one microscopic particle at a time.

This guy has to make at least ten rupees a day, Hanna thought. *The only way he is going to feed his eighteen kids and wife was to keep his day job as a beggar.* Hanna made certain that the door to the closet that contained his luggage located in the nose of the aircraft's first-class section was closed and locked.

The cleaner moved on, and Hanna returned to his repose. He was vaguely aware of the sound of the buses arriving at the bottom of the stairways and slightly more aware of the sound of a couple of people moving through the cabin to their seats. There were only a few, and the conversation was hushed. They had to be Indians in their saris and Nehru jackets, Hanna thought. He had a passing question in the back of his mind as to why they had to land in Athens. There obviously were no Greeks on board in first-class, and if there were any in steerage they could always open a back door and let them parachute out as they flew over the city.

Hanna continued to doze for a few moments. It didn't last long. A member of the crew came on the aircraft's intercom to announce that they were all bright eyed and bushy tailed and ready to respond to Hanna's every need. It wasn't long before the flight attendant sweetly asked him to raise his seat for taxi and take off after which he could return to his sleeping position.

Hanna complied without comment through closed eyes.

Hanna breathed a sigh of relief as they lifted into the air. The monocoque frame that the aircraft was built around had survived one more time. With any luck at all the flight would actually land in Rome without further incident.

Hanna had to look around one last time before heading back to the land of nod. There were only five people in first class. An obviously married older couple and two fat and ugly European singles all by themselves. Hanna was the fifth.

The flight attendant had dimmed the lights before takeoff and almost immediately everyone in the cabin was asleep. Hanna rolled over on his right side. He could now face the other seat since the departure of the German's breath afforded him the luxury of making use of both his seat and the one adjacent.

It was at this point that Hanna began hearing a conversation next to his seat, and even though his Italian was atrocious, out of the corner of the one ear that had not yet fallen back to sleep, he thought the conversation he was trying to comprehend ended with the one flight attendant saying, "I don't care. He is mine. You take care of the other passengers tonight, and I will return the favor on our next flight out."

Hanna opened one eye and looked at the flight attendant claiming his body. Something stirred in his memory.

There was a time when Hanna maintained offices in both New York and Atlanta, between which he shuttled on a weekly basis. One Friday night on his way home for the weekend, he stepped on board his Delta flight to a greeting from the flight attendant.

"Good evening Mr. Hanna. I'll serve your Chivas and water just as soon as I have seated the other first-class passengers."

Hanna decided right then that his wife was right. He was traveling far too much.

And now it was happening again. For some reason, although he could not remember why, this flight attendant looked familiar.

Okay, Hanna thought, *there's a problem here.* The flight attendant had sat down in the seat next to him and was staring at him longingly.

Hanna was as dumbfounded as he had ever been.

"Excuse me," Hanna said, "but do we know one another? I am very tired, and if we don't, I need to get back to sleep since I have a very long day tomorrow."

"Good evening, Signore William. My name is Lana. You will not remember me, but you were on one of my flights last year with your wife. The two of you were flying the same route, and I could not stop looking at you and thinking how lucky your wife was to have you as a husband. I said to myself at the time that if I ever got you alone, I would do my best to try to get to know you better. When I saw your name alone on the manifest for tonight's flight to Rome, I couldn't wait to see you again. I guess I have, how do you Americans say? A crush on you. It is very obvious that you do a lot of international travel."

Hanna's mind rolled back to his wedding day. His wife was standing there at the entrance to the church, thirty minutes late as she always was. He sucked in his breath as he looked at her: Her blonde hair gleaming in the sun filtering through the colored windows from behind where she was standing. He had never seen anything more beautiful in his life. She embodied everything positive that Hanna had ever come to deem as such.

Now, he looked across at this body that was turned facing him, and he immediately concluded that this event was in the running for the Top Ten. The only difference between this thing and his gorgeous wife was that the one sitting next to him had long, jet-black hair. At the moment, that was the only thing keeping this body at arm's length. Hanna didn't have a great appreciation for dark hair: his weakness was blondes.

For the third time on this trip around the world and all within the space of the last ten days, Hanna could not talk. What he was looking at was a young Sophia Loren. The only difference between the actress and the body seated here was that this one was more beautiful.

"Where are you staying while you are in Rome, William?" Lana breathed, the slightly accented words dropping from her painted lips like early morning dew.

"How many times have you been to our fabulous city? I am sure that a man who has travelled as much as you has been there many times to take in its romantic sights and sounds. People say Paris is the City of Love, William. They are wrong. Rome is the City of Love."

Christ! Hanna thought. *This woman was better than the Chamber of Commerce.*

Hanna rolled this conversation over in his mind and decided not to lie to this Venus.

"Lana, first it is a profound pleasure to get to meet you. It is not often that the opportunity presents itself for two people to meet as we have been able to do this evening." Actually, Hanna could never recall meeting anyone this way.

"I must confess," Hanna said, "that despite all my travels around the world, which might very well compete with your own, I have never stepped onto Italian soil. I have been through Leonardo de Vinci airport many times, but I have never been through customs.

I have only ever gone from the arrivals to the departure in-transit lounge."

"No, no William, that cannot be true. You are more Roman than Roman men. When I saw you sleeping quietly after we boarded to relieve the crew in New Delhi I thought, this is a man for the ages." Lana moved closer to him as she said it.

Hanna was beside himself. The only other thing that had ever gotten to his libido like this was his gorgeous wife. Where was she when he needed her? Hanna thought. He couldn't get into an animated conversation with this flight attendant sitting here. If she touched him, he would blow.

"Could we possibly have a glass of wine back in the jump seats, Lana?" Hanna said. He had to get up and walk for a minute. They got up and moved back to the jump seats next to the first-class doors with their windows. Lana didn't walk, rather she glided with the polished touch of Sophia, his notion of the ideal woman since childhood. Lana brought two drinks over to the jump seats. She disguised hers in a paper cup as coffee.

God, he loved the Italians, Hanna thought.

Lana sat down next to him, grabbed his hand, put it on her knee, and began to stroke it.

"So William," she said, "you didn't say, but, how long are you going to be in Rome?" She slowly started to breathe more heavily as she talked.

"Well, Lana," Hanna said, "I don't have any plans to spend time in Rome on this trip. I am going straight through to Malaga. I will only be in the in-transit lounge for an hour after we arrive before leaving for Spain."

"You have never been in Rome, William, and you have no plans to visit on this trip?" Lana looked at him with incredulity. "This cannot be possible?"

Hanna tried again. "Lana, I have never visited Rome. I have never been in the city. Moreover, I have never been in Italy. I'm sorry but that is the truth."

"Well, William, if that is the case it is only more reason for you to visit the city on this trip."

Hanna was getting desperate.

"Lana, if I possibly could I would stop in Rome and visit the city and you. My problem is I have commitments in Malaga tomorrow afternoon that must be kept. Besides, I have no reservations for a layover in the city. It's the tourist season. I wouldn't be able to find a hotel room within fifty miles of the city center. We will just have to postpone my visit until my next trip."

Great reasoning, Hanna thought. *She can't get around the logic of this one. I'm saved for another day.*

"William," Lana replied, "You do not need a hotel reservation; you can stay with me. I live with my mother, but I have a separate suite in our home and we will not disturb her at all. Besides, she loves Americans, especially good-looking Americans and, you are a good-looking American."

Hanna was looking out the window at the refineries below burning off natural gas, wasting it because at that time there was no way to collect it and make use of it. They were flying up the middle of the Persian Gulf between Iran and Saudi Arabia. You could plainly see the refineries from thirty-five thousand feet; as one disappeared to the rear of the aircraft another appeared up ahead. The shoreline for hundreds of miles was lit up like it was daytime.

At some point, Hanna thought, they would have to turn northwest towards the Mediterranean and Greece. He wondered, as he always did in this part of the world, which alienated state would send up its fighters to shoot them down as they crossed their territory.

Hanna went back to his seat to think. *Let's see: He had to be in Malaga tomorrow afternoon in the hotel by four. His boss loved him very much and paid him a lot of money to be his point man around the world. Disappointing his boss would cause the latter to become upset. And Mr. Llewellyn didn't tolerate his staff not complying with instructions. On the other hand, Lana was quite capable and would probably (next to his wife) provide him with the most erotic seventy-two hours he had ever experienced in his lifetime. Hanna figured that showing him Rome was just a ruse hiding her true intentions, which were to abuse his body incessantly until he screamed out with pain.*

What was a poor boy to do? he thought as he sat back down in his seat. Lana had just served him a coffee and sat down next to him to resume the conversation.

"William," she said, "I want you to know that I have never done before what I am doing tonight. I have never in my life propositioned a man on an airplane. I am always the person being propositioned. But tonight is different from anything I have ever experienced. You are the most handsome man I have ever seen, and I want to get to know you. I don't care that you are married. All I want to do is spend some time with you."

Lana had grabbed his hand again and put it back on her knee. She leaned over towards him and waited for the embrace. Hanna put his hand on her lips, and like a man extracting himself from under a car wreck, he slowly pulled away from underneath the gaze of this incredibly tantalizing woman.

On the other hand, Hanna thought, *he could always call forward and advise his boss and his entourage that his flight into Rome was late and he wouldn't be able to get there before Saturday, a day from now. On second thought, that wouldn't fly considering the fact that there was a flight every hour between the two cities. Besides, Rebecca would check to verify the legitimacy of the excuse and find it wanting.*

What in the hell was he going to do? He had to be in Malaga later this afternoon.

The two of them were both leaning in toward the center of the two seats. Lana had snuck in under his arm, and her breath was warmly fanning the side of his neck. She moved even closer to him and took the dangling end of his arm and put it around her waist. Hanna wasn't sure but he thought he heard a quiet moan escape from her lips.

Then again, Hanna thought, *he could say he had developed food poisoning on the flight and had to disembark to be taken to a hospital. Crap, that wouldn't work either. Rebecca would have two-hundred dollars worth of flowers delivered to his hospital room within minutes, only to find out that he wasn't registered.*

The other first-class attendant came on the intercom. The sound of the engines had changed, and Hanna realized that they had begun their approach into Athens. Lana gave him a kiss behind the ear.

"I have to go help, William. I will see you again after we leave Athens for the short flight over to Rome."

Thirty minutes later, they were on the ground in Athens and taxiing to the disembarkation area where buses would pick up departing passengers and take them to customs. None of them in first class got off. Obviously, everyone was a good Catholic making a pilgrimage to the Vatican.

Hanna got up and walked the length of the cabin, doing a circuit that ended up back at the aircraft's stairwell in the first-class section where he could feel a fresh cool breeze blowing through the cabin. Looking off in the distance beyond the airport perimeter one could tell it was going to be a warm day with plenty of sun, dulled slightly as it came through the atmosphere of dust, pollutants, and humidity. His gaze shifted back across the tarmac towards the terminal. The crew and a cleaning staff that had come out from the terminal on the buses that picked up the arrivals and were finishing restoring the plane to its earlier self, when Hanna noticed passengers at the terminal being loaded on buses to come out to join them for the onward trip into Rome.

A lot of people, Hanna thought. *Unusual.*

Hanna stood idly by while the buses slowly crawled out to the waiting aircraft, the drivers, observing the five mile-per-hour speed limit under pain of being fired or executed.

As the buses stopped at the foot of the stairwell sufficiently far away that they would not clip and damage a wing or engine nacelle when they left, Hanna took a look at what was coming up the stairs. For some reason, these people looked familiar Hanna thought to himself, or at least most of them did. What was going on?

It didn't take long to find out. Hanna had moved back to his seat so that he wouldn't interfere with passengers boarding just as Lana's partner in the first-class cabin came on the intercom to welcome everyone on board their one hour and thirty minute flight to Rome, including those passengers from Alitalia's nonstop sister flight out of Singapore, which had left an hour and a half after Hanna's plane but developed mechanical troubles in flight and had to divert to Athens.

Hanna looked around him. Every seat in the cabin was occupied, mainly by angry, glowering people whose revere had been disturbed an hour and half short of their destination after having had the crap scared out of them because of an emergency landing.

Hanna looked on the positive side of it all. At least he wouldn't have Venus sitting next to him the rest of the way into Rome with those long sensuous fingers and manicured nails sliding through his shirt to slowly stroke his chest. He needed some time to gather his thoughts, Hanna reminded himself. He needed time to think and weigh his options.

Lana came by just before they had to sit down and fasten seat belts.

"William, there is an Alitalia official on board. I will have to use discretion between here and Rome. Please forgive me. I will talk to you later, before we begin our descent into the city."

Hanna looked up and winked. *Thank God,* he thought. *Now, he had some time to think about what he was going to do.*

The flight was off the ground in minutes. They were obviously not carrying fuel for eight hours like the first two segments of the flight. It went airborne like a bird despite its size.

Seven Forty Sevens were fourth generation DC-3s, Hanna thought. The workhorse of the sky. Three engines could quit no problem. Two tires blow on takeoff on the same side of the aircraft, no problem. A door blows off in flight, no problem. As long as you made a hot landing, the plane just acted like a glider and once again brought you safely to rest on terra firma.

Everything was happening around Hanna as though he was on a British Airways flight between Heathrow and Glasgow. Coffee and breakfast were being served: orange juice, bacon and eggs, toast, hash browns, and fruit. Efficiency ruled the moment. Lana had broken a sweat she was moving so fast. Then everything had to be quickly picked up as they began their descent into Rome's Leonardo da Vinci airport. The flight wasn't long enough to do decency to first-class service.

At this point, the crew was advising everyone to lift their seat backs "to the full upright position and fasten their seat belts." Lana was coming through the cabin placing customs forms on everyone's tray since Rome was the termination of the flight. She served everyone else before she brought Hanna's to him.

As she placed the form on the tray in front of him, she leaned over and put her lips to his ear.

"William, the flight crew goes one way when it leaves the aircraft. Passengers go the opposite way to proceed to customs. When you come to the point where the sign says in-transit passengers, you will turn to your right to proceed through customs. I will wait for you outside the door to customs. I can't wait for us to be alone together."

She gave his ear a peck as she moved back to the first class kitchen area where the first-class crew's jump seats were located.

The perceived promise of this woman to realign all of the body parts Hanna claimed ownership to from the disjointed fashion they now occupied was overwhelming his ability to reason. He filled out the customs form in the expectation of disembarking in Rome.

Lana came by one last time to check that passengers had their seat belts fastened and their seats in the full upright position. She allowed her hand to drop and stroke the back of Hanna's neck before she moved on while she checked his customs form.

Jesus Christ, Hanna thought. *At best, I'm dead on arrival back* home when I enter the corporate offices Monday morning; at worst, I'll just die sooner. The second option sounded better.

Thirty Four
There's Trouble Right Here in River City

The flight was quickly on the ground and even more quickly taxiing to the terminal. Fifteen minutes after landing, the engines had shut down, the jet way had moved up to the doors, and passengers had stood up, grabbed their luggage, and were now crushing forward to be off the behemoth as quickly as possible as though it were about to explode and melt into the tarmac.

Hanna stood back amid the panic. After the crowd had passed him by, he quietly moved up to the first-class closet at the nose of the first-class section, retrieved the two pieces of luggage he had brought on board, grabbed his third piece, which was always stowed beneath his seat and headed for the door.

He loved being the last person to disembark first class since no one from the rear of the aircraft, not even business class, were allowed to disembark before all first-class passengers had done so. Being the last person off first class always allowed him extra time to survey the masses herded in the cattle-car section of the aircraft getting more and more pissed off at him for keeping them waiting to disembark.

Lana was at his side as he moved to the exit.

"William," she whispered. "I will be outside waiting for you after you clear customs. I can't wait to take you home and introduce you to ma ma. We'll see you in a few minutes."

Ma ma? Hanna was beside himself. All he wanted to do was feel his body self destruct as this goddess beat it to death, and here she was, wanting to introduce him to her mother. It was becoming apparent that Lana wanted ma ma's confirmation that he would be an ideal candidate to provide her with grandchildren.

Once he was beyond the turn where the crew went one direction and passengers went another, he stopped, propped his luggage against the wall of the corridor and let the pack of passengers in the back of the plane go by.

Sophia (otherwise known as Lana) was now disembarking from the plane. In a moment, she would be standing outside the door to customs waiting for him to join her. She would be moving slightly from one foot to the other, and Hanna knew what that meant.

Hanna had not had a tryst with an Italian woman since he had moved from New York to Houston. But the memory of what they were ready to offer had his brain in a half nelson.

He started to walk again. Another thousand feet and he would hit the point where he had to turn right to go through customs.

He could do it, Hanna thought. He didn't have a solid reason why at the moment, but he would think of one. If nothing else, his excuse was going to have to be that the devil made him do it.

God! he thought. *He could not leave this piece of ass to languish without his company. It was as though Michelangelo, in addition to all his other works, had molded this woman's ancestors into the form that would ultimately generate this sculpture he had been looking at all night.*

He started to walk slowly forward again. He hated airline terminals that led to customs. The country you were entering obviously wanted you to be so thankful when you arrived at the custom's personnel booths that you would confess to any lies you had made on your customs-entry forms and hold your arms out to be handcuffed so that you could be led back to the in-transit lounge for shipment back to your country of origin.

Hanna had exaggerated to Lana a bit while they conversed

on the flight in. He had been through Rome several times, but he had not been through the airport as often as he had let Lana to believe. All that notwithstanding, he had to make a decision that was crushing his brains and his balls at the same time.

All of a sudden, he was standing at the decision point. The sign to the in-transit lounge arrowed down an escalator. The sign to customs pointed off to the right.

Goddammit, Hanna thought, *what do I do now?*

Lana was a seventy-two-hour piece of erotica. Jason Llewellyn was Hanna's lifeblood, and at the moment he needed a transfusion.

Despite the fact that he would not be able to respect himself in the morning, he started down the escalator to the in-transit lounge.

Strange things happen to people when their brains pop out of gear and slide into neutral. It was like the old manual stick shifts used to do back in the fifties. Hanna knew this, because at one time he had owned several antique autos, with license plates proclaiming them as such, and, they all came into his shop with a transmission that slipped out of gear. The point is that once one's mind has been made up regarding a random meeting that promised a weekend's worth of delight versus meeting with one's boss, the brain slips into neutral with the result that there is no active thought process. The only thing that functions is motor activity, which keeps the lungs breathing and the heart pumping.

Hanna was half way down the escalator on his way to the in-transit lounge, not knowing why he had decided to go on rather than spend three days in Rome with Sophia Loren's daughter, when he chanced to look up.

Leonardo da Vinci airport has an odd layout, although some other airports have the same architectural design. People behind customs are going one way, while people who have cleared customs (or who do not have to clear customs) are going the other. The only thing that separates them is bulletproof glass.

Hanna looked over with his mind in neutral. There was Lana

on the far side of the glass. It was obvious that she had already cleared customs. She was banging on the glass. As best as Hanna could discern reading the lips of a gorgeous Italian female trying to speak English, she was saying, "No, no, William. Go back up the escalator and turn to your left. You are going the wrong way."

There was no return escalator, and Hanna knew it.

Hanna's last vision of Lana was of an irate Italian female screaming while banging the glass between people planning to go through customs and those planning to never enter the country.

Hanna gazed down at the army guard at the bottom of the escalator, a Belgian FN slung over his shoulder, and gave a sigh of relief. If Lana came after him from the other side of customs, she would be gunned down like any other terrorist.

The unfortunate part of this horrifying event in which Hanna had opted for his future well-being rather than a weekend's worth of afternoon delight was the thought in the back of his mind of his never again being able to visit Italy.

He had a momentary vision of his stepping off a flight to Italy at some future date and proceeding through customs to be met outside by Lana's brother Bruno, whose only desire was to show Hanna the welcome afforded every enemy of the Cosa Nostra.

Rule Nine for Avoiding Infidelity While away from Home on Extended Business Travel

Italian women exude a level of female sensuality that is similar to the siren call of a mermaid. The American on extended business travel, therefore, must at all times ensure that their business commitments are so onerous that they will enable the traveler to overcome the hormonal demands of their loins when such a body appears, thus allowing them to ignore the allure of the finest example of womanhood the world has to offer.

Thirty Five
Quiet Delights

Hanna always marveled at the way some things begged description. If you were not there, no number of pictures or litany of words would ever give you the sense of what an observer's eyes were beholding. Niagara Falls was a perfect example. There wasn't any way to describe a six-foot deep wave of water spilling over a half-mile long precipice, dropping one hundred and fifty feet to the river bed below, draining North America's watershed where fully 20 percent of the world's supply of fresh water existed: doing it since the dawn of recorded time in unending fashion.

Hanna had once spent a weekend there with his beautiful very best friend ever. That gorgeous piece of feminity eventually became Mrs. Hanna and he had never regretted the decision he made that weekend.

He would never forget the experience.

The same could be said for the Grand Canyon. Standing back from its edge, leaning against the railing that terminated the pathway leading back to the El Tovar Hotel, which had been there forever, became a sight burned into the brain for recollection the remainder of one's life. Within the mind of any human being, Hanna acknowledging that his own mind could be included. It was impossible to contemplate that this land, although six-thousand feet in the air, had once been below the ocean's surface. The fossils in the walls that dropped sheer for over a mile, however, provided testimony to this fact.

Hanna's mind was really wandering now. He recalled the time, way back in his youth, having just graduated from high school and wanting to further his education, he had decided to hire on to a mining geophysical exploration team in Alaska for the winter. The recruits didn't need experience, they were hired as grunts but the money was good.

The work post had several advantages. First and foremost it kept him parted from a senior female in high school who wanted nothing more than his body for the rest of her natural born life. Hanna shuddered at the thought. Upon reflection, it probably contributed to the reason why he had eventually come to travel as much as he did. Getting away could keep him out of trouble as much as it could immerse him in it. Secondly, all of his Alaskan paycheck went into a savings account, which was designed to pay a substantial part of his tuition, since no one else had volunteered to do so. When you went to work for mineral exploration companies, they paid for everything, so there was no need to have money around unless you wanted to blow it in a good poker game.

Besides, the location was so remote that everyone on the crew was flown into the camp, and not even Superman could have found the place. This meant that the nearest bar was at least two-hundred miles away. The only problem was that when you returned to civilization, if someone said "Hi," you were stuck for an answer.

As far as Alaska was concerned, he would never forget the night that, on a bet and a dare, he had taken his five-star fartsack (sleeping bag to the uninitiated) outside the main tent where the four men of the team slept and proceeded to spend the entire night out in the cold. He loved it. He had left his clothes on including his parka and zipped the bag completely up over his head. The crew didn't work the next day because they all took turns going outside every thirty minutes to make certain he wasn't freezing to death. He quietly smiled to himself forever after over the incident.

There was nothing finer than really screwing up someone's brain that way.

But this wasn't the main point, Hanna thought. These crews always set up their tents on the edge of a lake. It was there they landed in the fall before the ice froze everything over for winter, and it was where they stayed until a strong wind blew the honeycombed ice down to one end of the lake in the spring, allowing the pontooned aircraft to resume their monthly resupply visits to the camps.

And it was the lake that fascinated Hanna. The night he had picked to prove his bet was a day after a two-foot snowfall and there was a full moon without a cloud in the sky. The ice was grinding as the sheets shifted by each other at the point where the flows had cracked. The snow was completely undisturbed in any direction you looked. Hanna also marveled at how few people realized or ever stopped to consider why ice would grind. Not that people cared, but to Hanna water stood out as a singular unique example of the chemistry of nature. Whereas all other liquids continued to shrink and become heavier as the temperature dropped, water was at its most dense at four degrees. Below that temperature it began to expand, which was the reason why water froze from the top down rather than from the bottom up. And the colder the temperature went, the more ice expanded to grind against itself.

But that was only part of the reason Hanna's mind was in a reflective mood. His third most unheralded moment of personal truth came with lying in his bag before he went to sleep that cold night in Alaska. It was the Northern Lights. They were everywhere, moving with slow, then lightening, speed, crackling across the heavens in unending vivid colors that no man or machine could create on earth.

And the final tidbit was that Hanna didn't zip himself into his bag to keep warm. He did so because the night was so bright with a full moon out that he could have read a newspaper at a time of year when the sun never rose above the horizon.

Today, Hanna was on the verge of another one of those

moments. The flight had left Rome's Leonardo de Vinci airport and set its course southwest headed straight for Marbella. He wouldn't even have to transfer in Madrid; the aircraft was nonstop to Spain's southern shore.

Hanna had stepped back in time when he stepped onto the aircraft. He didn't recognize the name of the airline company and initially cursed Rebecca who had set his itinerary. But then he realized that he was on an old Boeing 720, one of the first commercial jets ever put into service, and he instantly realized he had flown it years before in another life. The TWA couch in first class was still there, intact and inviting one to enjoy the camaraderie that came with possibly passing the time talking with others who might have a similar desire.

As air travelers leave the ground, headed southwest from Rome, they are immediately over the coast, headed out to sea, as when leaving Los Angeles. The coast drifts off to the horizon in both directions, and if the traveler is sitting on the right side of the aircraft, the coast begins its curve towards the west to become the French Riviera and then Spain. It doesn't take that long to get to Malaga, an hour and a half or so, but the views are spectacular. Sicily is on the horizon to the south. The flight path crosses Sardinia, and within the hour, the coastline begins to appear to the northwest. The coastline is the preserve of the wealthy, and the yachts that ply the waters contain nothing but the beautiful people: suntanned and ready for anything the world had to offer as long as it doesn't involve work.

Coming in to Marbella was uneventful, although the mountains to the north and the Mediterranean to the south with the African coastline faintly visible on the horizon had always held a certain fascination for Hanna. It wasn't as though it was a daily routine; however, he did go through this place on occasion.

Landing, baggage claim, and customs were all routine and Hanna found himself walking out to the curb in forty-five minutes. Regardless of all the bullcrap one heard in the press stateside, Europeans loved Americans, and Hanna could almost feel the female customs agent giving him a pat on the butt as he passed by her station with the entry stamp to the country firmly implanted on his passport.

His driver was standing just to the right of the door holding a small sign with "SEÑOR HANNA" written on it. Hanna waved at him—"Buenas dias, señor"—and was instantly assisted by redcaps, who had obviously been instructed to grab his luggage as soon as he was recognized.

Hanna allowed himself to be guided to the limousine awaiting his arrival in temperature-controlled comfort for the hour ride down the coast to Marbella. The windows were smoked so dark that no one was going to snoop into this toy. Hanna was beginning to feel like a drink, hopefully the bar in this mega machine wouldn't hold out on him.

The driver was at his side as he got to the door, grabbing the handle and silently swinging it open for his entry.

"Señor, please enjoy the ride. We will arrive in Malaga in an hour."

Hanna didn't want to burst the driver's bubble over the fact that he already knew this, deciding instead to just express his thanks and take in the scenery as the ride along the coast to the west unfolded. He hopped into the car.

"Bienvenidos, Señor Hanna," the voice said, "I am Mercedes. Would you care for a drink?"

Again, Hanna's mind went into lockdown for about five seconds, then he pushed his space bar and everything came back into focus.

"I'll have a Bloody Mary please, Mercedes," Hanna said. *There was no need to introduce himself,* Hanna thought, *this attendant already knew his name.*

Hanna's eyes slowly began to adjust to the darkened interior. He noticed that the rearview window from the driver's cabin was completely blacked out. The private limo attendant served his drink just as the car was thrown into gear for the trip to town.

"Here is your Bloody Mary, Mr. Hanna. Is there anything else you would care for? Perhaps something to eat? I have some beluga caviar, which can be served with chilled vodka, should you wish. I have also been informed that you have the taste buds of any virile American, so there is also a selection of sandwiches, roast beef, turkey, ham should you wish to be reminded of home along with an assortment of seafood fingers with their sauces including shrimp, lobster, and crab claws."

The car was floating down the road without a bump or a roll. *It was obviously designed to allow him to avoid attack in comfort in a hundred-mile-an-hour chase*, Hanna thought.

"I'll have a very small serving of the caviar with chilled vodka," Hanna responded. "Thank you Mercedes."

Since stepping into the car, Hanna had been taking stock of his personal waitress. The boss as usual had excelled in providing the finest in creature comforts. Hanna quickly realized that he would be incapable of truly evaluating the woman providing him with these in-transit personal services. All the blood in his body had drained to his feet causing him to lose all sense of touch.

Mercedes quickly prepared and served his order.

"Is there anything else that I could do for you?" Mercedes inquired.

Hanna had to do something to compose himself.

"Not at the moment, Mercedes, thank you, but why don't you join me in enjoying this little snack? After all, it's only a bit after lunch time, and I would love it if you would do so."

"Thank you very much, Señor Hanna," Mercedes said. "If you don't mind, I believe I will. I too, enjoy the caviar."

Hanna's mind was racing. Llewellyn had paid this girl so much that she was intent on ensuring that Hanna got everything he wanted, even though no one would ever have known it if she didn't. It was obvious to Hanna that Mercedes didn't care. He was going to be taken care of if he displayed the remotest desire to be taken care of. Hanna had to keep the conversation going, since he would have to register in the finest resort hotel in Malaga before he could change his clothes. Nothing untoward could happen in this car between now and then. Any strenuous activity now would be immediately obvious to his boss and the entourage traveling with him and Hanna couldn't afford to arrive in that condition.

"What do you do, Mercedes?" Hanna asked with a slight rasp in his voice. *Goddammit*, Hanna thought, *get your mind back in gear.*

Mercedes replied instantly.

"Well, Mr. Hanna, I have been on tour around the world for the past year as a goodwill ambassador. I just turned over my tiara awarded at the time I became Miss World last year to a new younger, more beautiful, woman at this year's host country, the Philippines this past weekend. But enough of me. Is there anything else you might wish for? We still have forty-five minutes until we arrive at the hotel."

Her skirt had ridden up her legs to the point where there was little left to the imagination, and she was gently dabbing his mouth with a linen napkin after each bite of caviar he took.

God damn his boss, Hanna thought. He was about to hit his third straight weekend out-of-town in the sexless environment into which he had been thrown, and his company had just arranged for him to be serviced by what the world, three hundred and sixty-five days ago, had adjudged to be the most beautiful woman on it. His boss had to be paying a five-figure amount to hire her for the six hours the round trip would take of her time and whatever other "anything elses" Hanna might desire.

The aura being exuded by this stick of dynamite reminded him of the scene in the movie where Dean Martin walked into the all female-run barbershop and the sign saying shave ten cents, haircut twenty-five cents, miscellaneous twenty dollars prompted the guy to say: "I'll have a little of that miscellaneous."

It was so true that love and hate sat right next to each other on the circle of emotions one could experience. He had this sudden desire to hug his boss while, at the same time, putting a bullet between his eyes.

Hanna's biggest problem was that there simply wasn't enough

time left to properly attend to Mercedes. Spanish, Italian, and French women all demanded extra attention when it came to matters of the flesh. The thirty minutes they had left on this trip into town wouldn't come close to satisfying this whirling dervish. *Hell, it wouldn't even come close to satisfying him in the weakened conditioned he was now in.* Hanna decided he had to talk his way through the next thirty minutes.

"Tell me, Mercedes," Hanna said, "Are you entered in the World Backgammon playoffs this weekend? You look like the sort who might do very well in such a competition."

Mercedes leaned back into her corner of the limousine's rear seat and talked the tournament nonstop until they reached the hotel.

Thirty Six
Saluting: The Ultimate Form of Respect

The limousine pulled into the driveway of the resort. Hanna had been here before, but he never ceased to be amazed. Despite what everything people thought they knew about Spain, it continued to be the world's best-kept secret.

Most of the resorts along this part of the Costa del Sol were four star, but several were graded five star and they deserved that status. Furthermore, at this time of year, their suites housed every pretender to the throne on the European continent. Arab sheiks who had not as yet completed the construction of their $100 million vacation retreats could be found occupying a floor here and there within the best hotels. The only reason these places cost so much, in Hanna's opinion, was because these meatballs needed eighty-three bedrooms to house their harems.

What the hell, Hanna thought. He had always been able to summon up the courage to walk the five-hundred dollar per square yard carpet between the two unshaven behemoths sitting all night on each side of the main entryway to some massive suite, despite the fact that these butt heads held an AK-47 in one hand and had an Uzi laying on the table in full view staring at you as though you could easily become their next victim of mistaken identity.

Resorts in this part of the world were very open. Wide-glass, floor-to-ceiling windows disappeared back into the walls, offering beautiful vistas. First beyond the wall, there would be a dining area with cushioned, wrought-iron furniture. Beyond that would be a pool with patio bars conveniently located at both ends behind the second or third row of chaise lounges, which would always completely encircle the swimming area. Beyond that lay the beach with perfect sand and beauty, unmatched in the world regardless of what the chain hotels paid the credit card companies to say about their private beach on Lukiewanahoki (sic) in the Hawaiian Islands being the best.

Finally, came the yacht basins, except that in this part of the world they were not called yachts. No, the behemoths resting at anchor in these berths were ships. There wasn't a home, palace, or castle in the world that could brag of having more amenities or artwork than these babies. The full-time crew usually consisted of somewhere between forty and fifty people, which would make the monthly payroll run somewhere in the $2 million range. Hanna's definition of yachts always prevailed: they were inanimate objects that made large holes in the water into which one poured money.

There was always a refreshing breeze wafting through the huge lobby of the resort, and while the weather was warm, the air was Mediterranean dry. Hanna was always confronted with the quandary as to why the Spanish had wanted to explore other parts of the world when they already lived in the best spot on the face of it.

Of course, there was always the ultimate coup de grace: the beautiful people. This jet-setting, polo-playing, horsey crowd languished around the pool, bejeweled and tanned to perfection. Occasionally, a group would stroll up to the patio restaurant for a campari and soda along with a cold lump-lobster and crab-meat cocktail. Most of the men wore abbreviated Speedos, which allowed the complete examination of all their equipment by every afternoon delight seated around the pool, with gold chains around their necks and waterproofed Rolexes on their wrists to accent their nearly perfect bodies. Polo on the weekends, water skiing a couple of times a week, and sex with some goddess at least once a day usually kept them hard, tough, lean, and looking like Adonises. In keeping with the Paris look du jour, most of them had a day's growth of beard on their face and wore fifteen-hundred-dollar sunglasses.

But the ultimate prizes were the women. They were the exact opposite of what Hanna had found when, at one time while traveling through the backwoods of a State ranked as one of the more obese in the country he had formulated the rule of ninety nine. Hanna's rule asserted the proposition that if a man spotted a good-looking woman sitting or standing anywhere with her friends, there was one chance in a hundred that any of her companions were also good looking. Thus, if two sex-starved males were traveling together, only one would get lucky.

Here, things were exactly the opposite. Hanna's gaze wandered out to the horizon, attempting to seek out with those sunburned eyes of his, the skin surrounding them wrinkled by years of watching nubile bodies go dancing daintily into the ocean, with the objective of locating one female dog. There were none. To a person, every woman tanning herself on a chaise, with the top of the bikini brassiere on, brassiere off, the bottom half of the outfit covering the bottom or a thong leaving nothing to the imagination, was ugly. Neither did any look over fifty, which really meant nothing since there was thousands of dollars invested in these bodies. Finally, few weighed more than 118 pounds. Hanna was all too familiar with that weight: it was the weight his wife carried. *God, how he wished he could talk some of these people into returning to Houston with him.*

Hanna knew it was coming. The question was when, and the suspense was killing him. He had arrived at the resort almost spot on four pm, checked in, and arranged to have his luggage taken up to his room. There was really no sense in going upstairs and checking out the suite which would be immaculate. He knew that, Jason Llewellyn, his boss, would be walking into the lobby within minutes. The DC-9 that had been customized for extremely long-range travel would be on the ground at Malaga at this point after having flown ten hours nonstop from Houston.

The aircraft could carry a hundred and fifty people in a commercial configuration. Jason's plane was outfitted to hold twelve. There were three double bedrooms, two showers, four bathrooms, luxury seats for all, and a complete kitchen on board. The company's chef at their headquarters in Houston usually accompanied the entourage on longer trips.

Hanna set himself up at one of the patio tables serving lunch and positioned himself to look towards the lobby with his back to the pool. *The New York Times* he had ordered from the concierge arrived at the same moment as his gin and tonic. Hanna opened up the paper and began to read. It was five minutes after four.

"Hannasan!" came the bellow from the boss.

Hanna looked up to see everyone approaching. Jason led the pack. There were three women walking behind him, followed by the chef and the aircraft's three-man crew in uniform.

Once again Hanna was bedeviled. Not only was he Jason's point man he was also his financial advisor on many things and Jason usually took his advise on federal income tax law regardless of whether he liked it or not.

Hanna had told him time and again that he had to quit being so ostentatious when travelling or the IRS was going to start denying the company's travel expenses. Yet, while he had always before been able to get along with two flight attendants to respond to his every whim, now he had gone to three. Jason did not uniform his women. As a matter of fact, he insisted that their wear be from one of the world's top-ten designers, and each dressed in their own look. Hanna recognized one from some other story. *Tuesday was her name*, Hanna thought. She was probably slightly over thirty, mature, educated at Vassar, and at some future date, destined to become the trophy wife for some extremely wealthy male. The second bettered the first slightly—a little bit sexier but that did not take anything away from the first.

The third, however, outdid both of them. She was younger but truly outstanding. She was capable of being Mercedes's successor's, successor, if one could follow that logic. Indeed, she was Miss World material any time she chose to run. Hanna was thankful they were in a very public area. It kept him from allowing his mind to wander too much.

"William," Jason started out. "You are my person when I can't be there. The work you did in Singapore was faultless and puts us in a position to dominate our industry when we finally sign a deal with the Chinese. Be looking for a little bit more in the old paycheck starting immediately."

Hanna smiled.

"I knew we could do the deal, Jason, and with your guidance and support of my negotiating position, I felt our success was guaranteed." Hanna's confidence had flooded back and he was holding sway over the group that had surrounded him. Everyone was gazing at him with admiration. Actually, Hanna thought, the flight attendants might possibly been gazing at him with a little bit more in mind.

Mental note to self, Hanna thought. *Determine which of the three Jason had bedded on the flight over and then concentrate on the other two.* No sense pissing off the man, he figured.

"Well, William," Jason went on, "we have come together here at the heart of opulence where frugality died a millennium ago and people can no longer pronounce the word let alone understand its meaning. So let the games begin. You are looking at the person who by Sunday evening will be the new backgammon champion of the world. No one in the motley crew of moneyed disasters gathered around us for the coming weekend has the wits to outmaneuver yours truly."

Hanna loved his boss. Jason was the only one he knew who had more arrogance than he when it came to describing how good he was.

"But enough small talk, William, let me introduce you to the reason I had you join us for a few hours."

Hanna's antenna immediately went up. What was this crap about introducing him to something?

"William," Jason went on, "this is my daughter, Misty. I think that probably the last time you saw her, she was a junior in high school."

Misty, the youngest of the three "flight attendants" immediately stepped forward and extended her hand.

"Hello William, it is such a pleasure to meet you again. It has been too long, and I was rather the ugly duckling the last time we saw each other."

Jesus Christ, Hanna thought to himself. He looked around for the nearest exit; too late. Misty had moved over to stand beside him. Her left hand was grasping his left arm. Her other arm she had brought around to grip his waist.

"In any case" Jason continued, "we must get registered and up to our rooms to have a shower before we meet for dinner. Your mission, William, should wish to accept it, is to escort my daughter around until her mother arrives late Saturday evening. You can then take your airline ticket and fly back to Houston. All I need you to do is ensure that my daughter does not run into any malingering, horny, young male whose only desire is to bed her and escape with her virtue."

"Daaaad!" Misty said. "I'm a grown woman, and I can take care of myself. I must say though that William is an excellent substitute for a horny, young male."

"Do you accept the mission, William?" Jason asked.

Hanna realized it wasn't a question. It was an order.

Just as the words came out of Jason's mouth, Misty dropped her right hand behind Hanna's ass and gave it a grab.

"Startling" is not the exact word one could use to describe this action; however, suffice it to say that Hanna's right arm came up in a perfect salute as he blurted out, "Yes sir, Mr. Llewellyn."

No one in the group saw the grab. They were all in the process of turning around to head over to the concierge to register as Hanna came six inches off the floor.

Misty had thrown both her arms around Hanna's neck and was swinging her body against his—certain of her lower body parts rubbing against his leg as she did so.

"Oh, William, I am so glad that daddy chose you to be my escort for the next day and a half. You bring just the experience I need to truly become a woman. How about we go up to my room and change into bathing suits to go for a swim? We can have sex before we come down to get the evening started."

There was no way to describe the panic that was settling in on Hanna's psyche.

He looked at his watch.

It was nine minutes after four.

Time had just developed a bad case of the slows.

Thirty Seven
You Only Live Twice

Once when you are born and once when you stare death in the face, Hanna thought, finishing the sentence that Ian Fleming had penned. To the best of Hanna's knowledge the rest of the world was completely unaware of the insight the author had offered the world that day since he had never heard anyone else quote it.

It was 4:10 on a Friday afternoon. Hanna had to keep the boss's tower-dwelling, celibate daughter from getting laid, either by him or anyone else, until his tour of duty ended early Sunday morning at approximately two am. That was the time at which her mother was scheduled to arrive to assume this responsibility.

Hanna calculated that, allowing for potty breaks, this amounted to an elapsed time of approximately 1,911 minutes. There was no way on God's green earth that Hanna was going to be able to conceal the panting vagina implanted in the body of a young Posh Posh for that length of time. Sooner or later some young, virile, suntanned Adonis was going to pick up the scent, and then Hanna was going to be in real trouble.

All of the forgoing, however, remained secondary to his own internal brain spasm, which had launched a physical reaction that would prevent him from standing up until someone came at him full frontal assault in a karate-chopping frenzy.

"Well Misty," Hanna said, "since we have been thrust together

[Hanna almost choked as he said it] for the next day and a half, I think we should celebrate the very agreeable circumstances in which we find ourselves by having a glass of wine together."

"Huh," was Misty's response.

"Are you saying, William, that we should postpone sex until after we have a drink? God, Hanna, did you not have a childhood?"

"What kind of wine would you enjoy Misty: a red or a white, possibly a campari and soda?"

"Jesus, William" was the instant response, "God, you're a disappointment. I had such super plans for us. Go upstairs for an hour of hard sex, then dress for dinner with Daddy and the others, then back to my room for more sex, then go out to the pool and enjoy the band and the drinks until we got horny again."

"Look, Misty," Hanna responded, "your daddy was very clear about the fact that he did not want you falling victim to some roguish lout whose only ambition in life was to extract your virginity before throwing your character under the bus. Being a father, Misty, I understand his concerns completely. Please help me here."

Hanna gave the waitress an order: the white for Misty, a merlot for himself.

"Oh, William," Misty lamented, "I don't want to get you into trouble. Please don't blame me for that. I just need a man before the night ends, and so far, you are the best I have seen. Besides, you come highly recommended by my father. You really must try to rethink your position, William. Please."

Posh Posh had her hand resting on Hanna's knee slowly stroking it.

"Don't worry," Hanna replied, "You and I have the full evening after dinner to get to know one another. I'm sure that between the two of us we will think of something."

Misty put her arms around his neck and gave him a deep hug and kiss.

"Oh William, I knew you would come around. I can wait."

Hanna gave a wry internal half smile, half sob.

He had just figured out how he was going to extract his ass from the extracurricular activities Misty was contemplating for later tonight.

"Damn your eyes, Misty, for making me lust like Jimmy Carter. I just hate it when demands are thrust upon my body and my brain requiring that I ignore all my internal instinct to act out my rogue-elephant alter ego, which would otherwise require that I mount anything animate within reach."

"Ah, William, there you are."

The voice was unmistakable; Jason and company had returned.

"And how has my very charming daughter been acting? I hope she has made me proud as she always does," he said as he leaned over and gave her a buss on the forehead.

"She has been every bit a credit to the Llewellyn name—" Hanna replied, "a perfect lady and an example for all young people of her age to follow."

"Good, good, William. You are my personal connoisseur on life. If you say it, I believe it."

"Why thank you," Hanna replied, "that is a wonderful complement, and I am going to take it in all seriousness."

"Not to worry, William."

Then moving on as though they were all starting over at the beginning Jason said, "Everyone, we will have to enjoy a late afternoon 'linner.' My first game is seven thirty this evening, and, after I win that one, I will be playing again at nine thirty. We can have supper after that before we call it a day."

"Linner" was Jason's expression for a meal somewhere between lunch and dinner. Hanna hated the word, but like any good brownnoser, he had taught himself to live with it.

It was five thirty, and Jason elected to have them eat poolside, which wasn't a bad choice. The sun was getting low in the west going down behind Gibraltar, the temperature had dropped a few degrees that later would require wraps for the ladies, and a lot of the afternoon group were beginning to head upstairs to get it on with whatever body they had chosen to be with and then have a nap before preparing for dinner about ten.

You didn't describe meals served anywhere in a five-star hotel, you just sat back and enjoyed them. Every type of entrée served in any form preferred was available. To top it off, one could order any form of drink, salad, dessert, or aperitif ever invented by man. If it was solid, it tasted like the Houston Brennan's bread pudding with brandy, and if it was a liquid it had the consistency of mother's milk. It was difficult to stop eating.

This evening, the meal had the essence of a Cajun dinner at Curvee's in New Orleans. The only difference here was that the servings were small and light so that no one looked like they were trying to become obese. After having a cocktail (Chivas and water for Hanna), the meal began with a remoulade-covered shrimp and a light fragrant wine. This was immediately followed by grilled diver scallops and a spinach puree that everyone washed down with a white La Lezardiere unparalleled for taste. A light salad came next with greens, cucumbers, and one tantalizing olive served with one's choice of dressings. Hanna chose homemade honey mustard that was like nothing he had ever tasted before. He only wished that he had been served more than one olive. Olives were his weakness. Bread, baked that day in the hotel's ovens, with thick crusts and olive oil was then served with bay scallops, tomatoes, and a white Henri Brecht. Lamb chops with mint served over a bed of mashed potatoes were the entrée accompanied by a St. Emilion Beausejour-Becot. At any given sitting, Hanna could eat six of these chops. There wasn't a way in the world to describe how delicious they were. The problem here was that only one per guest was served. A fruit compote then came, served with a sorbet and Champagne to freshen the palette. The meal finished with cheeses and grapes washed down by a 1910 South African Port.

In thinking about it, Hanna began to realize that the group of them made a pretty good-looking table. The pilot was a hot ex-

NASA astronaut that had decided that Jason's $250,000 annual stipend coupled with the lifestyle it offered were preferable to armed-forces pay offering a one in sixty chance of dying on takeoff or reentry. Lookswise, she could give Sally Ride competition, and Houston took care of its own.

Then there were the male copilot and navigator, both of whom were in their fifth year of flying with a major U.S. airline when Jason hired them and single, which kept them broad at the shoulder and lean at the hip.

Of course, you couldn't overlook the two personal flight attendants who were capable of attending to all of Jason's needs through the simple act of walking by his chair on the aircraft.

Finally, there came Hanna and the berserk daughter who, had they been in the middle of heavy supper-time activity rather than late afternoon quiet, would have embarrassed everyone since she had touched every part of Hanna's body since sitting down to eat. "Misty," Jason had said once, "for god's sake try to leave William alone long enough for him to eat."

"Yes, Daddy," Misty said.

Thank you Jason, Hanna thought.

"Oh, don't worry about it Jason," Hanna said, "Misty is just showing how likable we all are."

"Well, everyone," Jason said, "Time to go and rout that first opponent. Misty, you must come by at some point. You're my good luck charm."

"I'll have her by in a few minutes, Jason. We'll let you get underway before we come by. Good luck, sir."

"Good luck, Daddy," Misty said. "See you soon."

Everyone got up to leave. Hanna was just beginning to really enjoy the evening, and it was obvious Misty was as well. She had just pulled up her skirt and stretched her legs out straight on the chair next to her. All Hanna could do was shake his head.

"Misty," Hanna said. "The evening is beginning to really turn beautiful. How about another glass of that wine you have been enjoying?"

"That would be great, William. Gosh, I like you. Don't do me too good tonight or it'll be love."

Her chair backed up to Hanna's. Her hand gently played with his hair. The yacht owners were being served hors d'ouvers and martinis (they liked their buzz extra fast), and the sun had drifted below the horizon bringing on twilight. Misty continued to practice her deep breathing exercises while massaging the back of Hanna's neck. God did not have to poke his head out from behind the single puffy cloud in the sky to explain how good he was tonight: Hanna had already complemented him.

"Y'know Misty, it's time to go over to the hall and wish your daddy good luck. What do you say?"

"Ah, William, it's such a beautiful evening that I just don't want to move at the moment, but you're right—we should go over and wish him well."

Hanna ordered refills and asked for the check. It came back at $3,154.09. *Jesus Christ*, Hanna thought, *thank you guys, thank you guys. The damn tip for this thing (linner) would be double what a good meal at McCormick and Schmicks in Uptown Houston would have cost him.*

Hanna sighed, added 30 percent and signed the thing. *Someday*, he thought.

They slowly worked their way over to the hall. It was eight o'clock, and the tournament was well underway. A quiet bedlam was the only way to describe the action in the room. The cream of wealth, power, and position roamed idly about, drinks in one hand and cigarettes in the other. (No one denied the elite their smoke when such was their desire.)

"There he is," Misty said. "Daddy, good luck, Daddy. How are you doing?" Jason's opposition looked up in a very unsettling manner, which suggested that if Misty said one more word he would be on his feet tossing a double-bladed knife for her to catch.

Jason had put his finger to his lips. "Sssh Misty, there will be time to talk after the game is over."

"Okay, Daddy," Misty replied and turned to leave. Hanna followed.

"Sheeesh, what a stick in the mud," Misty said, "why does he have to play that guy?"

Hanna was tempted to explain but decided against it.

"Let's go over to the bar and relax until there is a break in the action, Misty," Hanna said. "I want to show you something."

They picked a table with curved, well-cushioned, bench-seat chairs on the back facing out. The set up was a little like the Brown Derby in Hollywood used to be. The view was unobstructed across the very large room. Misty had been well trained by her mother and others concerning the principles of etiquette and she carried it well, but Hanna thought he saw just the suggestion of a slight imbalance as she sat down.

"Misty," Hanna said, "I know you enjoy fine wines but how about extremely aged fine scotches? Have you ever had one? I'm not talking about your eight-year-old Chivas Regal; I'm talking about a fifty-year-old Scottish single malt. The drink is very smooth, and I'm sure you'll enjoy it immensely for a change of pace."

"Why not?" Misty replied, "With you by my side, I am ready for anything. Just one thing though, after this we are going up to bed, right?"

"After this, Misty, my body is yours for the rest of the evening," Hanna responded.

Hanna ordered two scotches, neat. He knew they would be served in very large sixteen-ounce brandy glasses, and he knew there would be somewhere in the neighborhood of six ounces of deadly fluid in each.

The drinks arrived, and they toasted to each other. Fifteen minutes later, Hanna had paid a five-hundred dollar bill, and they were headed out of the bar slowly making their way towards the elevator. Misty was still in animated conversation with no more indication that she had had a lot to drink than some sixty-year-old matron who, over the last thirty years, had never enjoyed less than three double gin martinis for lunch.

The elevator door opened. Hanna hesitated. Not for long, as Misty jerked his elbow and, by extension, his body onto it.

Hanna was beginning to sweat. Something had to break he thought. He had run out of excuses, and the body now dragging him down the hallway was demanding recompense.

However she did it, Misty had her electronic key out as she hit the door.

The door swung wide open. Hanna found himself being dragged across the room to the bed as his shirt was removed, revealing that rippled muscular chest that Hanna always prided in himself. Misty then removed her dress (if you could call something designed to be a skirt a dress). She had her arms around his neck. Hanna was off balance.

Not good, Hanna thought. They started to fall back onto the bed, which had already been turned down by night service. Misty's legs curled out, wrapping themselves around his waist in an attempt to provide his loins with a glimpse of the heaven that awaited them. A hand had unzipped his fly, and was beginning to stroke something that didn't need stroking.

Hanna began to think: *Ten hours between Houston and Marbella; jet lag approximating eight hours; six hours in the sun; a long meal with family; five glasses of wine and six ounces of Black Velvet. When would events start to lay waste to this body writhing underneath him?*

For the first time in his life Hanna had begun to curse himself for the blunder in calculations he had made.

"Oh ,William," Misty sighed as she pushed her crotch up into his groin, an extremely pleasant experience despite the fact that neither of them had yet undressed to that level. "Please be gentle with me, I have never done this bef..."

Snore.

Misty was gone. She was undressed except for her underwear.

Hanna pulled the sheets and blankets back, puffed the pillows and replaced them under her head. He then closed the patio doors, turned down the air conditioning to sixty-two degrees, covered her back up, and turned around to redress himself. Hanna was hoping the low temperature would add a few hours of suspended animation to her beauty sleep tonight, giving him some extra time to figure out what he was going to do to get through this ordeal.

He sat down in one of the large overstuffed chairs in the suite for a full fifteen minutes while his breathing and his body returned to normal. Misty was dead to the world.

Christ, he thought, *that was close, nevertheless, it once again proved his philosophy that, in times of high crises, booze was the only answer.*

Hanna adjusted the room lighting and closed the drapes in the hope that Misty would sleep until noon, if not longer. He then collected and gently folded the handkerchief-sized outerwear that Misty had removed from her body before collapsing and laid everything out on the back of a heavily cushioned chair.

In a final act of masochism he pulled back the bedding one last time to view the almost naked body of Posh Posh. He then slowly replaced the bedding and headed for the door. On the way out, he grabbed the "Do not disturb" sign hanging on the door knob inside the room and placed it on the outside knob. Unless Misty woke up to an atomic device exploding outside her window in the morning, this should guarantee Hanna's peace and quiet until at least two o'clock tomorrow afternoon. That would leave him with a remaining in-charge time of one-half day. Twelve hours. Seven hundred and twenty minutes. A whole bunch of seconds.

Hanna needed a plan. As he walked a bit unsteadily down the hallway, he came to the realization that he had just lived twice. The problem was that he was still debating if death might not have been the preferred alternative.

Thirty Eight
Life Must be Viewed as a Series of Challenges

Said the son of the self-made, millionaire CEO of Enormous Company, Inc. puking up the standard jargon of the Harvard MBA program. *Not as,* Hanna continued, *the bouncing around from pillar to post in some unrecognizable form of controlled chaos, which brought with it a new bruise and scar that would be recognizable in every poolside photo taken of the perpetrator for the rest of his life.*

Hanna wondered how he was going to survive the last twelve hours of this chamber of horrors Jason had handed him?

He stepped off the elevator on the main floor. It was eleven thirty, and things were just starting to get going. The entertainment establishments were in full operation. The five bars were all open and packed with guests. One could forget about eating unless he had a reservation. Hanna knew there were three dance floors strategically placed around the huge main-floor layout; however, the building was so designed that you could never hear feedback from one dance area overriding the sound of the one closer at hand.

Assuming that Jason had won both his backgammon rounds, Hanna calculated that the entourage would be sitting down to supper shortly. Knowing the boss as he did, Hanna decided to walk to the most expensive restaurant located on the premises and conduct a quick search for his clan.

He had no sooner approached the maitre d' than the voice boomed out across the frozen wasteland that lay between them.

"William!" Jason hollered to the annoyance of every segment of royalty seated in the room, "Come join us. Where is Misty? By the way, I won both my games. It will make tomorrow a long day."

Hanna, noticing the irritation of the assembled diners (the ugly American has struck again) as he slipped quietly into his chair.

"Good evening Jason, good evening everyone. I am sorry to say that a short while back Misty succumbed to jet lag and too long a day. She is now asleep in her room. Her last words were to ask me to apologize to all of you for not being able to join you for supper this evening. Congratulations on today's wins Jason, as if those were in order, since, we all know we will still be saying this when the tournament is over."

Hanna had not yet placed a drink order so he raised his very chilled glass of Evian and toasted, "A votre santé, Jason, and good luck over the rest of the weekend."

The entourage followed with the toast to their supreme leader.

As Hanna had expected, the food was indescribably good, and Jason's conversation excruciatingly boorish since it consisted entirely of a move by move replay of both games he had been in this evening. Hanna could not have cared less. He knew absolutely nothing about the game or its rules.

It was one-thirty in the morning when they finished. The room was beginning to quiet down a bit, but there were still more tables occupied than empty.

God, the Spanish knew how to live, Hanna thought.

Everyone got up quietly joking and enjoying the spirit of the evening meal. This was a microcosm of their Houston office, since the office tended, more or less, to exude the same characteristics. This was not going to be a late night for anyone. The entourage had been up for over a day and a half, having flown in straight from

Houston, and Hanna, it finally occurred to him, had not closed his eyes since before Lana had accosted him on the Alitalia flight after it went wheels up a day and a half ago in New Delhi.

Everyone headed straight for the elevators as soon as they left the restaurant. Hanna excused himself when they passed the newsstand, explaining that he had this sudden desire to immerse himself in a newspaper before going to bed.

"Good evenings" were exchanged all around, and the entourage continued on while Hanna made a detour.

Hanna had just formulated a solution to his dilemma, but he needed time to set it up.

Why not try the bar and disco out on the far side of the pool? Hanna thought.

He moved out onto the patio and into a sea of bedlam. Almost all the chaise lounges were in use, the pool was full, everyone had a drink in their hand, and the band was playing a reggae tune. The bar itself, right off the edge of the dance floor, was very large with at least a dozen stools to sit at and the dance floor had at least a hundred people on it, each rubbing as much of their body into the person nearest them as they could.

It also had the mix Hanna was looking for. There were men dancing with women, women dancing with women, women dancing with men, and men dancing with men. The diversity of the moment was a feast for Hanna's scheming eyes.

Everyone looked the same—young, beautiful, eager for life, and absolutely in love with themselves in the best definition of a true narcissist. Hanna's eyes slowly scanned the talent pool finally settling on a tall, blond, olive-skinned, six footer, bred to satisfy the desires of the beautiful people. All it would require to activate the body would be an admiring glance of some gorgeous male or female. This honey dew, Hanna surmised, leaned more to the male persuasion if Hanna was sizing him up properly. Perfect!

Let's check him out, Hanna thought as he slid in between the stools next to cool man.

"A glass of merlot," Hanna flipped to the bartender, then

turned to the boy with "Jeeeezz, you would think tiny butts would remember after having served me the same all afternoon."

"Well," cool man replied, "I heard from someone that his mother was very sick, but she lives in Montreal and he doesn't have the money to take the time to go see her. I understand she may not make it. Of course it could be that the bar is just really busy tonight, and he is off his game."

"Oh no, that is just not fair. He should be at his mother's side," Hanna said. "It is such a shame, and he's so young to."

Hanna had reached up and placed his hand gently on cool man's arm rippling with gym built up muscle and attached to a body beautiful deciding that he had his man.

Hanna withdrew his hand quickly. *No sense getting too friendly,* he thought.

"I just wish there was some way I could help tiny butts," cool man replied. "He's such a nice boy, and I can't stand watching him hurt so badly."

"What's your name" Hanna asked, "Mine is William, but my friends call me Bill."

"Oh, William, it is such a pleasure to meet you," cool man said taking Hanna's hand with a limp shake. "My name is Bruce. May I call you Bill?"

"Of course you can," Hanna replied. "May I suggest that we find a table somewhere that is a little less busy and maybe we can figure out a way to help tiny butts?"

Bruce jumped he was so happy about the prospect. "Oh, that is so very nice of you, Bill. Let's do it."

Hanna was amazed that the place was still so packed, considering it was approaching three am. Still, it didn't take long to find a table, and they both sat just as the waiter arrived with a new round of drinks Hanna had ordered before they left the bar.

Hanna asked about Bruce's family and especially his mother and got a ten minute reply dealing with the current status of all of them. He was almost crying by the time he finished with his mother. She was currently undergoing chemo for some form of cancer, and Bruce couldn't wait for his vacation to be over this coming week so that he could return home to be by her side. He didn't have enough money to change his reservation. Bruce lived in Brooklyn.

Hanna shook his head. He couldn't believe what he was hearing.

"Well, Bruce, I have a bit of a dilemma," Hanna said, "and I was hoping that you might be able to take some time out of your day tomorrow to help me out. You see, I have a very young, innocent lady that I have been asked to escort until such time as her mother arrives about an hour after midnight tomorrow evening. She is a virgin, but she sees in me an answer to her status since she does not want to remain that way. I, unfortunately, cannot allow myself to engage in activity of this sort, so I need a proxy to fill in on my behalf from early afternoon tomorrow—say two in the afternoon until about two the following morning. Since friendship rather than the flow of adrenaline to your loins seems to drive your relationship with women, I think you would be a perfect stand-in for myself, and I don't think it would be necessary for me to tell you that the preservation of this young lady's virginity is the only goal of this operation."

"How about it, Bruce?" Hanna asked. "The mission is all yours, should you decide to accept it."

Hanna could see Bruce getting coy.

"Well, I guess I wouldn't mind performing this deception you are proposing, Bill, but how does that allow me to help my friend tiny butts?"

"Oh, my goodness Bruce. I forgot to mention some means of thanking you for the time you would divert to this little sidebar activity. How about I pay you a thousand dollars now for your help and give you another four thousand after you have completed the job at two the following morning when you are done? Let me see, that would work out to about four hundred dollars an hour for your time."

Hanna figured that Bruce the golden boy was probably living

at the two-dollar-a-night hostel ten blocks inland and was probably making ends meet by offering "services" to men of a similar persuasion attending the backgammon tournament, but he still was not quite prepared for Bruce's reaction to his proposal.

First, Bruce's jaw dropped a good three inches. After that, in order, he jumped up and ran around to give Hanna a hug and kiss, he then thanked Hanna for helping not only tiny butts but also his own fate, stating that now he would be able to afford the penalty charge to change his flight reservation to take him back to Brooklyn early. He was holding Hanna's hand and sobbing as he sat down.

Careful Hanna, he thought, *you don't want this guy thinking you're part of the gay community.*

"So you are agreeable to the arrangement then Bruce?" Hanna asked, "and I can expect to see you about two pm tomorrow out here on the patio?"

"Yes, yes, Bill," Bruce replied.

They spent the next thirty minutes, while sipping a second drink, going over the details as to how tomorrow would shake out. The last thing Hanna did before he stood up to leave was to take his wallet clip out, peel off ten one-hundred dollar bills and hand them to Bruce.

Bruce's hand was shaking so badly he could hardly take them.

"Bill, what you have done literally offers me the chance to better myself and I can't thank you enough. Are you sure you don't want a little companionship later in your room? I would be so happy to accommodate you at no charge if you do?"

The offer sent a chill down Hanna's back. His guess was that Bruce couldn't quite believe that he was straight.

"No, Bruce. I started off today a long time ago in Singapore, and I need some sleep. You go back and enjoy your friends. I'll see you tomorrow."

"Until tomorrow then, Bill." Bruce turned and did a gay lope back to the bar.

God, Hanna thought, *I hope he doesn't buy more than one round of drinks on the house. If he does, he'll find out how little a thousand dollars can buy.* He just hoped that by tomorrow night Bruce would have enough in his pocket to get both tiny butts and himself home.

On his way through the lobby, he stopped at the newsstand and bought the *New York Times*. Ten minutes late, he was in his room, bed turned back, resort-supplied kimono on, sitting out on his patio with the doors open, gazing down from the sixth floor at the pool he had just left below him, sipping on a Chivas and water he had just poured from his mini bar while sitting there reading yesterday morning's paper at three am.

Ten minutes later, the time, the booze, the jet lag, the water lapping at the shoreline, the crescent moon high in the sky, and a dozen other soothing sounds and views washing over him, the paper slipped slowly from Hanna's hand as he dropped off to sleep while laying on the patio's chaise lounge.

Thirty Nine
Planning: The Key To Success

Hanna woke to the sound of voices. He looked down from the balcony to see pool life guards with bronzed bodies and motor activated loins cleaning the deck and pool before the start of the day's activities. There were two older couples who had taken up residency poolside, at what was obviously their favorite tanning spot, but other than that the pool was vacant. Hanna looked at his watch. It was nine thirty. Apparently, everyone was still trying to recover from last night's drunken soiree.

God I love the Spanish, Hanna thought.

The first thing he did after setting up the in-room coffee maker to brew some of the good stuff was to order breakfast and the morning's *London Financial Times* from room service. He then showered, shaved, and did everything else appropriate to those arising to greet the day would do.

He dressed in his finest resort-inspired haute couture and was about to move outside to catch some early morning rays when the door rang.

"Room service," said the voice in a feline tone with a bit of Spanish accent.

Hanna opened the door to view, as usual, one more feminine product of the Spanish Main.

God, Hanna thought again, *why did the Spanish ever have any desire to go off and explore for new worlds? They had it all right here. It had to have the same logic behind it as the reason why movie stars with gorgeous wives got photographed by the paparazzi while being blown by some hooker while parked at the corner of Hollywood and Vine.*

The Spanish miniskirt with tiny white apron set out breakfast on the patio table after insisting that Hanna sit down and enjoy his morning paper while she did so. Hanna knew it, and Hanna knew she knew it that this put her in the best possible position to display every moving part of her body to see at what point his brain would explode.

He mused as to whether or not the CIA had ever used this torture technique.

Hanna began his meal about ten minutes after the maid left. His pulse rate had dropped to ninety, and at this point he figured he could proceed without serious damage to his body. His breathing was still raspy; however, he figured that would return to normal in the next half hour.

Breakfast was delicious. Fresh fruit, berries, toast, and boiled three and one-half minute eggs. Grapefruit juice and coffee finished off the morning ritual.

Hanna stood up, walked over to the chaise lounge he had come to know and love overnight and sat down to read the paper. He couldn't. His mind kept reverting to the plan he had concocted with Bruce for the day.

Let's see, Hanna thought, *have I thought of everything?* No one among the entourage would be awake before noon. Jason would use the personal services of whichever flight attendant was currently in favor, order breakfast in room for the two of them, and then clean up to head down to the tournament room for today's events, which were to begin at approximately two thirty this afternoon. The rest of the group would spend the afternoon playing tourist up in the center of town. They had no desire to continue paying twenty-five dollars for a Bloody Mary when they could buy a local beer for fifty cents up in the town square. Nothing to worry about with the Houston set.

Misty's normal wake up time was about one in the afternoon. Hanna had heard this from her father on several occasions when they had an early takeoff planned, and Misty was a no show at the time to leave for the airport. Misty was incapable of taking care of herself, therefore she would head downstairs to find somebody to feed her after she cleaned up. That would make the timing about two. Hanna had arranged for the hotel staff to look for him on the main floor patio restaurant to receive any phone calls to his room after one o'clock this afternoon. Misty would be trying to contact him somewhere during the next hour with a request for him to solve all of her problems both actual and perceived. She had to know where to find him.

If they sat down and ordered lunch somewhere in the two o'clock timeframe, they would be about to begin to eat at roughly 2:20. Bruce would walk out through the lobby doors at that point, and Hanna would wave him over.

Bruce was the ideal male phallic symbol if you didn't mention his mother. His entire body was gym perfected; every muscle revealed itself not in outrageous overabundance, as was the desire of the Mr. World contestants, but rather as a subtle reminder that it was there and capable of revealing itself. His shoulders dimensions, whether it was an optical illusion or not, appeared to be far wider than his hips and his head had those features that were about as close as anyone could get to the male sculpture throwing the discus. Blond and tanned, he would be able to hold Misty in one palm, raised arm's length above his head. Hanna had encouraged him to do that at least once during the course of the afternoon so that she could dog it over everyone else on the beach.

Hanna had already made all the arrangements so that whatever the two of them ordered was to be charged to his account.

Later in the evening, when Misty wished to change clothes for the night's activities, Bruce was to remain staunchly coy, not making promises of any sort and to mention only the delights to be enjoyed later but not now. He would remain in the lobby while Misty went upstairs and changed.

Shortly before two in the morning, Bruce was to talk Misty into moving to the upper patio area. Hotel reception was about two feet around the corner, out of view.

As soon as Mildred Llewellyn entered the registration area, Hanna would greet her and point out the fact that her daughter was out on the patio around the corner waiting to hug her with open arms.

At that point, Hanna would head for a small alcove back in a corner to sit unseen until it was two thirty and time for him to catch his car to the airport in Marbella. He would be joined there by Bruce to whom he would pass the final four thousand dollars to complete the deal and then watch as he pee-peed his pants.

By previous arrangement, of course, Hanna would be checked out of his room and his luggage removed to the temporary porte cochere storage to await his departure.

Hanna sighed. If only he had been around to be in charge of the European theater operations in World War II instead of Eisenhower. The war would have ended two years earlier. Despite Hanna's concerns about Bruce's ability to appear and carry out the plan they had hatched together, there came Bruce walking across the patio at exactly two fifteen.

Misty, while in the middle of berating Hanna for not satisfying her desperate hunger for sex last night, had stopped to ravenously mouth a double-size portion of her omelet not even noticing Hanna waving at Bruce. She only turned once he had invited the hunk over.

As Bruce approached the table, Hanna said, "Bruce, so good to see you again. Please meet my friend Misty."

Bruce said, "How good to see you again William, and certainly how pleasant it is to be able to touch the hand of your friend. A pleasure to meet you, Misty. May I call you Misty?"

Bruce was at his godlike best, standing there in an abbreviated Speedo, which left nothing to the imagination.

For the first time ever, Misty was speechless. She just stood there marveling at this piece of Nirvana she had just been handed.

Finally, after regaining use of the motor-control part of her brain which allowed the heart and lungs to resume their normal activities she said, "How delightful to meet you, Bruce. Please sit down and join us for lunch. William and I were just going to lie around the pool for the afternoon and we would love to have you join us. Do you have any plans?"

"I don't have any plans that I can't break," Bruce responded. "But what's this lying around the pool all afternoon? Why don't we get some jet skis and spend some time out on the Mediterranean?"

"I think that is a wonderful idea," Hanna chimed in, "The only problem is that I do have a bit of business to attend to. Why don't the two of you just go out and enjoy yourselves, and I will catch up with you later?"

"That's fine with me," Misty said, "How about you, Bruce?" Bruce nodded his agreement, and Hanna could see Misty's mind rolling over at all the opportunities she was going to have to disrupt the flow of this guy's penile functions over the course of the afternoon and evening.

Good luck, Hanna thought.

"Well, if you don't mind then, I'll be leaving," Hanna said. "Bruce, could you please arrange for the waiter to add 30 percent to the check and have it charged to my room? Thanks much."

Hanna quickly stood up and moved away back into the lobby. He ran all the way to the elevator, closed the door, and did a one-man polka all the way to his floor.

Damn, it felt good. He had put in place a plan whereby he would not have to be felt up all afternoon by a horny Cleopatra demanding nothing less than the opportunity to suck all the fluids out of his body. All this after his having promised her boss that he would see to it that she remained celibate. Then, he had delivered to her the body of an Olympic god, who, unbeknownst to her, had absolutely no interest in her sexual needs or desires.

He opened the door to his room. Everything had been cleaned and made up.

Hanna was going to take a nap.

He was then going to pack for the trip home.

He was then going to order dinner in, on his patio.

At one am, he was going to request a red cap to take his luggage down to the porte cochere. He was then going to go down to the main bar from which he could see the registration area and the patio seating outside the glass walls.

Now here he was. It was 1:30, and he was seated at the bar sipping quietly on a last Chivas and water. He had not seen any of the entourage all day let alone this evening. Jason would be busy pleasuring himself at the moment with his current toy: The rest of the crew were probably all asleep having paired off earlier in the evening with something to their liking.

At 1:50, through the cherry wood room divider he saw Bruce come up to the patio with Misty in tow. She was bubbling.

Goddammit, Hanna thought, *if that guy had changed her status, I'm going to be really pissed.*

Nah, Hanna thought, *at this point the guy was as reliable as the sun rising in the east. Besides, if he had, what the hell difference did it make?*

It was 2:07, and suddenly, there she was. Mildred Llewellyn had just entered the lobby and was heading for the registration desk.

Hanna took one look at her as he paid his check and began to walk out around the bar area to greet her. It was times like these that he really pitied Jason. Mildred had the voice of an opera singer somewhere in the middle of *Aida* and a body resembling that of a beer-swilling Susan Boyle.

Hanna came up behind her. From a safe distance he said, "Mildred, my goodness I can't believe it's you. Good to see you again. How is everything?"

Mildred had turned around towards him as soon as he began

to speak and with outthrust arms she motioned for him to give her a warm hug and a buss. Hanna did.

"William, my friend of friends, how are you? It has been so long, and now we have to meet like this half way around the world."

Hanna was in no mood to explain that this was only one quarter the way around the world.

"Yes, yes," he said, "so true. By the way, your daughter is close by. Would you like me to take you over to see her?"

"Oh, please, William."

Hanna immediately extended his arm and began walking Mildred out to the patio. As they rounded the corner he saw all the smiles and pleasure of the evening disappear from Misty's face.

"Well, hello mother," Misty said. "How was your trip?"

"Oh, Misty, it is so good to see you again. Have you made any progress on tatting that doily for your father's study? He is going to be so happy and proud when he receives that from you for his birthday next month."

"Well, Mrs. Llewellyn," Hanna said, "it is with great pleasure that I return your daughter to your care. It was a delight to be able to spend some time with her."

"Oh, William, you are so perfect in your complements. Thank you for the time you have set aside to be with our very wonderful daughter. When do you leave for Houston?"

"In twenty minutes, Madam. I have a seven o'clock flight leaving Marbella for Paris from which I shall proceed onward to Houston later this morning."

Bruce had disappeared. Misty, who was so pissed and hung up at having been cornered this way, just stood there with her mouth open. Mildred, who always thought the world revolved around her, had not even realized there had been someone sitting with Misty when she walked out onto the patio with Hanna.

"Well, you have a great flight then, William, and we will all see you back in Houston in a week or so," Mildred said. "Come Misty, help me arrange for assistance in taking my luggage upstairs. We can then sit out on the patio, sip wine, and have a grand old conversation. Where is your father by the way? It's just awful the way he leaves me to fend for myself."

Hanna just hoped that Jason had not fallen asleep in his mistress's arms and managed to get back to the conjugal bed before Mildred's arrival.

God, what a letdown for Jason her arrival had to be.

"Thank you very much, Mildred, and welcome to Malaga. Enjoy yourself in every way possible while you are here. It's a beautiful place."

Hanna headed back to the nook in the lobby. There was Bruce. He handed him the four-thousand dollars in an envelope.

"You didn't decide you were heterosexual and nail her this afternoon I hope, Bruce."

"Are you kidding, Bill? The more beautiful and feminine they are the more of a turnoff they are to me. I did have to drag a couple of horny toads off her body before the day was over, however. But don't worry, they didn't get anywhere."

"Bruce," Hanna said, "Have a good life, and thank you for helping me out today. I hope both you and tiny butts are able to do what you have to do. You earned the money to do it with my thanks and blessing. Good luck."

"Thank you, Mr. Hanna," Bruce said as he shook his hand. "I truly hope we will meet again sometime."

Bruce was gone.

Hanna headed for the porte cochere.

Rule Ten for Avoiding Infidelity While away from Home on Extended Business Travel

The sexual exploitation of children ranks among the most vile of crimes, and a new global community is beginning to understand and appreciate the need to protect the young among us from themselves. This may be performed through the administration of large quantities of liquor to knock them unconscious for extended periods of time or placing them under the supervision of personnel who will, if paid enough, physically restrain them from attempting to inflict such sensual pleasures on themselves. Therefore, the business traveler must constantly be alert to these temptresses willing on a moment's notice to inflict themselves upon the innocent bystander's body. In addition, it is recommended that the traveler enroll in training classes that will teach the techniques outlined above as proven methods by which to avoid the coy wiles of the oversexed young and the raging hormones with which they are infected.

Forty
At Last, on the Road to Home

Hanna quickly moved to the edge of the curb at the broad porte cochere to wait for his limousine to pull around and load his luggage. It would take a little time getting schedules adjusted since it was two thirty Sunday morning, and Hanna was an hour early. He shrugged off the added wait time: he didn't give a crap. The nightly appearance of the beautiful people was just starting to get under way. Nothing got going on the Costa del Sol until after dinner, which was usually served about eleven. Of course, no bar closed before the sun came up either.

In twos, fours, and every other sized group they came and went. People bar hopped all up and down the beach. It was like Las Vegas.

The men wore sleeveless tops with three buttons undone at the neck to reveal hairy chests, the trousers at least one size too small, designed to unabashedly outline their privates to anyone who might be interested. At least a day's worth of whisker growth and sunglasses completed the ensemble. It didn't make any difference that the army would have been using their night vision goggles for five hours now: sunglasses were mandatory.

To a person, the women were made up, jeweled, slim, and tanned. All wore dresses with hardly any top and skirts sufficiently short that they were a quicker short cut to the treasures they hid than one's laptop could get them to the Internet.

Hanna could have cared less. He was headed for home, and not even the bulls of Pamplona could stop him now.

Five minutes later, with the hands of the hotel help having been fed and the limo moving away from the town center, Hanna propped himself in the corner of the car's rear seat and tried to get comfortable for the hour long ride back to Marbella airport. His conscious was so clear that he would have been asleep in ten seconds except that a voice came quietly over the intercom from the driver.

"Ah, Señor Hanna, sir," the driver said, "Mr. Llewellyn made us arrange for a pitcher of Bloody Marys to be on board for your transit to Marbella airport. If you just reach inside the refrigerator, you will find a fresh one poured."

Hanna dragged himself over to the rear-facing seat and opened the door to the cooler. There sat a Bloody Mary looking like a bowl of Hagan Daz ice cream. An executive-size envelope was propped up against this delecto with "Mr. Hanna" typed in script across it.

Hanna took a long slow draught on the Bloody Mary and opened the single sheet of paper inside.

William:

Mr. Chou and I both agreed before you left for Singapore that if you could close the deal between his company and our company it would be worth $100 million in terms of the leverage it would provide our partnership moving forward. To that end we decided that the person who was able to close the deal, keeping in mind that every time the partnership had previously been negotiated it had fallen through, should receive a 10 percent commission.

The $10 million was deposited in your payroll account the day we left for Marbella.

You will also find a note on your desk when you arrive

in the office Monday morning, which is a buy-in agreement providing you with a 5 percent ownership interest in my firm.

Every time you turn around, William, you just reconfirm my good luck in having hired you in the first place.

Congratulations, best regards, and have a safe flight home

Jason

At twenty minutes to four the limo pulled up in front of the departures entry way. Hanna was sound asleep in the middle of his third Bloody Mary.

God! He was good, was his last conscious thought. *Ne plus ultra as the French would say.*

"Señor Hanna, sir." The driver was gently shaking his shoulder. "Señor Hanna, we have arrived at the Marbella airport, Señor Hanna."

Hanna was beginning to get the picture. He had just completed the first step on getting his ass back to the U.S.A.

A hundred-dollar bill here and another one there, and he was on his way to check in for Paris. Twenty minutes later, his passage was cleared through Iberia Airlines and customs. The flight was scheduled to leave at seven. Hanna decided to have breakfast in the first-class lounge. His greatest ambition in life at the moment was to be able to sleep the hour and a half to Paris uninterrupted—a decision that was exquisite in its simplicity.

First-class lounges outside the U.S.A, were different than their counterparts in country. They were first class.

Hanna dined with poached eggs on toast, ham, and a large bowl of fruit, all washed down by two mimosas as the sun slowly began to rise on the eastern horizon.

The day was perfect, Hanna thought. *Big sky, like Texas, without a cloud, like Texas, a slight breeze off the ocean with no humidity, unfortunately, not like Texas.*

The announcement to board the flight came at twenty minutes

to seven. Hanna was curious as to why the flight was being boarded so close to take off time until he took his seat and the door closed. There were only three people in first class and no more than twenty in steerage. One of the two other first-class passengers had smiled pleasantly at him as he turned to place his luggage in the overhead bin. It was obvious this aircraft was needed in Paris each morning to meet the schedule for some onward flight. There wasn't any way one was going to talk those Broadway Babies down on the Costa del Sol into getting up in the middle of the night to catch a flight to anywhere.

The flight was airborne at exactly seven. Three minutes later, the first-class flight attendant was up and walking down the aisle to where he was seated to enquire as to any creature comforts he might need.

Now that he had been released from the talons of the boss's daughter, there were several Hanna thought to himself.

"¿Quieres una bebida, Señor Anna?" she asked as she leaned over in front of him to arrange his table and provide him with an opportunity to admire the upper portion of her perfectly formed body. "Would you care for a drink?"

It was at times like this, thought Hanna, *when confronted with one's principles, that a person had to be steadfast in one's beliefs.*

Hanna was fed up with being poured off the aircraft at his destination, and before he got on this series of flights that would end with him being back in Houston, he had sworn on granny's bible that he was not going to over imbibe on this flight home. For just one time, he was going to be stalwart in the face of adversity, which would permit him the opportunity to recall at least some details of the flight.

"I'll have a Bloody Mary, Senorita. Thank you for asking."

What the hell, Hanna thought. *One more drink wouldn't hurt all that much.*

He had turned around and was admiring the long shadows cast across the fields and vineyards 35,000 feet below, when he heard the voice.

"Bonjour, Monsieur Hanna. What is bringing you to our fair country today? I trust we will have a little time to get to know you better before your travels move you on to your final destination," the woman said as she sat down in the aisle seat next to him and made herself comfortable.

Somewhere during this exchange, Hanna could no longer recall when, the flight attendant had returned with his drink which as he gazed down at it now, was half gone.

How did things like this happen ? he thought.

"By the way, Guilliame," his new seatmate continued, "my name is Brigette. Brigette Marsailles. I have to extend to you an apology since I took the liberty of asking our hostess what your name was."

"I'm very pleased to meet you, Brigette," Hanna replied. "I regard it as a great honor and privilege that you decided to sit and entertain me with a brief discourse on this very short flight into Paris." The panic had once again set in, replacing the placid demeanor Hanna had managed to surround himself with earlier in the evening. He couldn't even remember what he had just said.

"Here you go, Señor Anna," the flight attendant said. "I noticed your drink was empty and decided to bring you another."

It was an ambush, Hanna thought to himself. His boss had seduced him with money, causing him to consume vast quantities of booze. This lead to breakfast with copious quantities of booze. Now, here he sat land locked in a window seat being drugged with still more booze by a Spaniard and claim jumped by an extremely mature, handsome, and demure French woman of evil intentions who, it would appear from an outward glance, lived full-time in a suite at the Georges Cinq and was just returning from a too short month long period of "alone time" away from her husband. He suspected there were no tan lines on this body.

"Guilliame," Bridgette said (she refused to call him William), "what is your native land? My English is not good enough to recognize accents. Are you British, Slavic, German, Russian, or

Italian. Please don't tell me you are Russian. You are much too polite to be one of those beasts."

Hanna had a problem. He hadn't heard the most obvious guess. What was that supposed to mean. Was the oversight caused by excitement, love, indifference, apathy, or hatred.

"I'm American, Bridgette. I would have thought that would have been your first guess," Hanna said.

The pitch of the engines changed and the nose of the engine dropped as they began their descent into Paris.

"Oh, no, William" Bridgette said, "Americans are more pompous than the British monarchy. They are conceited, loud, gauche, obnoxious, self-centered, egotistical, fat, and boorish. Please don't tell me you are American, William. I am attracted to you too much."

"I must apologize for being an American," Hanna said, "It was an unfortunate whim of fate, but if you will allow me this one final safe passage through the birthplace of the age of enlightenment, I will promise to never again defile the soil of your nation by setting foot on it."

The lights had come on in the cabin for their final approach to Charles de Gaulle airport.

It was 8:35.

Bridgette had stomped back to her assigned seat.

The aircraft landed.

Forty One
There's No Place Like Home

It took the usual forty-five minutes to get to the terminal. In-bound aircraft are parked so far away from the terminal at Charles de Gaulle airport that you need binoculars to locate it upon arrival. Since there were only twenty five or so people on the flight, it was assigned only one bus. Hanna stood up front near the driver and everyone else populated the rear. No one wanted to be associated with him by proximity, because he was American and had admitted it.

The time went by quickly after they hit the terminal despite the boring surroundings, and he was soon on his way to board the flight to Houston. This part of the airport was fascinating. The aircraft were all lined up in a row at successive gates. There was the United flight to Chicago. There was the American flight to Dallas and a second one to Dulles in Washington, D.C. Then there was a Delta flight boarding for Atlanta.

One Christmas eve when he was returning from Romania to Houston, he had walked right by the flight carrying "El Estupido," an Englishman on a flight to Boston who tried while over the Atlantic to set his shoe on fire and blow the explosives located in them to bring down the aircraft. Two passengers sitting next to him had strongly dissuaded him not to do that by taking his head in a hammer lock. The only problem was that, since then, every passenger boarding a flight anywhere in the world had to remove their shoes and have them scanned.

Hanna could tolerate the boarding process in Paris because there are normally two lines: one for first class (the chosen few he liked to think) and a second for all the peons. The flight attendant had taken his arm as he looked back one last time. They would be on their second drink before all of steerage was seated. Hanna wasn't sure that was a good idea; however, it was too late now.

In no particular order, seating in the back of the plane, as far as Hanna was concerned, involved such things as children and babies being torn from their mothers arms and men being taken to the rear of the plane to be ejected for no particular reason. Maybe Hanna's experiences with the no-class section in the back of the bus were a little extreme: however, to him that was always the way it seemed to be whenever he was forced to sit back there.

Hanna was transfixed by the moment.

It was a Continental flight, and the first-class flight attendant knew the names of everyone flying in the cabin long before they boarded.

Hanna stepped onto the plane.

"Good afternoon, Mr. Hanna," was his greeting. He always relished this moment and fantasized often about testing the flight attendant's attentiveness by suggesting that the two of them retire to her sleeping quarters below the main deck to see if they could become as one before they arrived at their destination.

Hanna decided he didn't have to. The lead flight attendant had already handed him a Bloody Mary, which fulfilled half his desire. He sat in one of the two center seats in the middle of the first-class section on the Boeing 747. He took his first sip of his morning eye opener just as Willie Nelson's "My Heroes Have Always Been Cowboys" from "The Electric Horseman" began to play.

"Welcome home," Hanna said to himself. This is one of those times when being an American was its own reward and nothing else mattered. Every time Hanna got on an aircraft knowing the next stop was the USA he felt an elation that was as good as sex.

When the opportunity presented itself, he called over one of the first-class staff and presented her with a gift of about three dozen porcelain bracelets he had acquired in China specifically for this purpose. They were not cheap, but neither were they terribly expensive. He motioned the flight attendant (a stunning brunette with a body that as far as he was concerned had been cut by an expert from Waterford crystal at Tiffany's in New York) and spoke as she leaned towards his mouth.

"These are for you and all the ladies serving us on the flight home today. Should you wish them all, be my guest. Should you wish to share, you can do that too. Just enjoy them with my good wishes."

This small tribute to our often maligned heroines of the skies usually elicited exquisite service from the attendants for the duration of the flight with frequent conversations from them to help break the ennui of the ensuing eleven hours in the air. Hanna had never received anything in return for this gesture other than fabulous service. As far as he was concerned that last overseas flight home before he set foot on real American soil, as opposed to one of its airline representatives, which by Congress, had been deemed to be American soil, was well worth the small price he paid in terms of his making like the Magi bearing gifts.

The doors to the flight closed after what seemed like an eternity. By this time, everyone in first class knew one another having hobnobbed, joked, made idle conversation, and drank two, maybe three cocktails in an effort to find some meaning to life before passing out for the balance of the flight. Hanna was probably representative of what most of the assembled group in first class had experienced during the course of the day.

"Let me see how well I can recount," Hanna said to himself.

Actually, he didn't say it to himself; he slurred it to himself. The meal last evening with Misty and her "date" Hanna had arranged accounted for several. Two and a half in the limo, two at breakfast in Marbella, two or three on the flight into Paris (he couldn't remember how many), and a final one upon entering the first-class cabin. Hanna couldn't add that far and no sleep last night didn't help.

The doors to the aircraft closed, the engines started, and they began taxiing to the runway. It took another thirty minutes, but slowly and surely they lined up for takeoff.

The takeoff on small domestic flights is normally a simple task. Ten million Americans do it every day. You turned down the runway, the engines spooled up, the aircraft began to rotate— twenty-five seconds later at stall speed then lift off in seven more as the craft hit its take off speed of approximately 135 knots.

Taking off for an eleven-hour flight in a two-level 747 loaded with fuel and riding on landing gears outfitted with about forty tires the size that grandpa's tractor used to use was a slightly different situation. A 747's weighted approximately a million pounds at liftoff, and even though Hanna was once a trained pilot in another life, when this behemoth began to roll down the runway he always had a few reservations.

Hanna always had his eyes on his watch. Fifteen seconds, and the roll had barely begun; if lucky, they seemed to be up to fifteen miles an hour. Twenty-five seconds, where on a domestic flight they would be starting to rotate, the damned craft was moving at about the speed of those tour buses taking you by the houses of Hollywood's rich and famous. Forty seconds and you sensed a bit of movement in the nose of the aircraft. Hanna always had visions of both pilots straining on the yoke together trying to get the bastard off the ground before someone screamed "abort." The nose usually came up within the next five seconds, and, if you were lucky, you missed the lighting posts off the end of the runway as you literally grunted the thing into the air. Hanna had this vision of the only way they got the thing airborne was by retracting the wheels at the last moment to reduce the drag sufficiently that the plane would fly.

"In the air once more," Hanna sighed to himself.

Hanna ascertained that he was close to maxing out. The amount of booze that he had been forced to consume in the past twenty-four hours was beginning the metabolic process of melting his body into a small stain of fluid on the floor of the aircraft. It was sort of like the German officer in Harrison Ford's movie who began to melt when he dared to look at the sands of the sacred temple as it reassembled itself after being violated by everyone's need to take a look.

In a word, he was beginning to feel pretty crappy.

The staff began to serve dinner. Summer, which was the nametag on the breast of the brunette to whom he had given the bracelets, leaned over him and, smiling, slowly breathed the question. "Would you enjoy some beluga caviar and chilled Russian vodka before being served your salad, Mr. Hanna?"

"That would be delightful," he replied.

What the hell, he thought; their arrival time was one o'clock in Houston this afternoon. He'd have almost twenty-four hours to detoxify before hitting the office Monday morning. "Mai won tee," as the Chinese said, "no problem."

The serving was elaborately set with linen table cloths spread across the very large tray that disappeared into an arm of the oversized seat when not in use. Eating utensils were sterling silver, and the glass was crystal.

First, the salad arrived served with whatever dressing one might desire and your choices of white or red wine. Hanna usually chose the white at this juncture. It always seemed to be more appropriate for the time of day. Thirty minutes later, the residue of this dish having been cleared away, the entrée appeared. Hanna had ordered the duck a l'orange today with sweet sauce, chickpeas, pan-fried potatoes, and white asparagus. With this, he chose a glass of a very fine merlot and accepted a refill when the first serving ran out before his meal was finished. The meal was followed up by a choice of one of many deserts ranging all the way from crème brulé to cheese and carrot cake. Hanna always declined these health hazards, preferring instead to finish up with green grapes and a variety of cheeses served with excellent coffee and a liquor, which, for Hanna had to be a fine Amaretto de Saronno.

Hanna's final act of the day was a quick trip to the bathroom. Back in his seat, he converted it into a bed, asked Summer for a pillow and blanket, and allowed her to tuck him in. Sleep came in the same form as an anesthesiologist injecting you just before surgery. Hanna slept the next seven hours without waking once.

"Mr. Hanna, would you like to come with me down to our private sleeping quarters where we could become comfortable and visit for a while? There's no one down there at the moment, so we would have the whole place to ourselves."

"Mr. Hanna," Summer was standing over him gently shaking him awake. "We are two hours out of Houston. Would you care to freshen up, shave, and maybe brush your teeth and clean up a little before breakfast?"

"That would be very nice," Hanna responded.

Goddammit! He'd been dreaming, he thought as he pulled out the dopp kit he always had in his carryon for this purpose.

Events went quickly after that. A shave and teeth brushing combined with stripping to his waist in the john and giving himself a cold sponge bath had reinvigorated him. As usual, Hanna always carried with him a change of clothing he dressed into for the balance of the flight. Breakfast was the usual ham and eggs with cinnamon rolls, coffee, and orange juice. By the time Summer cleaned up his tray, the aircraft was already on its glide path into Houston, and he was filling out the usual customs crap.

He took a quick look around for the one foreigner who was sweating the most and wondering how many dollars over the ten grand limit he was planning to sneak into the country.

"DO YOU HAVE ANYTHING TO DECLARE?" the form requested. It also described the laws that would be broken and the penalties that one would incur if they were not absolutely 100 percent truthful on this form.

Nothing, unless you want my headache, was Hanna's only thought, as he wrote "no" on the form.

Hell, he traveled so much they knew him in customs. He wouldn't have any trouble.

The aircraft landed without incident, and then spent ten minutes taxiing up to the jetway. This device, very common at American airports, had yet to be invented in most of the rest of the world where a bus was the usual way of entering airport facilities.

After walking the mandatory fifteen miles (or so it always seemed) to get from the inbound arrival gate to customs, Hanna picked up his luggage and headed for the agent's desk. He was through it in a second.

"Welcome home, sir" were the agent's only words.

Hanna walked through the custom's area doors, and there she was smiling, waiting for him behind the line. As soon as she saw him, she started walking around to the end where you could actually greet the passenger coming out the door.

She was wearing a very summery St. John knit (and Hanna knew this one was real when he got the charge on his American Express bill). Actually, that happened frequently. *What the hell*, he thought, *he paid more for insurance coverage on her fur coats then he did for her Jaguar.*

The hemline came one inch above the knee. Her blond hair was perfectly combed and sparkled in the light of the sun streaming in through the huge windows that ran along the outer wall. She was wearing three-inch stiletto heels that perfectly matched her purse and belt.

All five-hundred people waiting in customs for their relatives to appear were looking at the two of them. Movie stars they guessed. Hanna walked up to her, standing about one inch in front of that gorgeous face and the pretty nose attached to it.

"Hi, big guy," she said, giving him a kiss that was a hint of what was to come. "See anything you can't do without?"

"Hi, gorgeous. Do you ever mess around?" Hanna said.

"It all depends," she said, "You got any money?"

Ah, Hanna thought, *life is good.*

They walked to her Jaguar convertible in the parking lot, threw his bags in the trunk, and got in. The car's twelve cylinders rumbled to life as she slowly eased it out of the lot, paid the attendant, and headed for the freeway.

"What did the flight attendant pass out for a take-home sip today?" she asked.

"Chartreuse," Hanna answered. "I put two of them in my carry-on."

"How long you going to need?" She asked.

Hanna thought. Last weekend's disaster was putting extra pressure on his neurons, and it had been a long time. "Probably about four hours," he replied.

"Yeah, I figured about the same myself," she replied. "We had better stick the Chartreuse in the freezer. It always tastes better chilled."

Ultimate Rule For Avoiding Infidelity While away from Home on Extended Business Travel

It is always recommended when selecting one's soul mate that there is genuine assurance that her only concern in life is your well being and that, more than anything else, she is the most gorgeous woman in the world. Of course, the business man with this sort of relationship has already realized that, with other women, the fun is only in the hunt and that beyond that the psyche is always seeking ways to fail at closing the deal because he is not really interested in the kill.

Epilogue

It's strange how an issue of no importance can slowly assume the opposite status. I have encountered more of a problem writing the Epilogue to this book than writing the book itself.

At first, I was baffled by the block, until I realized the crux of my problem. Simply put, I was concerned as to how my family would react to the book, notwithstanding the fact that they had urged me to write it for years. They all know, since I have lectured them at length on the subject, that travel is its own reward and an education unto itself. This evolves from the fact that leading such a life of travel involves a person in many situations, most of them thought provoking, educational and, in many cases, extremely humorous.

At this point the question becomes, how does one explain the colorful prose and somewhat intimate situations described in the book—especially when the words "colorful" and "intimate" might be considered understatements?

When I sat down to write this book, I had a problem with my age. How does the patriarch of the family, with one foot in the grave and half responsible for a brood of kids, all very successful in their own right and all in their middle forties, explain to them what he has written?

There is a simple answer: once you get beyond the morality of the issues that should be addressed (but aren't) and totally ignore the fact that you are the senior in the family that should be setting the example, it's easy.

I envision all the family, each retiring for a sleepless night once they have read the book, since they will not be able to get beyond the issue of how much of it is fact and how much is fiction. Fortunately for them, that is one secret that their father, grandfather and husband will take to the grave.

While the family has seen plenty of evidence to affirm in their own minds the love and admiration their parents and grandparents have for one another and the sacredness with which they regard their brood, they still may not realize what soul mates they are. Suffice it to say that Pop Pop's head will be resting on Mee Mee's lap as he lies dying, and none of the events described on these pages ever reached the point where they overcame Pop Pop's love for Mee Mee and the way he has always cherished her company.

I should add that this book was difficult to write only because the author was laughing so hard most of the time that typing became a challenge. If there is anything keeping me in good health for my age it is the fact that life is so funny.